EX LIBRIS

Claude O. Winans
California Collection

AMERICA
IS GOOD TO A
COUNTRY BOY

AMERICA
IS GOOD TO A
COUNTRY BOY

LELAND W. CUTLER

STANFORD UNIVERSITY PRESS
STANFORD, CALIFORNIA
1954

STANFORD UNIVERSITY PRESS, STANFORD, CALIFORNIA

PUBLISHED IN GREAT BRITAIN, INDIA, AND PAKISTAN BY GEOFFREY CUMBERLEGE,
OXFORD UNIVERSITY PRESS, LONDON, BOMBAY, AND KARACHI

THE BAKER AND TAYLOR COMPANY, HILLSIDE, NEW JERSEY
HENRY M. SNYDER & COMPANY, INC., 440 FOURTH AVENUE, NEW YORK 16
W. S. HALL & COMPANY, 457 MADISON AVENUE, NEW YORK 22

Library of Congress Catalog Card Number: 54-7162

To

E. P. C.

Whose understanding over the years
has kept my memories alive

ONCE UPON A TIME

Once upon a time
Children played;
Played as God thought children ought to play—
In dirt, and not with ribboned arms of nurses at their call.

Once upon a time
Men led ladies in the minuet,
And wore their kerchiefs at their sleeves
To mild their braggart hearts.

Once upon a time
There was a girl with eyes so gentle and so clear
You sometimes had to drop your own.

That was once upon a time,
And all has changed—
Except your girl and mine!

◄◄◄◄◄◄◄◄◄◄◄◄◄◄◄◄◄◄◄◄◄◄◄◄◄◄◄◄◄◄◆►►►►►►►►►►►►►►►►►►►►►►►►►►►►►

FOREWORD

LELAND CUTLER is not unaccustomed to passing judgment on matters of consequence. In this volume of memoirs, he holds that America has been good to him, a country boy. The judgment is supported by worthy evidence. But other evidence supports another judgment, namely, that Leland Cutler has been good to America, especially to the City of San Francisco and to Stanford University.

Leland Cutler is a builder: of a business, a bridge, civic enterprises that include an Exposition and a World Trade Center, and of innumerable friendships. None of these has he built singlehandedly, and he would be the first to say so. Indeed, he would not have been happy building by himself, because too much of his pleasure has come from association with others in joint undertakings.

He will tell you, if you know him well, that he is a simple man. But if you know him well you will hesitate to accept this self-judgment. True, he has no "side"; he is not pretentious. He knows that the shortest distance between two points is a straight line, and he would prefer, in his straightforwardness, to pursue the most direct course toward his goal. But he is also schooled in the ways of men, by virtue of which he knows that there are occasions when the longest way round is the shortest way home.

And you would be deceived if you accepted his self-characterization as a simple man to mean that his is a case of still water running deep: the water runs deep enough, in all truth, but Leland Cutler has seldom been still. The reservoir of energy that has sustained him seems to have been inexhaustible, and his competence and joy in oral communication are self-evident to his friends and associates.

Yet he is meditative. He doesn't apply that adjective to himself, but he admits to dreaming dreams and claims that dreams have value. He has dreamed on the high seas and in the air as he has traveled far and wide for civic benefit; he has dreamed in his study as the sun rose to find him at his desk ; and he has dreamed on horseback among the hills that rise behind Stanford, the alma mater he has loved and served long and well.

And who can fairly dispute his claim that dreams have value? So many of his dreams have come true. And they did so because Leland Cutler gave them little choice to do otherwise. His dreaming was not idle. So when he asserts that dreams have value, I for one would not dispute him, because his dreams have produced achievement.

All who know Leland Cutler will join with me in gratitude for his friendship, for his good works, and for his abiding faith that the good in men far outweighs the evil. The pages that follow record many of those works and bespeak that faith, but no printed word can do justice to the fountain of friendship and fun that is in him, because these must be experienced to be appreciated. I write this Foreword with all the affection of one who has experienced them both.

J. E. WALLACE STERLING

STANFORD UNIVERSITY
March 27, 1954

PREFACE

AS I look back upon my childhood, I realize that I was the biggest hick in Colusa County, California. My clothes, as I remember, were good enough but mostly handmade by my mother, or secondhand, given by neighbors or relatives and I was conscious of it. My father was gone and I did not know him. I was trained by my mother, who worked and fed my sister and me and I grew up in the United States of America. Until I went to college, and even then for a time, I felt inferior to my fellows, but tried to cover my timidity as best I could. I read everything I could get my hands on and was passionately fond of the history of my country. I played over my head at sports and the drama and tried to keep up with my fellow students while I worked my way through college. In time the impress of the culture and love and soundness of my elders and the leadership of my teachers steadied me and brought me to manhood, and I realized that America was being very good to me and was the greatest country in the world.

At no time in my life did I ever come to feel that I was a hero; I wanted to help and make the dreams of others come true, just as I want my grandchildren someday to help my dreams come true. Looking back I can't think of anything I have done that was my own idea—I just helped. Frank J. Taylor wrote an article for the *American Magazine* in April 1939, when I was president of the Golden Gate International Exposition, entitled "A Dream That Came True." He said in part: "Poor old Le. He always ends up being the fall guy—which is right. Le Cutler can no more say 'No' to a civic job involving San Francisco than he can dictate like Mussolini, and being an easy-going willing gent whom everybody pushes around, he can't dictate at all. He couldn't say 'No' when the town singled him out to head the Community Chest, or the Chamber of Commerce, or the Board of Trustees of Stanford University. He couldn't decline the job of front man for the town when it came to promoting the San Francisco–Oakland Bay Bridge," and so on. Mr. Taylor probably never read the beautiful poem of Dana Burnet—

> The dreamer dies, but never dies the dream,
> Still shall the Vision live! Say nevermore
> That dreams are fragile things. What else endures
> Of all this broken world save only dreams!

In 1934 John Henry Nash, almost without my knowledge, printed privately some things that I had said from time to time and called the book *Once Upon a Time*. He insisted that I copyright the book and the copies were gone before I knew it, and I have only five—one for Mrs. Cutler, one each for our three children, and one that I lend to friends. My friends have urged me to have *Once Upon a Time* reprinted so that it might have a wider circulation, but no one else could emulate Nash in his workmanship and so I just set down my experiences over the years.

I can't dismiss John Henry Nash with a word. He was one of the great printers of the world and universally recognized as such. When he was an apprentice his master printer made him promise that he would not ever print anything that he would not set the type for with his own hands. He had his own building which still stands in San Francisco as the John Henry Nash Building. He had a magnificent library, always wore a smock at his work and stood before his case and set the type by hand. I paid thirty-seven dollars and a half for one of my own books which I located as a collector's item in New York, and I am very proud of the fact that John deemed my words to be worthy of his printing and fashioned them with his hands. Nash was a poet at heart and like the poets of old had some angels who financed him in everything he did. He toured Europe for special paper and made arrangements there with masters of type for special and new type. He even had an architect, who too was a poet at heart, design his home high on the Berkeley hills. The contract price was twenty-five thousand dollars. The eventual cost was seventy-five thousand. Nash used to point to the books in his library and say, "Nothing can ever happen to me. If I start to get hungry I can take any one of those books and sell it for enough to last me for a year or a lifetime." Of course hard times came first to John's angels and then to him. He had Stanford and the University of California appraise his library and they both agreed on approximately $200,000. Universities, however, haven't money for such purposes. Milton Ray, of Ray Burners, who was a poet at heart as well as an inventor and successful manufacturer, purchased the library and gave it to the University of California, where it now is. Wisely Ray arranged payment to Nash on a monthly basis, so that he and his family were taken care of. My copy of *Once Upon a Time* is inscribed, "To Leland W. Cutler from John Henry Nash, the Maker of this Book."

I have written my memoirs principally for my grandchildren in the hope that someday they will read this book. I even thought of titling it "Reveries of a Grandfather" but what I write are not reveries at all, but things that have happened in my life, which has been a strenuous and a happy one. I hope my grandchildren will at least have a happy life and I tell them stories of mine all the time. They are not afraid of me, and the thing I love about our family life is that their parents take time out to explain everything and play with them and keep them happy. It may be that they will read these words someday and know that grandfathers aren't old fossils but children themselves inside.

I used to think that men who wrote the story of their lives were supreme egotists. I don't any more because I have so many friends who have made my life happy, and my accomplishments possible. I tell the story because I have had a part in many things and with many people. Most of them were good and I enjoyed them. Those I did not think were good I avoided and often thought of Marshall P. Wilder's book, *The Sunny Side of the Street*, which I read in my youth. The opening paragraph was: "I live on the sunny side of the street—the shady people live on the other side."

CONTENTS

COLUSA, CALIFORNIA

NOW and then my grandchildren climb on my knee and entreat me to tell them another "remember" story. Then it is I realize that I have been telling them things that happened in my memory of a long time ago; memories of my own two grandfathers and my childhood with them. As I look back, grandfathers were men who wore whiskers and were very old, and yet I smile when I realize that they were probably younger than I am now.

When I was six, my Grandfather Durham drove me in a buckboard from Irvington, California, to Stanford University, where President Benjamin Harrison planted a tree, with Senator Leland Stanford presiding. I never will forget the great pride I had that my grandfather's whiskers were longer than the whiskers of the President of the United States and of the Founder of Stanford University. Of course, I did not know that particular memory would cling to me for more than half a century, or that radio would come and that as President of the Board of Trustees of Stanford I would broadcast that trivial incident on the fiftieth anniversary of the University. I did not know either that another President of the United States and a fellow Trustee, Herbert Hoover, would stand beside me on that occasion and tell me that my story was the best part of my speech!

Recently, Thomas A. Maloney, speaker pro tem of the California Assembly, said at a dinner in San Francisco: "Le Cutler is a city slicker like the rest of us, but he goes to the Legislature and is listened to because he tells everybody he was born in Colusa." Although my great friend, Richard Barrett, used to say that I was born in more towns than any man he ever knew, the fact is that I was born in Colusa, California, and lived there until I was nine years old. My Ethel Jane, who is Mrs. Cutler, says to this day that the world must have started when I was nine because I mark everything of my telling as before or after that yearning age.

My father died when I was a year and a half old; my sister Georgia was three, and my mother was twenty-two. I like to think that I have a memory of my father giving me some candy as I sat on the sitting room floor. I later described to my mother the pattern of the carpet as I remembered it and it was the carpet we had when my father died, but I guess I was just too little for it to be true. I have to this day, however, a memory of my father which came to me from those who knew him and which will be with me to the end. He was a great gentleman, and from writings which he left for me I know how high were his ideals and how greatly he wanted to live and have a full rich part in the living. He was a student and knew the history of our country and many languages, ancient and modern. Judge Burnett of the Appellate bench, who had gone to school with him at Santa Rosa, told me one time that when my father spoke you could not tell where Shakespeare left off and Cutler began.

My father was eleven years older than my mother. They met when he went from Elmira, near Suisun, California, where he was born, to Santa Rosa to live with my Grandfather Durham and go to school to him. There were many denominational colleges in California in the early days and my Grandfather Durham, at various times, was president of several which were sponsored by the Christian Church. My Grandfather Durham was a minister of that church, and my Grandfather Cutler was a stalwart member all of his life, having come to California from Missouri, where the denomination was very strong.

My father graduated from Santa Rosa College in 1880 and delivered the valedictory address. That same year he moved with the Durhams to College City, Colusa County, where my grandfather Durham became president of Pierce Christian College, the site of what was Pierce Union High School, later moved to Arbuckle, California. Two years later he and my mother, Elda Durham, were married in College City. My mother was then eighteen and my father twenty-nine. My mother was a gifted girl with a great talent for the piano and music in every form. She had a lovely voice, and from childhood had painted in oils and water colors. My father was now principal of the high school in Colusa and studying law with Richard Bayne, who was best man at the wedding, with my Grandfather Durham officiating. The newly married couple went immediately to Colusa, where my father had purchased a home, and there my sister and I were born. The house is still there, but moved a block away nearer the river.

My father and mother had only four years together, and he died at the age of thirty-three. He had been admitted to the bar and was practicing law at the time of his death. I have the newspaper clippings which my mother kept in an old scrapbook, and I had a long life close by her to learn from her own lips of their great happiness together. My mother did not marry again nor did she mourn unseemly. She was always proud of the love she had and she was the happiest woman I ever knew. She died peacefully in 1945 at the age of eighty-three after a beautiful and extraordinarily useful life.

One of the fine lawyers of California, U. W. Brown of Colusa, who died last year well in his nineties, studied law in my father's office and spoke reverently and gently of him whenever we were together. Mr. Brown was with me at the Colusa cemetery on the times I needed him most and I will never forget the comfort I had from him.

My Grandfather and Grandmother Cutler, my mother and father and my sister Georgia, are buried there. Colusa has a meaning for me that no other town or city can ever have.

I have before me an address delivered by my father in 1881 at a State Teachers' Institute, when he was principal of the Colusa High School. I found it last year in an old trunk of my mother's. The address is written out in his own hand, and he said in part:

We must teach that truth is valuable for its intrinsic worth; that patriotism is a debt we owe to the State; that happiness is more than money-getting, and wisdom more than great riches. I would impress upon my pupils that they are preparing not for recitation but for life and for the good of themselves and those with whom they have to do. I would instill in them daily the broad and humanizing sentiments of philanthropy and charity; teach them to venerate the law as they would the protecting hand of fraternal love. I would guide them along the pure streams of classic literature and direct them to the fountain head for yet purer draughts so that in the end the great practical result of education would be obtained—that they would be better men and women. The great beauties of Horace, of Virgil, of Shakespeare and Longfellow are as close to the humble as to the mighty. The humble man should be a man of culture because nature is very near to him, and the classics close to his single chair. Thus he can associate himself with the nobility of the ages and its royal line as illustrious and soul-filling as the lineage of divinity.

The work of the teacher, if well done, is like the work of the parent, silently done; silently our influence will be felt in the coming years as silently through their circling tracks go the worlds above us. Our star of life, like the parents' star, may go down in the lengthening shadows of the night, but the radiance of its rising will beam brighter on some other shore. And if we are true to our trusts, the results of our labours with those we teach, shall be as a pillar of cloud by day and a pillar of fire by night to guide our children and our children's children and our Nation's destiny.

And so at twenty-two, my mother began her long life alone with two children to support. She had no money, but she had talent and great courage and a greater faith. She had friends from her childhood and she made new ones every day of her life. She gave painting lessons and music lessons and studied and practiced these arts by herself at every opportunity. She took lessons from her betters whenever she could and kept abreast of everything that was good and stimulating. Many of her early friends have told me that they took lessons from her not only to learn but to be with her and have the benediction of her personality and her patience. She told me one time that at first the neighbors tried to sympathize with her and would say "It's too bad, Elda, you have those two little children," and my mother would say, "I couldn't make it without them and all I ask is that they remember their life as a happy one."

I think the burden of all of her prayers was that my sister and I might have a happy life. A great part of my mother's life was devoted to making other people happy, and of course in the doing she herself was happy. If I would take her to a movie that turned out to be pretty terrible and would suggest leaving, she would say, "You sit right here, son; we paid our money to enjoy ourselves—now settle down and do it!"

In a play I wrote one year for the Family Club in San Francisco, I wrote these lines, with music for the verse by William Lawrence:

I've loved a lady all my life—she rocked my trundle bed with love and when I could not sleep, she used to stroke my tousled head with her cool hands. Why—my mother had the prettiest voice, so soft, so sweet, that from the memory of those days it seems to me she always sang. And though I was too young to understand the words, I never will forget the prayer of her fair cheek against my own.

That lady always waved to me when I trudged off to school and if I thought to turn around, I saw her cheerful by the door. I didn't know of course that when she went inside and was alone, something strange and tearful touched her eyes and heart with hope.

And after school when I stubbed home my square-toed shoes through dust, the lady would set a little table with a pastry she had baked and while I ate she'd give to me her sweet soft voice again and ask me of the day. And when my telling was all done and quiet came, she told me of great gentlemen and ladies who loved each other and she would say, "My son, if ever you grow up, please be a gentleman as men know such—and please remember wild flowers and the spring and clear bright pictures of your youth."

And do you know that to this day when I sit by an opened window and have the fragrance of the wild flowers and the spring, I think I will be always young and even though I know my lady is close by, if only through a picture frame I can see her twinkling eyes and her smooth gray hair, the tired days ahead I think will be as youth.

My lady lives in sweetness and to the end she will love me like she did when I was young. Her voice is still so soft, her hands are yet so cool, she stands so cheerful by the door, I wish my tousled head might be the same—for that great lady.

> When I was a laddie a long time ago
> My mother would whisper so soft and so low,
> "Be a good little laddie as upward you grow,"
> When I was a laddie a long time ago.

> "You're just a wee laddie," my mother would say,
> "I wish that forever you're little this way,
> It's easy to spank ye for which ye will thank me
> When no longer a laddie," my mother would say.

> When I was a laddie the spanking, heigh-ho,
> Was light as the spun thread and all of you know
> That where it hurt most was in my heart-o,
> When I was a laddie a long time ago.

> When I was a laddie my mother would sing
> While she swung me up high in an old-fashioned swing,
> "You're up there, my laddie, as high as a king,"
> Those were the words that my mother would sing.

5

"My laddie, a king can not ever be high
Like king that ye are in your mother's blue eye,
I'm dyin' to thrash ye and surely to lash ye
If you're not still a laddie the day that you die."

When I was a laddie the scolding, heigh-ho,
Was light as the spun thread and all of you know
That where it hurt most was in my heart-o,
When I was a laddie a long time ago.

I'm no more a laddie, for laddies do grow
But I'd give the world if my mother could know
I remember her songs with her cheeks all aglow,
When I was a laddie a long time ago.

Remember her telling me please to be good,
The spankings she gave in the way that she would,
God knows that I need it today if I'd heed it
Like when as a laddie a long time ago.

When I was a laddie my mother, heigh-ho,
Was sweet as the spun thread and all of you know
That where she lives most is in my heart-o,
Like when as a laddie a long time ago.

Many of the things that happened in my early boyhood remain so closely in my memory that in raising our own children I tried to be mindful of the age at which they would remember too. The companions I had—those I liked and those I didn't like and what I liked or didn't like about them; the adventures we had and the games we played and the make-believe that was so real and has grown more so with the memory of those years.

The people in Colusa County in the 'eighties and 'nineties were very close to each other. Rich or poor, many of them had come by ox team, as had my Grandfather Cutler, from Missouri or Kentucky or Virginia. Most of them were Democrats. My father was, and my mother used to say that he could tell you why he was a Democrat. There wasn't any Glenn County then—it was all a part of Colusa County, and an empire in itself, rich in wheat.

6

In Colusa we lived just a few hundred feet from the Sacramento River, which was the greatest body of water known to any boyhood. My earliest recollection is of sitting on its banks and watching a steamboat nosing its way around a bend in the river. At the first blast of the whistle in the distance, the little boys and girls of the neighborhood would scramble to a vantage point of the levee and strain their eyes for the first glimpse of the white prow and follow the slash of the stern paddles till the boat was tied up at Jackson's warehouse. We were forbidden to go there and Mr. Jackson did not like us to get in the way, but he was kind to us so we went anyway. Some of the boats had been to Red Bluff, and we were awed to hear the deck hands talk about the snags in the river. We didn't know what snags were. I remember I thought they were a big fish, because I heard one of the hands say they caught a big snag just out of Red Bluff and were delayed several hours. One summer the river was very low and on a dare two of us waded across it. We fell into a big hole and I thought we were going to drown. We made the opposite bank but we came back on the bridge two very scared and dripping youngsters and torn by blackberry vines from the other bank. We dried ourselves as best we could before we dared go home. I am sure we did not give a full and true description of our adventure or the cause of our plight. I wasn't nine years old and I shudder to think what I would have done to my children or would do to my grandchildren if they should ever try such a thing.

On the far bank of the river was a dense interlocking of wild blackberry vines, and one day, without telling my mother, I took my bucket and set forth on a berrying expedition. I had just started to gather a few when I came face to face with a band of Indians, Coluse Indians from the reservation nearby. This I did not know until years later. To me they were savages and my tow hair stood on end, ready for the scalping. The Chief grunted, "You show us your house, they buy blackberry, you no pick." I noticed then they all had buckets filled to the brim. I had a wild idea that if I was polite and led them to my mother my life would be spared, at least until I got home. So the procession of one scared little white boy and a dozen strapping Indians started out. At our house on arrival was Will S. Green, editor and publisher of the *Colusa Sun* and later treasurer of the State of California. My mother bought a bucket from the Indians and Mr. Green said his family would take the rest if I would guide the Indians there. That was several blocks away and although I received from him the first nickel of my career for the job, I earned it because I was in mortal terror all the way and continued my disarming politeness as a safety measure until the Green home was reached.

Colonel John T. Harrington, newly arrived from Kentucky, planted an orange grove—one of the first in California. The little boys of Colusa knew where it was and how to get there and it was in that grove that I tasted my first orange. There can never be another one like it. Almost every day in San Francisco I see Mrs. Meyer, Colonel Harrington's daughter, and when I go to Sacramento, I revel in the companionship of Edwin Bedell, the Colonel's grandson. Always do I think of the oranges we thought Colonel Harrington didn't know we ate.

I remember most the older people who were kind to me. Ed Bedell's father was one of them. Of course the escapades of a boy under nine weren't very terrible, but Ike Bedell rescued me from several which were real to me. He fixed our front gate which I had been forbidden to swing on and in swinging had thrown it clear off its hinges. The good part about it was that he fixed it before my mother found out about it and he also turned off a faucet in the yard which I had been explicitly told should not be turned on, but which I did, and the water gushed until Ike Bedell came along. The crowning kindness was when he gave me twenty-five cents for some empty bottles that he didn't need but which my mother had asked me to get rid of.

That front gate was a great vantage point for me. I would sit on it and see all the passers-by. When our children were young I was telling them one night about an episode of the gate that still frightens me to remember. I told them a large colored man, the biggest in Colusa, and certainly the biggest I ever had seen, came by and chased me through the house into the kitchen where my mother was. As I dashed for the wood-shed, I heard him say to my mother: "Your boy called me a coon," and my mother's reply, "I'll take care of him." I told my children that it took an hour or two for my mother to find me. The day after I told the story, my mother in response to questions from the children told them that it wasn't a man at all who chased me for calling him a coon, but a little

8

pickaninny about my own age whom I played with daily. It hasn't been easy to live that one down.

And still before I was nine, with all the boys and girls and grown men who could be gathered, I wore a red shirt and carried a torch light for Grover Cleveland. The parade started at the depot of the Colusa and Lake (narrow-gauge) Railroad which connected with the main line at Colusa Junction ten miles away. Some noted speaker was marched to a carriage and escorted to the Opera House. I remember very little except the marching and the smoky smell of the torch. Not only for his deeds but from the memory of that night, Grover Cleveland has been one of my heroes. When I first read Nevins' *Grover Cleveland—A Study in Courage*, I halfway expected to find some reference to the Colusa parade and my torch-carrying and was disappointed to find that it was overlooked.

Wild geese and ducks were as thick as blossoms and farmer friends who had grain fields would have us over to stay all night in the fields and scare the birds. The older boys had guns and I guess the rest of us slept intermittently, but I liked to think that we stayed up all night. Anyhow, we had fun, a good breakfast in the morning, and ten cents apiece for our adventure. There was no limit on wild duck or geese in those days.

Colusa had a large and active Chinatown and for several years high-binders were on the loose. All of our parents impressed upon us that we must stay away from it because there was no doubt that it was actually dangerous. The result of course was that we visited it at every opportunity and always walked through Chinatown on our way home from school for lunch or after school. As a boy, I saw many shootings there and stabbings, and once on the levee with other boys and girls and elders too we sat and watched two Chinese fight it out with hatchets until Marshal Scoggins and his deputy, Johnny Crosson, arrived. Shootings were not confined to Chinatown in those days. I saw several on Colusa streets and we always followed Marshal Scoggins down the middle of the street as he led assailants off to jail. He was a brave officer, served Colusa faithfully for many years, and was the hero of all the boys. He was killed about 1920 by a criminal he had just placed under arrest and he will always have a place in the affection of old Colusa-ites.

9

The one thing that struck terror to all of us children was the Sacramento floods. There was no such thing as flood control and the levees were uncertain at best. When the town bell rang sometimes in the middle of the night it meant that we must get up and take to higher ground. My Grandfather Cutler lived alone after my grandmother's death a few miles from us up the river. He came to us one night at midnight wet to the waist. He had been reading on the second floor of his house and said he felt his feet getting cold but was so absorbed in his reading he paid little attention. He became colder and colder and as he leaned over to turn up the light a bit saw that the water was up to his chair. He barely got out. Such is the power of concentration and a good book.

While we were living in Colusa, my Grandfather and Grandmother Durham and my uncles and aunts moved to Irvington, Alameda County, where my grandfather became president of Washington College. My Grandfather Cutler and my father's brother and my Cutler cousins stayed in Colusa. At Christmastime and in the summers when my mother could afford it we went to Irvington where our Durham relatives were. We did not always have the money to travel. Train connections could not get us there in a day and the trip generally meant a stopover in San Francisco. At Christmastime rains and river overflow prevented us a time or two from going to Irvington at all. The first Christmas I remember was at home in Colusa with a tree which my mother set up at night under the big clock after my sister and I had been put to bed. In the morning a sheet covered the tree and the clock and we were told we must stay away and not peek. That old clock now is on the wall of my home with its pendulum still swinging. I never glance at it without thinking of my first Christmas and how my sister and I peeked every chance we had as Christmas Day wore on.

I have a clear warm memory of my Grandfather Cutler. He had crossed the plains from Boone County, Missouri, with my grandmother and settled in Solano County, where my father and his brothers and sister were born. Apparently my grandfather did not come to California for gold. He was a farmer and not only farmed for his own account but supervised several large holdings for others, notably Colonel Moulton of Colusa. The Moulton Break, now a concrete bypass for Sacramento River floodwaters, bears the Colonel's name. When I was learning to read the *Colusa Sun*, I asked my mother what the abbreviation "Col." meant and she replied "Colorado." I thereupon read aloud that "Colorado Moulton has gone to San Francisco." He was known as "Colorado Moulton" forever after in our family.

Colonel Moulton was a man of great consequence in early Colusa history, and his big white colonial house, the scene of early old-fashioned hospitality and gay parties, was still standing a few years ago in the middle of a rice field, and chiefly inhabited by wandering tramps.

The association of my grandfather with the Moulton enterprise made him well known in the county. From all I have heard about him and as I knew him in my boyhood, he would have been well known anywhere. He was a well-read, kindly man, with a hearty laugh and an inexhaustible fund of stories. With all of it, I remember him as a reserved, dignified person, who gave no encouragement to backslappers. Except when he said grace at meals, I cannot remember him without a twinkle in his eyes.

The use of the word "liquor" in our household was as taboo as the substance itself. My grandfather liked to slyly refer to his uncle, J. H. Cutler of Kentucky, who he said invented one of the first steam stills in America. His product was J. H. Cutler whiskey. It was greatly in demand in Virginia, but in the shipping the stencil became blurred and it was known as J. H. Cutter Whiskey. My grandfather would end his story with a smile and with credit to Providence for blurring the stencil and thus sparing the Cutler name and keeping intact the influence of Alexander Campbell.

In Kentucky my grandfather knew Alexander Campbell, the founder of the denomination of the Disciples of Christ, later known as the Christian Church. He also knew Alexander's brother. He resented the use of the word "Campbellites" and expressed the view that it was presuming considerably to appropriate the exclusive name "Christian" for the denomination. My wife, a good Presbyterian, holds the same view as of this day and tells me about it now and then in her own way. Grandfather subscribed to most of the Campbell beliefs, particularly baptism by immersion, but he did not accept their frowning on organ music in church and their barring other musical substitutes for the tuning fork.

Grandfather Cutler had a true, if not particularly musical, voice and many an evening he sang old songs with my mother at the piano. Some of them were hymns and sentimental ballads of the day and some were campfire songs of many verses, which I asked for over and over again.

Grandfather had white whiskers and he used to give them a little tug when he was laughing at you and telling a story that needed a little extra stress. From the clippings my mother saved which expressed his views on local and national issues, I know he had a clear, progressive mind and was a sturdy fearless thinker. In 1858 he had gone to the California Legislature and did not run for re-election. This gave him an oracle's place in the community which, from his writings in the *Colusa Sun* and from what has been told me, I am sure he enjoyed greatly. I knew him until I was thirteen and heard him address several meetings, church, political farm associations, and the like. As I remember, his speeches were always pleasant to listen to and punctuated with homely stories and incidents which gave the impression of simple relaxed conversation. He had had many experiences with life in Missouri and crossing the plains, and with his reading and his humor he could put a very good speech together.

My grandfather addressed the California Legislature in 1858 and prophesied that one day there would be a bridge across San Francisco Bay. Seventy-four years later I came back from Washington, D.C., as head of the Financial Advisory Committee appointed by Governor Rolph to assist in negotiations with the Reconstruction Finance Corporation for construction of the San Francisco–Oakland Bay Bridge. We had obtained a conditional initial commitment of $61,400,000, later to be increased to $75,000,000. A parade and brass band up Market Street from the ferry to City Hall was arranged by Mayor Rossi and the citizens of San Francisco. My mother was at the ferry too and she gave me there an old faded newspaper clipping which she had kept all the years, telling me of my grandfather's prophecy of three-quarters of a century before, and it was captioned "Cutler, the Dreamer."

It was more than half a century ago that my Grandfather Cutler died, but he is much more than a memory to me. Not long ago I was telling a friend about my grandchildren and how greatly I enjoyed them and how I spent all the time I could with them. I asked him if he had grandchildren and he said, "Yes, four, but for their sakes I stay just as far away from them as I can because I still remember what a damned old nuisance my old grandfather was." I enjoy the story, but my two grandfathers were such a part of my early life and I have such clear bright pictures of my youth with them that I am impelled, whether I succeed or not, to give my grandchildren something of the same experience. A good part of my early fun was with the connivance of my grandfathers and much of it was instigated by them. They seemed to know what boys wanted to do and I guess that is a good part of what grandfathers are for.

When I had nearly reached the important age of nine, my sister and I came into the house from play one day and found my mother in tears and with a letter in her hand. She quickly smiled and hugged us and said she had great news and a surprise for us. We of course were excited while she asked us to guess what it was, and then she told us we were all going to move to Irvington, where our Grandfather and Grandmother Durham lived. I still can feel the tug inside of me at the thought of leaving Colusa, but Irvington was associated with a ride on a train and holiday visits, and my mother was laughing now as though she were happy and so my sister and I jumped up and down and were happy too.

Grandfather Durham was well established in Irvington as president of Washington College. He was also the minister of the only church there, the Christian Church, and he had bought a farm just outside the town. J. H. McCollough, who was associated with my grandfather in the college, was a Christian minister also and owned a farm adjoining the Durhams'. It was only natural therefore that the road leading to the Durham and McCollough farms should be known by the unde-nominational name of "Christian Alley." As a boy in Colusa, I thought I had learned something about fighting, but some of the best fights of my career came out of the taunts flung at me as a denizen of Christian Alley. At times I had the cowardly thought of withdrawing my young membership from the Church and I read the story of the martyrs with a new respect.

Irvington was first known by the undignified name of "Nigger Corners." This was in honor of two Negroes who kept a saloon at the crossing of the roads from Mission San Jose to Warm Springs and Centerville. Later the scattered residents of the settlement changed the name to Washington Corners and again to Irvington. It was in 1871 that Washington College was built by the citizens of Washington Township—an attractive group of buildings on a sloping knoll and in the town of Irvington. The school opened in the summer of 1872 with Rev. and Mrs. S. S. Harmon as principals. It was a coeducational institution. Albert Lyser followed the Harmons for a year and in 1883 my grandfather, Reverend Judge Durham, became its president. It then was a denominational college under the auspices of the Christian Church. Rev. J. H. McCollough joined my grandfather in the administration of the college the following year. I go into this detail because Washington College made a real contribution to the early educational progress of California and attracted students from far and wide.

Grandfather Durham was an unusual scholar. He had been head of Eureka College in Illinois and a college in Abingdon in that state, from which he had graduated and where he met my grandmother. He was a student of the sciences and humanities and particularly versed in mathematics, astronomy, and botany, and taught both Latin and Greek. On the long winter evenings at Irvington he used to read passages of the Bible to me and explain the various shades of meaning involved in translation from the Greek. Those evenings are very vivid in my memory. He would tell me many stories of his life in Illinois; of hearing Lincoln and Douglas debate and how he followed them from place to place as they talked to thousands out of doors and beneath the trees, near Galesburg. I wish I had listened more attentively to my grandfather's telling of those days. I never hear a speaker of today or make a speech myself without wondering how Lincoln and Douglas got along without a loudspeaker or the radio.

My grandfather and my grandmother, Elvira Whitman, were married in Cameron, Illinois, just outside of Monmouth, and my mother was born there. It seemed to me later that everybody in that section of the country was related, because sooner or later they all came to visit us at Irvington. And they were wonderful, inspiring people. They didn't come for just a day or two. They stayed all summer or winter, as the case might be, and they were all cousins and uncles and aunts

14

of some degree, and not one of them but I remember with affection because they were patient with me and kind to me. They told of adventures beyond anything I had ever known or heard and jokes I remember now and which are funny to me still. Between the college and the farm, we had lots of room and nobody was ever in anybody's way. Some of the younger relatives or near-relatives came to study at the college. Some of these fine people of those early Irvington and Washington College days are living now and as close to me as are my own. Those who are gone are firmly in the pleasant memory of a happy boyhood.

Such was the place to which we were going and for which we were leaving Colusa. I learned later of course that much correspondence between my mother and my grandparents at Irvington preceded the decision. My grandfather was well established there and Washington College was a going institution. While my mother had many dear friends in Colusa, her mother and father and her two brothers and sister were in Irvington. The latter, my Aunt Mary Durham, had graduated from the Boston Conservatory of Music and was teaching music at the college. My grandfather urged my mother to join the faculty and the family and teach art. Several of her earlier friends were on the faculty and in some cases studying with my grandfather.

When it was known that my mother was moving away, Colusa-ites gave her a big party at the home of Mr. and Mrs. Oscar Robinson. Mr. Robinson later and for thirty years was mayor of Colusa, and he and Mrs. Robinson were among my mother's earliest friends. (Mrs. Robinson outlived my mother and was at her funeral services a few years ago.) My sister and I were included in the party and managed to be conspicuous enough to almost be the guests of honor. I remember well that it was a musical evening, with my mother at the piano and an effective orchestra made up of guests who knew well in advance that they would be called upon. Home entertainment hasn't changed in this regard. We all know ahead of time when we go out for an evening that we will be asked to do our bit. I remember the cornetist at the party particularly—Will Frank. He was the local jeweler, who played that great instrument beautifully and was the leader of the Colusa Silver Cornet Band which gave concerts on Saturday nights in the park across the street from our house. I had long hoped that I could be a cornet player, and the night of my mother's party I determined I would be. I spoke to Will Frank about it, and although he laughed he said he would speak to my mother about it and see what could be arranged. The transaction took two years to materialize because I had to keep reminding people of my ambition. In due course, in Irvington on the tree one Christmastime was the beloved instrument. My mother had purchased it from Will Frank, who had a gold one for himself and gave us a bargain. The only lack of understanding I can recall on the part of my grandparents was their insistence that I do my practicing in the barn.

My mother was given a gift at the Robinson party. Although quite a few speeches were made, as I remember, the gift was no surprise as she had been allowed to pick it out. Her pre-party choice had narrowed to a gold slug of early California minting, which I had very strongly urged. To my disappointment she chose amethyst earrings, necklace, and brooch, and they were her most cherished adornments as long as she lived.

My Grandmother Durham came to Colusa to get my sister and myself and take us to Irvington. My mother was to stay on and to dismantle the house, sell it if she could, and pack our things. About all I remember of going with our grandmother was the fried chicken which we had in a basket and the train which was always an adventure. I remember too a feeling of loneliness at Colusa Junction while we were waiting for the big train and the Colusa and Lake wood-burning engine with its two coaches going back home again. Will Harrington, the engineer, was my friend. I don't suppose he knew or cared that I was going away for good, never to live in Colusa again, but he waved to me and tooted the whistle of old Number 1 and to me it was a benediction.

It was night when we arrived in San Francisco. I cannot recall any of the early-day acquaintances of our people who ever spoke of hotels. They always stayed with friends, whether it was for a night or a week. That seemed fair enough because friends always stayed with us, and over the long course I suppose it balanced out. My grandmother took us in San Francisco to the home of Aunt Lydia Luse. Of course she wasn't an aunt at all, but she had been in our home many times and

16

was on the Christian Woman's Board of Missions with my grandmother. She had a big house which I have since learned was in the neighborhood of Rincon Hill and the only feather bed I have ever encountered. The household had gone to bed when we arrived. Aunt Lydia's husband didn't greet us laughingly. He had a lamp in his hand, a scowl on his brow, and not much of a covering for his body. I thought he was about the toughest looking man I had ever seen and for some reason I wished I were back in Colusa. Our train for Irvington left the next forenoon, but at breakfast, which was served by a Chinese in a white coat, Mr. Luse said: "Mrs. Durham, stay over a day and take these children to the Midwinter Fair." That was quickly agreed to by all parties and the stern Mr. Luse gave my sister and me each fifty cents "to enjoy the day." I remember my grandmother laughing when I remarked that Mr. Luse was the nicest-looking man of my acquaintance.

H. H. Luse was a remarkable man and apparently a wealthy man. I seem to remember my grandparents saying that he was in the lumber business. I know I heard them say that he loaned money at small interest and long payments to build churches at many places in California. Also that he gave the money to build a church in San Francisco. After his gift of fifty cents each to my sister and me I could not doubt it. I learned later that like so many of my grandparents' friends he was a strict prohibitionist and gave money to that cause, and when I was able to read I saw a sign on a stick in the front yard of his home, "No smoking allowed on these premises." One of his daughters, Rebecca, a lovely and attractive woman, taught at Washington College. As a youngster I was allowed to enroll in her elocution class along with my constant playmate, Raymond Ingram, my friend now of more than half a century and known and loved as "Blondie" Ingram throughout California.

The only thing I remember about the Midwinter Fair was riding a camel. My grandmother tried to dissuade my spending any of Mr. Luse's money for that, but a big scene was threatened unless she gave in. It was a terrifying experience, which started when the camel began to rise. I have never tried one since and neither sheiks nor the beasts they rode have ever had any element of romance for me!

I don't remember the ferryboat and train to Irvington; I just remember being there. No abrupt transition of my life from Colusa to

Irvington seems to have taken place. I wasn't in a strange or unfamiliar place because of my grandparents and relatives whom I had always known and Washington College and the town which I had often explored thoroughly as a boy. I loved the hills and canyons and either wandered over them on foot or rode bareback on a gentle horse. My grandfather had a big, black-and-white dog who answered to the name of Hix. Hix took up with me and we were inseparable, and he undoubtedly kept me two or three years later from going to the Spanish-American War. I was twelve when I decided to go as a bugler. I packed some lunch and started with Hix at my heels. We got as far as the fence which marked the boundary of the farm, when the dog sat down and refused to go farther. Of course I could not go without him and I was forced to continue my bugle calls in the barn.

I missed my mother, who was still in Colusa and would not join us until summer. Finally when she had arranged everything in Colusa and had sold our home, the great railroad strike of 1894 was on, but that did not maroon my mother. She boarded a river steamer at Colusa for Sacramento, where she landed a day and a night later, because the boat tied up at all the freight landings en route. There were no passenger accommodations so my mother made herself as comfortable as she could on deck. At Sacramento she took another river boat for San Francisco and there spent the night with our dependable friends, the Luses. The next morning she was aboard the old paddle steamer *Alviso*. This chugged down the South Bay and into the sloughs that eventuated at Alviso. The trip was timed for high tides in some of the sloughs that meandered toward San Jose. Alviso was about fifteen miles from Irvington and we met my mother there with a buggy and a spring wagon. My sister and I drove her home in the buggy behind old Puss, while my Grandfather Durham brought along the baggage and the freight in the wagon. Primitive transportation from Colusa to Irvington, which probably would not be thought of in this generation, but it seemed a natural one at the time, although a little slow. I remember as we crossed the railroad tracks at Milpitas between Alviso and Irvington we stopped while a locomotive went by with armed soldiers sitting on the coal tender. I was greatly impressed and that night at supper I told of the soldiers I had seen. My uncle remarked that the presence of

18

soldiers on the engine could be blamed on Olney, who was a more stubborn man than President Cleveland. Alice Olney was a mighty pretty girl who lived on the hill above us with her parents. It was several years before I knew my uncle didn't mean her father as the stubborn man, but Richard Olney, Attorney General in the Cleveland cabinet. I had a further misunderstanding of presidential activities a little later in the year. Manuel Venzela was a Portuguese worker on the farm whom I very much admired. He had a tent pitched in the orchard and did his own cooking. I spent a great deal of time with him and he started me off on the Portuguese language. I was greatly excited and worried, therefore, when my uncle exclaimed one night while reading the paper that Cleveland had made a terrible mistake with Venzela and that Venzela would probably never recover from whatever ailed him. At least that is what I thought my uncle said, and I rushed out to the tent to find Manuel in comfortable circumstances fast asleep. Upon inquiry it was explained to me that Venezuela was a country and not my Manuel.

IRVINGTON, CALIFORNIA

I SOON found that I hadn't gone to Irvington only to roam the hills with my dog and on horseback. Within a day or so of my arrival, I was assigned two cows which had to be milked morning and evening. My grandfather sat with me on a stool for several days and demonstrated carefully all of the intricacies of the operation. I soon became an accomplished milker although undoubtedly my elders strung me along at the start by telling me so and praising me until I really had the knack of it. I have a smug feeling inside of me that I could step out today and milk a cow with the best of them and secretly hope the opportunity will someday arise. When I had taken over the cow situation to the satisfaction of all concerned it seemed only natural that the horses should be added to my repertoire. It became my job to feed and water them and keep the barn clean. I enjoyed greatly working with the horses and everything about them. Care of the barn was another matter. From the start I understood and loved horses and they seemed to understand me and my boyish vagaries. Our horses were for work in season and to be hitched to the surrey or the spring wagon when occasion demanded. I rode them all at every opportunity. We had one bay mare, Daisy, which was reserved primarily for driving. I kept her curried and brushed and used her for my riding horse whenever I could wangle permission. It was several years before I had a saddle and instead of a bridle my grandfather showed me how to fashion a hackamore that served perfectly. Daisy had some mustang in her and lived to be about twenty. She was a lovely animal and on several Fourth of July occasions I won prizes with her. Days before the events I would rub her coat with coal oil until she shone, and then with a borrowed saddle and trappings she pranced through the parade like a thoroughbred. The oat bin went down considerably around each Fourth of July but my grandfather never complained.

I rode Daisy into the canyons and over the hills. I talked to her as

I rode and it never occurred to me that she might not understand. Later when I was ready for high school, I rode her daily to Centerville, a ten-mile round trip. By then we had been together—boy and horse—for five years. There cannot be any wonder that we understood each other and became closer as the years went by. When I see school buses carrying children to school and the youngsters suffering the hardships of being driven by chauffeurs and taxis, I think of the great joy of ten miles a day on Daisy's back. Come rain or storm it made no difference; a poncho was a sure safe protection. And to think that the children of today don't know what a poncho is!

Some of my earliest and most stimulating memories are associated with riding horseback. Fay Chadbourne's farm was a few miles from ours. Fay and his brother Tad were acknowledged to be the best riders in the township. Their brother Ben, who was younger than they, grew up to be an outstanding rider. Another brother Fred drove trotters on the Pleasanton track and later on the big circuit. Fay was an all-round athlete and an excellent boxer. He was older than I but our love of horses and my young hero worship drew us constantly together. He taught me much about riding and how to stay on almost any kind of horse, and as little as I was he put on the boxing gloves with me almost daily and trained me to defend myself. None of my family objected to my going with him on long rides. Only my grandmother looked at him askance because he was not a member of the Church and was, she thought, too much interested in my sister.

I obtained permission one day to ride with Fay to Rosedale in the Livermore hills, probably twenty-five miles away. He was going to see about some cattle and we would stay all night. I always looked forward to such trips and enjoyed them greatly. We slept out of doors but sat for hours around a campfire before we laid out our saddle roll. There was always singing and a guitar or a banjo. "Shorty" Scott, whom some of the boys called "Scotty," was, as his name implied, close to the ground. He had been a drummer boy in the Civil War. He knew all the verses of every song that had ever been written and he had one in particular which I have never heard anyplace else. It had countless verses and I still remember many of them. I guess the name of it was "Snagtooth Sal." Scotty would strum his guitar and amidst a hushed silence from his fellows would sing the verses in a serious quavering voice while others joined in the chorus after each verse. By the time the middle of the song was reached sniffles and sobs would be heard. It is hard for me to sing the song today without crying, for it was a touching ballad of love and life and death. It went like this:

> I was young and happy and my heart was light and gay
> Singing, always singing through the sunny summer day
> Happy as a lizard in the waving chaparral
> A-walkin' down through Laramie with Snagtooth Sal.
>
> CHORUS:
> Sal, Sal, my heart it broke today
> Broke in two forever when they layed you in the clay
> I would give creation to be walking with my Pal
> A-walkin' down through Laramie with Snagtooth Sal.

The final verse never failed to draw tears from every hardened eye:

> So bury me tomorrow where the lily blossoms spring
> Underneath the willows where the little robins sing
> Place a little stone above a little mound of sod
> And write "Here lies a lovin' and a busted heart," by God.
> And though you yearn to see me, Oh, never more you shall
> A-walkin' down through Laramie with Snagtooth Sal.

About fifteen miles from Irvington and on the way to Rosedale was the Hearst Ranch. It was known as the Hacienda and Mrs. Phoebe Hearst spent a great deal of time here. It was a fabulous place and much romance and legend had been built up about it in the minds of the countryfolk who had never entered its gate. Fay Chadbourne and I on our way to Rosedale decided to see the Hacienda for ourselves. We had left home about five A.M. and it was probably nine o'clock when we disregarded the sign "No Admittance" and rode in. A little lady whom we quickly sensed to be Mrs. Hearst, was walking across the lawn and stopped as we trotted up. We were embarrassed, in fact panicky, but took refuge in politeness and tipped our hats to her. Mrs. Hearst came over to us smiling at our apparent confusion and guilt and asked us who we were and where we had ridden from. We explained as best we could and she put us at ease by calling one of the men who was scowling at us and telling him to give our horses oats and the cook instructions for hot cakes. I carry the memory of a lovely understanding lady to this day. A few years ago on a wedding anniversary, I persuaded Mrs. Cutler to go there with me for a week end. She had heard my story many times and had come to have some of my sentimental feeling toward the place. The week end disillusioned us. The ranch is still beautiful but I could not recapture that morning of my boyhood or transmit it to my wife. I should have learned my lesson and let my memories alone, but once in a while still I try to bring them back. Of course it is trite to observe that it can't be done with those things that were so dear to us. I understand a small part of Browning anyhow:

> Never the time and the place
> And the loved ones all together.

One horseback adventure had to do with a Corbett-Sharkey fight in San Francisco. I was reading everything I could about boxers, and James J. Corbett, champion heavyweight of the world, was one of my idols. The battleship *Pennsylvania* was in San Francisco, and Tom Sharkey, a seaman with quite a reputation in the Navy, was matched with Corbett for an exhibition bout of four rounds. The principal purpose was to give Corbett's friends a chance to see him in action. Fay Chadbourne and I told our folks that we were going into the hills to see about some cattle "for a man." We left shortly after noon and rode to Hayward. There we tied our horses to a hitching rack opposite the brewery where the car tracks began and took the trolley to Oakland. We crossed over to San Francisco on the ferry and took the streetcar to the Mechanics Pavilion. This was my first experience with such a crowd, which was carefree and loud. It was made doubly so undoubtedly by the sailors present who seemed very sure of their man Sharkey. They had good reason to be. Sharkey was the first in the ring, a deep-chested broad-shouldered powerhouse who received a mighty cheer. Corbett was tall and lithe and graceful and his ovation was terrific and lasted several minutes. There was no doubt in my mind as to what Corbett would do to Sharkey. But he didn't do it. Sharkey rushed Corbett all over the ring and pummeled him relentlessly. Only Corbett's marvelous footwork, and part of that was real running, saved him. As I remember, no decision was given but there wasn't any question that Sharkey was the winner. The ride home was a long one, for one of my idols had been toppled. I had told my mother that I would stay with Fay that night, and the dawn was breaking when we rode into his yard and it was a cheerless dawn. The papers explained that Corbett had eaten a hearty French dinner just before the bout and was not in condition. Even that did not calm my disappointment.

(When I was president of the Golden Gate International Exposition of 1939, Tom Sharkey was in the cast of the Cavalcade of the Golden West. When I told him that I had been a boyhood spectator of his first meeting with Corbett, he was delighted and regaled me on many occasions thereafter with details of his victory over the champion. I could not gainsay him, but while the fight itself proved he was the better man, Sharkey's telling left no doubt about it and made him a complete master of every exchange of blows.)

My uncle, W. W. Durham, whom I called "Uncle W.," had watched Fay and me boxing and at Christmas gave me a set of boxing gloves. I had them for many years and became fairly proficient for one who had no punch at all. Fay was really good and won an amateur championship at the Olympic Club. He then tried out on a professional bout under an Italian name, Joe Angeli. As I remember, we repeated our horseback ride to Hayward and trolley and ferry to San Francisco. He did very well and knocked out his opponent. He would have been off to a good fighting career if the next day's newspaper had not published his picture. Although it was captioned "Joe Angeli" it was clearly Chadbourne, and at that point Papa Chadbourne put a sudden stop to his professional fighting.

Centerville, where I later went to high school, only five miles from the town of Irvington, had an athletic club. For a small community it was a well-rounded institution—clubhouse and gymnasium, circular bicycle track with banked curves, all necessary paraphernalia, and many excellent and enthusiastic athletes. These came from all over the township and Chadbourne was one of them. That meant of course that for a while I spent as much time as I possibly could at the C.A.C. Fay pitched for the baseball team, played on the football team, and was its star boxer. Only Henry Crosby was better and that might have been

24

because he was bigger and older. Henry was one of the most graceful big men I ever knew. He was a brother of Judge Peter Crosby and Dr. Daniel Crosby, and all of the Crosby boys played a constructive part in Alameda County history.

Bicycle racing was a leading sport. The hundred-mile relay race around the Bay, starting at San Francisco and finishing at Oakland, was an annual event and aroused tremendous interest. Many clubs had entries who trained faithfully for months. Each club had to have at least twenty riders for the ten relays of ten miles each, the main rider and a trailer and sometimes more. My Uncle W. had given me a bicycle and although I was pretty young I used to train on the Centerville Athletic Club track and on the road leading to Centerville and back. My chance came one year when I was picked by the Garden City Athletic Club of San Jose to trail a five-mile strip that led through Irvington, my home town. The race was always held on Sundays and there were complications in the fact that the race went through Irvington about the time that church was out. The church was on the main road and my grandfather was the preacher. Also, I was janitor of the church and was supposed to be in the congregation, and bicycle racing on Sunday was taboo. I had watched enough races to know that the congregation, including my grandfather, stayed around on one pretext or another until the race had passed. As I whizzed by the church, I had my cap well over my eyes and my shoulders hunched over the handlebars, but when I turned the corner by Clark's store I sat up so that all Irvington could see. I am sure they saw because a couple of days later my grandfather took me off alone and questioned, "Son, bicycle riding must be fun?" I said, "It is, Grandpa." "Well," he replied, "Do all of it you can but I think it would be better if you didn't associate with bicycle riders as a group on Sundays." He chuckled and that was all.

Grandmother would have approached it differently. She was stern and hewed close to her line and I was always a little afraid of her. She had been strictly raised and I couldn't make her laugh very often. Looking back, it may be that she didn't have much to laugh about. My grandfather was easygoing and not very provident. Families other than her own were centered in her home and countless friends as close as relatives were on continual visits. She cooked and worked long hours and the stove was a hot one and burned a great deal of wood. I know because I chopped most of it and carried all of it to the wood box. Everybody worked. My Aunt Nellie, Uncle W.'s wife, and my cousins Anne and Frank lived in their own home across the road. My Aunt Mary and Uncle Haley and the three Cutlers were in the main house and there were never less than a dozen or so relatives from Illinois and other places. Three meals a day, and hearty ones, had to be cooked. Fruit in almost unbelievable quantities was put up in season. Morning, noon, and night, there were always four or five people around the stove and my grandmother was the center of it. Between times she was presiding over missionary societies, temperance meetings, prayer meetings, Sunday school teaching, and church services. My grandfather did as much of it too and prepared two Sunday sermons besides, but he was always happy and cheerful with a story to tell and a chuckle to listen.

Family life at Irvington with my grandparents and uncles and aunts and cousins was one of the great experiences of my life. I had my mother close by to guide me in time of real trouble but I had so many bosses that my mother wisely kept out of a good part of the disciplining. I inwardly rebelled at being told what to do by so many people and more and more turned to my mother for the final verdict. The result was a secret but delightful understanding between us and I doubt that my many mentors knew the difference. But when I did anything that called for commendation, each one took the credit. Those that are living still do—which is all right with me.

Meals at our Irvington home were largely and promptly attended. Grace was said before every meal and visitors were always called on by my grandfather for a word of prayer. Later when I was in college and would take classmates home for the holidays I would warn them that they would be called on and I am proud to say that not a one of them ever failed me, although it was a brand new experience. Supper—or dinner, as we now call it—was a major experience. Plentiful food and lively conversation. Politics, world affairs, religion, articles in the *Chicago Tribune* were all discussed along with the minor happenings of the day. No one hurried and it was all interesting to me. Much of it of course was over my head, but I absorbed a great deal of it and pieced together to my own satisfaction the things I didn't understand. Everyone helped in clearing away the table and then my grandfather would have absolute silence while evening worship began. He would read a passage from the family Bible (a large one and no other would do) and then explain and comment for a few minutes in conversational but reverent tones. He would then call for questions and when they were disposed of we would all kneel in prayer and end with the Lord's Prayer. This was all very impressive to me and as a boy I did not shrink from it or dread it. Such was my training that I think I was an earnest and sincere part of it. There is no disrespect or facetiousness in recounting the fact that on the word "trespasses" of the Lord's Prayer I invariably yawned night after night. Not before or after, but just on that one word. Such is the habit of a lifetime that I still do.

When the evening worship was over my mother and sister and I would have a half-hour or so of music. We had two pianos and an organ at home. My sister played the violin and I was making substantial progress on the cornet. My mother had long been a student of harmony and she was able to give me a good idea of the various parts. I really loved to harmonize. The cornet was in B flat and to play with the piano or organ I had to transpose and play in C. The only lessons I had at the start were from my mother and she taught me from the standpoint of the fundamentals of music and how even the cornet must blend into the making of a harmonious whole. I looked forward to those evenings and we had great times.

Most of the family, my grandparents included, had good voices and I learned to subordinate my playing to the rich voices that had the lead. My mother had a beautiful contralto and it was therefore easy to learn a pattern of harmony to be adapted in many ways. My grandfather had sung bass in a male quartet in Abingdon, Illinois, and fifty years later when he was seventy I heard him sing with that same quartet at the state meeting of the Christian Church in Santa Cruz. Thirty minutes of the evening were given over to the old veterans and they were good. A male quartet always inspires the listeners to join in and every quartet singer resents it. One night at Irvington when my mother and aunt and uncle and grandfather were singing a quartet, I joined in on the harmony quite lustily. When they had finished, my grandfather whispered to me, "Son, don't ever forget there are only four in a quartet." I have used that line myself over the years and sometimes it is quite effective.

As of now I sing whatever part is missing in a quartet. One time I was singing bass at the Bohemian Club and Vail Bakewell, who had a true and lovely tenor voice, stopped me in the middle of a close one which we were rolling on our tongues: "Le," he said, "there is only one thing wrong with your bass; intead of changing the note, you just change the expression on your face!"

From the start, I was a steady churchgoer; there were several reasons for that. My Grandfather Durham was the preacher, my mother was the organist, my Aunt Mary Durham led the choir, and I was the janitor. I was so young that the elders figured two dollars a month would be about right. It didn't make much difference because I seldom got the two dollars. I did, however, have to be in constant attendance. I was pretty good at sweeping; a long rug or runner of woven burlap was down each aisle, and sweeping the dirt under the two of them where it was safely hidden was not difficult and didn't take long. I wasn't so good at dusting and was generally taken to task for the omission on Sunday morning. Coal-oil lamps had to be filled, wicks pressed even with a match, and smoky chimneys cleaned and polished with paper. The baptistry, which was in the center of the church platform hidden by a trap door, took a long time to fill. Once or twice I was able to borrow the town's sprinkling wagon, fill it at the town hydrant, and with our horses drive it to the back yard of the church. There I syphoned it with a hose into the baptistry. That was my own idea and I was commended highly by my elders. My salary, however, was not raised or more often produced.

I went to Sunday school in the morning and stayed through church services, which began at eleven. I rang the bell twice for Sunday school and twice for each further service during the Sunday. I was always being begged by the other boys to let them have a tug at the bell rope but generally managed to perform the rite myself and frequently had to be told to stop and that I had rung it long enough.

Junior Christian Endeavor was at six and called for more bell-ringing, with Senior Christian Endeavor at seven and a repeat performance

28

of the bell. Church service at eight, with ditto. Once I had forgotten to fill the big lamps that were suspended from the ceiling and they flickered and went out in the midst of my grandfather's sermon. That was a tragic night and my only hope was that I might be fired as janitor. My punishment, however, was that I was continued at the same rate and frequency of pay and would never forget the coal oil again.

My Aunt Mary, shortly after we arrived in Irvington, offered me a prize at the end of the year if I would commit to memory two verses of the Bible every day. I did this for three or four years, and as I have a retentive memory I recall most of them. The prizes were not much— in fact I have forgotten what they were—but I had great pride in learning the verses. I repeated them daily to my aunt or my mother or grandparents, and once a month some one of them would review me in what I had learned. Just recently I came across a little booklet, *The Nutting Party*, with an inscription by my grandmother, "To Leland Cutler—1897, for reading the Bible from Genesis to Revelation." I was then twelve years old and there must have been a few passages I did not understand and probably skippd, but no one can say the reading did me any harm. I don't read the Bible now as much as I would like, but I pretty well know where the passages are and where the comfort and the beauty is. The hundreds of verses I learned are fresh in my mind and heart and have grown in meaning to me throughout the years. I have often wondered whether my Aunt Mary really knew what she was doing when she started me on the Bible. Probably she did.

People seemed to gravitate to my Grandfather Durham and his teachings. Edwin Markham, the poet, author of "The Man With the Hoe," was with him at Christian College, Santa Rosa. Judge Albert Burnett, my father George L. Cutler, and A. W. Sanford followed him to College City. When he moved to Irvington, many of them went there to his college. A. W. Sanford taught me in the eighth grade at grammar school in Irvington and yet he had gone to school to my grandfather in Santa Rosa with my father. People liked to be with my grandfather. I did even when I had to work beside him. He had a great knowledge of nature and good stories to illustrate his telling, and even though the farm work was hard, he made it sound easy. He would awaken me at five A.M. and say, "Son, let's slip down in the orchard and thin those peaches." That sounded as though we would be back in a few minutes, but the job generally took a couple of weeks.

Shortly after we moved to Irvington, he gave up Washington College with the determination to live on the farm and devote himself to preaching and lecturing. But first he had to fulfill the secret ambition of his life and visit Palestine and the Holy Land. I really think he gave up Washington College just for that experience, and it was an experience. He probably could not afford it but he went anyhow. All of his life he had been a thorough and searching student of the Bible and the places where Jesus lived were very real to him. From the time that he left home until he returned, he wrote articles published twice a week captioned: "From the Golden Gate to Jerusalem." They were carefully and entertainingly written. My mother preserved them in a scrapbook which I still have, and my grandfather used them as a basis for his lectures on his return. He gave many such lectures for several years before religious and educational groups starting in Illinois, where he had taught and where many of his old friends were. The articles I read and lectures I heard showed clearly how spontaneously the sight of historical places not only in Palestine but in great cities like London and Paris stirred his knowledge of history to life and his philosophy of living to expression. The trip to him was probably the greatest experience in his life. It gave a richness to his fine mind, augmented by the reading and studying of his earlier years that sustained him in his older age. It made him good company for himself and for everyone around him.

One echo of my grandfather's Palestine trip is in the Cutler lore of today. There was of course no wireless and there was no telegraph office in Irvington. The nearest Western Union was at Mission San Jose, three miles away. Grandfather Durham landed in New York after what probably had been a rough voyage and he had been away a long time. Regardless of the great pleasure of the trip it was a relief to be home. About midnight we were awakened by a telegram brought by a man from Mission San Jose on a bicycle. It was addressed to my grandmother, signed by my grandfather, and consisted of one word: "Safe." Everybody in the household laughed even at that hour; everybody, that is, except my grandmother—she cried. My wife and children are well acquainted with the story and to this day members of the

30

family use the magic word to report conditions wherever they may be. It is now a code word which is thoroughly understood in our immediate family and sometimes covers a multitude of sins.

Grandfather Durham was a great power in the state meetings of the Christian Church in the Tabernacle at Santa Cruz. His hearty handshake was known as the "Durham grip." My Grandmother Durham died in 1912, and two years later my grandfather was killed in a railroad wreck between Clay station and Lodi on his return from his Sunday preaching engagement at the little church at Clay. That was nearly forty years ago, but the people there have a little room they call the Durham room and have a memorial service every year in his memory. One time at Santa Cruz a memorial was held for him, and I said:

> I knew a man one time who was so gentle he could waken children to their toil with smiles. A man who was so kind that dogs would whine outside the door for him to come and pat their moistened noses to a day of play. A man who was so stern in his belief in God that he made all his children bow their heads in thanks for food and kneel before they went to sleep.
>
> Of course he knew that some day lads would have to take the place of men and little girls would grow to be as good as the only woman that he knew.
>
> He was my mother's dad, and when he died, thousands felt that they had lost a friend and to this day, men grip their neighbor's hand in faith because of him.

Washington College later became Curtner Ladies' Seminary. H. C. Ingram had been on the faculty of Washington College and had married Miss Ingar Stephenson, a teacher of literature and languages at the college. They were the parents of Raymond Ingram, previously mentioned, and were chosen to head the new seminary. Mrs. Ingram was a cousin of my aunt, Nellie Durham (Uncle W.'s wife), and so Raymond was a second cousin of Frank Durham, who is my first cousin. While somewhat complicated, the significance is that though Raymond and I grew up together and are generally accepted as cousins, we are not related. The impression is understandable because Mr. Ingram, after his wife's death, married my aunt, Mary, my mother's sister. "Blondie" (Raymond) and I have been so close over the years that we have not thought it worth while to disillusion anyone. While Blondie is pretty rugged now, is well over six feet, and rowed on the crew at California, he doesn't like to be reminded that he had beautiful golden curls as a boy and played the piano at Curtner concerts. In fact, I played piano duets with him. I am a little older but we had one good knockdown and drag-out fight when we were very little. That called for a family conference with Blondie's mother as the chief witness for the prosecution. My mother did very well for the defense and Mr. Ingram was referee. As I remember it, Blondie and I were slightly embarrassed over the fuss made by our mothers but otherwise felt no concern. Mr. Ingram was on the spot and by way of smoothing things over took us both on an excursion to San Francisco the next day. We went to the park and rode in the boats and on the donkeys and the trains and ate all that was put before us. We quietly decided that we would fight again with our eyes and cunning for another trip to San Francisco. Raymond and I for sixty years have shared each other's experiences and he is a sterling citizen and to me as my own brother.

Curtner Seminary flourished as a girl's school with a fine attendance and several of the Washington College faculty. My mother continued in art and my Aunt Mary in music. The main building burned on the morning of July 4, 1899, and the seminary did not resume. A year later W. W. Anderson of Anderson's University Academy, Alameda, erected buildings on the site of the old college and seminary and transferred his activities to Irvington as Anderson Military Academy.

Farm work, horseback-riding and my other boyish activities of course did not keep me out of school. I started in the Irvington grammar school, then called the Washington Public School, the day after I arrived from Colusa. Daniel Crosby was my first teacher. He taught and helped put his brother, Peter, through Michigan Law School and later Peter taught and helped Dan through medical school. I liked them both and my boyish admiration ripened into a close friendship that lasted until the time of their deaths a few years ago. They were born in Centerville, where their parents had a little farm. One morning at recess I had to "stay in" due to some forgotten infraction of the rules. Dan stayed in too, and with his head on his desk, promptly went to sleep. Miss Rix and Miss Emerson, the two remaining teachers, woke him up when recess was over and I heard Dan tell them that it being a moonlight night he had plowed until three o'clock and had to catch up on his sleep because he had three or four more nights of it. Both Dan and Peter played baseball with us and arranged extracurricular activities that kept us always interested. I kept my boxing gloves at school during the week and whichever Crosby brother was teaching at the time frequently acted as referee. Also, the gloves were used occasionally for grudge fights after school, and all in all we had some active times.

Many Portuguese had settled in the Santa Clara Valley and particularly in Washington Township. They were hard-working and industrious and good neighbors. The majority of them were from the Azores and Madeira and a sturdy lot. Many of my schoolmates were Portuguese, as were the workers on the farms, and I quickly picked up a working knowledge of the language. The Amarals were a large family and lived fairly close to us. Mrs. Amaral was a superior woman and a graduate of the University of Lisbon. She was the only one from Lisbon that any of us knew about. She had Portuguese books and dictionaries and smilingly helped me with the language on every possible occasion. I made many such occasions because her boys and I were friends and she baked round bread with a thick crust which I very much liked. My people took to looking for me at the Amarals whenever I was missing. My grandmother had a secret fear that Mrs. Amaral would get me into the Catholic Church and frequently questioned me as to what went on between us about religion. Blondie Ingram and I began to talk English with a Portuguese accent and still do with each other when we get nostalgic. Many of the Portuguese idioms when broken down into English are laugh-provoking, just as is our English, I suppose, when translated literally into another medium. My first major recitation as a freshman at Stanford involved reciting:

> At Flores in the Azores
> Sir Richard Grenville lay.

I recited it with the circumflex over both e's:

> At Florês in the Azorês
> Sir Richard Grenville lay.

Of course, my English professor, Lee Emerson Bassett, and the whole class laughed at me because along with the circumflex I had a Portuguese cadence to the rendition. I flared up because I knew I was right. The

33

Portuguese of my acquaintance had all spoken of the Azorês. Professor Bassett and I had quite a few words on the subject which went beyond the circumflex and next day I received a letter from him, still preserved in my scrapbook:

> Your remarks and attitude yesterday lead me to believe that you are not getting the benefit from the course which might be desired. I therefore suggest that you withdraw from the course unless you care to apologize.
> Sincerely
> Lee Emerson Bassett

Of course I apologized. I needed the credits. I also took every course that Bassett ever gave and we became fast friends and are to this day. On the occasion of his joining the emeritus ranks at Stanford, Professor Bassett wrote me a delightful letter which I greatly cherish. He admitted that I was right and he was wrong and that the circumflex should be over the "e" in both Florês and Azorês. I like so much the thought of being vindicated after all these years that I won't admit even to myself that he was spoofing me.

School wasn't particularly hard for me and about the only thing that bothered me was "fractions." I read everything I could get my hands on. I liked geography because the textbook we had was large and flat and I could easily hide a small paper-back book between its covers while pretending to study state boundaries. I always knew where east was because the sun rose over Mission Peak. To this day I think of that and instinctively wiggle my right hand to indicate east and my left for west when once I have located north.

I had many chores to do before and after school. We had a real farm and everything that went with it. Now, of course, I always refer to it as a ranch, as do the men who were boys with me in those days. They speak of their ranches which adjoined the Durham ranch and we're serious about it even among ourselves. School was more or less adjusted to the work on the farm. I would be let out early in the afternoon if I had no recitations, and if my schoolwork was up would be allowed to go home and pull mustard out of the grain or hoe potatoes. As I grew older, I plowed and cultivated and pitched hay. At first I couldn't pitch it very far or very high but became quite proficient as I grew taller. I

34

drove the horse that went around in a circle all day long hitched up to a hay baler. I sewed sacks on a harvester rig one vacation at $1.75 per day. The day began at daylight and ended only with darkness. We ate in a cook wagon and slept under the stars. Beau Brummells of today go to golf courses and summer resorts without coats and with their flowered shirttails out. We inaugurated that fashion in the hayfields years ago to keep the burrs and barley out of our overalls. The bane of my life was picking prunes. It seemed as though I personally picked every prune that was raised in the Santa Clara Valley. I had to get down on my knees to do it for they were picked off the ground after they had fallen. I had a pad of gunny sack tied to my knees to absorb the hardness of the clods but there was precious little absorbing. I was paid four cents a box and it took twenty-five boxes to make a dollar. Now when I ride in a dining car and pay fifty cents for three prunes with a dash of cream, a vision of the ground purple and blue with them appears and I am glad there are only three prunes in the dish.

We rigged up a dryer and dried our own prunes. That meant a big cauldron for boiling water with lye added. A perforated bucket full of prunes was swung on a light derrick and dipped in the water. This perforated the skins to hasten drying and then the prunes were rolled out on a tray. These trays had to be spread on the ground to dry and they had to be stacked when the weather threatened. Also, when the prunes were dried they had to be hauled to our warehouse and stored until they were sold. If the selling was delayed they had to be shoveled to keep them loose and the sugar from packing. Frequently in those days they had to be carried over to another season. Outside pickers were paid first and I being home folks was put off till the last or not paid at all. I can't remember much money ever changing hands in all my years of working on the family farm. I grew up to dislike prunes and I never was enthusiastic about manual labor for myself. I made boyish vows that if I ever got off the farm I would stay away from farms forever. I did get off but in later years the pendulum swung back again and at various times I have tried long-distance farming. The money results have been not quite as good as when I was a boy and worked for my grandfather!

I had a very fine black dog, Gyp, who succeeded Hix. Gyp was a little fellow and went everyplace with me. He particularly liked to be

35

with me when I milked the cows and could catch and swallow a stream of milk from any angle. He went to school with me every day and the only way he could be kept home was to tie him up. Once or twice he scurried into the schoolroom with me, and Dan Crosby sent us both home, which was all right with me.

I finally reached the eighth grade, which looked as though it might mean graduation. My teacher then was A. W. Sanford, who had been a classmate of my father and a student of my grandfather at Santa Rosa Christian College. Mr. Sanford sent me home too one day because I had a fight with his son, Shelton, and knocked him out with a solar-plexus punch. That was before Fitzsimmons invented the blow but I remember I hit him in the stomach with a twisting curve to my wrist. I talked about going to Warm Springs to school (four miles away) where Dan Crosby had gone. That is, I talked about it for one consecutive day, when my Uncle Haley took me by the ear and led me back to Mr. Sanford's school.

As the time of graduation approached, P. M. Fisher, Superintendent of Schools of Alameda County, announced that he would take final examinations out of the hands of the principals and have them conducted under his supervision at central points throughout the county. Centerville was designated by him for Washington Township pupils. It can be imagined that this caused considerable consternation and frightened every eighth grader involved. We went to Centerville and amid strangers and strange surroundings were given the test which Fisher had prepared. I still think it wasn't a fair deal, but when the returns were in a few weeks later I had passed. No one else from Irvington did and many other schools in the township had similar fatalities. Such a cry went up that Fisher announced conditional admission to high school would be granted to nongraduating grammar-school students. All they would have to do would be to keep up a good high-school record. This alleviated matters somewhat but it didn't help graduation exercises any. I sat on the stage of Clark's Hall all alone and delivered the valedictory address. My subject, which I had chosen all by myself, was "The Price of Progress and Perfection"—pretty good for a fourteen-year-old boy! I didn't read it, but spoke it in good rhetorical fashion for I had rehearsed it on horseback for several weeks. I remember one

36

phrase which I particularly liked and, if I can ever fit it in, will probably use again some day: "Temples are not erected without a quarry's depletion." I probably had been reading Emerson's "Essay on Compensation." I still remember the smiles on the faces of the mature members of my audience. I thought then that it was approbation, not realizing that it had been a long time since any of them had been so thoroughly amused.

The lone diploma for the Irvington school had not arrived for the exercises. Mr. Sanford improvised a scroll and tied it neatly with red ribbon. He presented it with a little speech of congratulation and the audience didn't know the difference. I have his improvised diploma before me now and it reads: "This is to certify that Leland Cutler has squeezed through the Eighth Grade with credits sufficient to entitle him to promotion to the Ninth Grade. He is a squeezer of note and as such I cheerfully recommend him to any school where his lot may be cast." And I had spoken on the "Price of Progress and Perfection"!

The Union High School at Centerville was one of the fine preparatory schools of the state. As I look back and with the experience I have had with educational matters, I realize its teaching staff was excellent and that the school could be numbered among the best. I plunged into Latin, Greek, history, algebra, and English, and my training in those not-too-easy subjects proved later to be fundamentally sound.

The high school was five miles away from our farm and that meant very early rising because the cows had to be milked and the horses fed and numberless other chores attended to. Most of the time I rode horseback with a sack of hay tied on behind the saddle. Occasionally I would ride my bicycle, which was faster, but I reserved that for the times when I was having a late start. I much preferred the horse. Once in a while I would drive a spring wagon and take a load of neighbor boys and girls, but this would be by prearrangement and for some special reason.

I greatly enjoyed the going and coming and the fresh new experiences of my first year in high school. There was an independence about it that was very satisfying and opened up new adventures to me. When I first learned to write on a slate at Colusa, it was part of the prescribed routine to show what we had written to the teacher. I invariably wrote, "I like my schoolwork very much." I doubt that I knew what it meant because I had no particular affection for any kind of work. The phrase became so shopworn that my teacher directed me to learn some new words and put them together. At Centerville the words came immediately to life. I did like my schoolwork, the teachers were stimulating, and the result was that I got along very well. I have some of my report cards of the period and modesty forbids that I recount the marks I got. I wasn't the teacher's pet either.

Above schoolwork, riding to school and home again, and new friends—all of which I reveled in—football was my crowning passion. Centerville High School had a champion preparatory football team for several years and outstanding players. Centerville furnished the colleges with great players: James Whipple and Jack Whipple, Bart Thane, George Emmerson, Billy Patterson, Jack Blacow, Ezra Decoto and Lou Decoto—who played against Pop Warner's Carlisle Indians—and countless others. Washington Township had many fine men who played for the Centerville Athletic Club and the Olympic and Reliance Clubs in their games with Stanford and California. Football was in the air and young and old talked it and concentrated on it.

In 1899 Centerville High School defeated all of the schools in the so-called Amateur Athletic League, which embraced most of the schools in the Bay Area. We were then set to play Belmont Military Academy for the theoretical championship of Northern California. I played quarterback. I was very light but that was what a quarterback was supposed to be as the game was played in those days. It was the five-yard game: five yards in three downs and the ball had to go through three hands. The quarterback ran the team, gave the signals with both teams lined up (no huddles), and the quarterback always had to pass the ball behind him. Any forward handling was penalized and the forward pass of today was against all the canons of football. Every team had some variation of a quarterback play where the half or full would take the ball from center and pass to the quarter, giving him a chance to run. These plays were used sparingly, for their success depended upon the element of surprise. Otherwise the quarterback was used for generalship and relaying the ball and such interference as a light man could give. He was, however, invariably used as safety when the opposing team had the ball.

38

No one at Centerville thought of training rules. We were all farmer boys and had plenty of workouts at home. We played two zero-to-zero games with Belmont at the old Sixteenth and Harrison Street grounds in San Francisco (where the playing field was sand), and the night before the games the high school gave us a dance in the Centerville Town Hall. We caught the seven o'clock train next morning for the scene of battle. It was not until many years later that the playing time was divided into quarters. We played two thirty-five-minute halves and a tackled player wasn't down until he yelled "Down." Goals after touchdowns were kicked on a line from where the touchdown was made and this sometimes entailed very different angles. Of course, from the vantage point of years, I can't recall that we ever missed the points after touchdown and I have very little patience with those who do.

Some of us played on club teams after the high-school season was over. I remember particularly one game against Pleasanton, where a self-collected group of us challenged the whole Livermore Valley. We had previously beaten a Pleasanton team at Irvington but this particular game at Livermore should never have been arranged. It would have been much better for us if we had "stood" at home. The score I think was 32 to 0 the wrong way. Our club won a game at Vallejo against a team from Mare Island captained by Pete Kaarsburg of University of California fame. We played the Suisun Athletic Club and had to wait for the tide to go out to have a playing field.

My mother and the Durhams didn't approve of my playing and I'm not so sure they knew of the club games, particularly the Mare Island one, which was played on Sunday. My grandfather, however, saw most of the high-school games played on the Centerville grounds and enjoyed talking them over with me afterward.

That year at Centerville High School passed all too quickly and I have nothing but pleasant memories of it. I did not dream that it would be the only one I would spend there. As the end of the school year approached, William Walker Anderson of Anderson Academy, in Alameda County, announced he had arranged to move his school to Irvington on the former site of Washington College and Curtner Seminary. It was to be a military school for boys. Mr. Anderson was a well-known and admittedly fine educator and had long been principal of the Santa Cruz High School before organizing his own private school. On one of his visits to Irvington he came to see us and talked to my mother and me about my entering as a day scholar. Mr. Anderson was a remarkable Scot, six feet three or four, straight as a ramrod, with short well-trimmed white whiskers and twinkling blue eyes. He knew everything about boys, what they thought or might probably do under any set of circumstances. He was most convincing and, as much as I thought of Centerville and my friends there, I was persuaded. I knew I would see them as frequently as I chose and unconsciously or consciously was swayed by the thought of myself in uniform among my old cronies. The principal of the high school, Professor Liddeke, tried to dissuade me and was most uncomplimentary in his remarks about private schools. My other high-school teachers advanced various arguments against the move but to no avail. I entered Anderson Academy in 1900 and finished all of my preparatory work by 1902. Thus I saved a year and did the ordinary high-school course in three.

Those two years at Anderson brought still further interest to my growing life. I did not like the military drill and setting-up exercises day after day but I did like the uniform and I thought it looked particularly well on horseback. The academy was immediately accepted by the community and the township. Mrs. Anderson and her daughter saw to it that the academy became the social center for the young people, with dances, dress parades, Arbor Days, and the like. Young ladies thereabouts preferred the newcomers because they knew me as about the same sort of person in uniform or out. Unbeknownst to my family, I had learned to dance so I stayed in the midst of things anyhow.

I kept on with the subjects I had started at Centerville and added some new ones. Professor Anderson was particularly good at Latin and Greek and he permitted me to go as fast as I could. Greek was difficult for me but I was taking it because Richard Bayne, my father's former law partner, had told my mother it was good "mental discipline." I will certainly vouch for that. To help myself along I did what I am sure no other student in the history of any school has ever done, I decided to get a Greek "pony"! I ordered the book through Bobby Crowell who had a little bookstore in the village. I had cautioned him so thoroughly about the transaction being kept secret that when the book arrived he delivered it personally to Professor Anderson. When recitation time came the Professor with a twinkle in his eye said that Mr. Crowell had delivered a most interesting Greek book for me but as it had the English words too, he would keep it and make doubly sure that my translation was correct. He held the pony under lock and key for two years and spread it out before him at recitation time. I had to pay for the book and suffer while Professor Anderson sat smugly above me and enjoyed himself.

Anderson Academy had very good football and baseball teams. The boys on the average were older than those I had been with in high school. The star players at Centerville had graduated and when we played them we regularly defeated them at both football and baseball. Every Saturday through both seasons we played some team and generally in the metropolitan area. That meant week ends in San Francisco or Oakland or Alameda. Many of the students lived around San Francisco Bay and I would stay with them in their homes on these trips. I remember vividly the parents of many of the boys, for they always made us feel at home and extended themselves to see that we had things to do. Frequently we were taken to the theater, which was a new experience for me. I saw many fine actors and acquired the habit early of paying ten cents for a seat in the gallery of the Orpheum whenever the opportunity presented. We played several games in Berkeley against Berkeley High School and Boone's Academy and were permitted the use of the University of California field. Also we were kept overnight and dined at some of the fraternity houses, which was a new experience. On one occasion our football team went by river boat to Stockton to play the Stockton High School. Our commandant was in charge of us and Professor Anderson had made quite a speech to us before we left. The game had been negotiated by one of the star pupils whose home was in Stockton and very much against the wishes of Mr. and Mrs. Anderson. We all knew about it early in the season but knew also that we would meet with opposition from the Andersons so kept it quiet. The boy who had arranged it was a big favorite of the Andersons and in fact of everyone, and after a long and wheedling session, permission was granted. Unknown to the professor, it had been advertised in Stockton for several weeks. It was the overnight trip and return on the river boat that

Professor Anderson feared because he knew his boys pretty well. Our commandant was new and, while he had a formidable air, he didn't frighten us a bit and we had little use for him. Except for a lot of skylarking which the commandant tried in vain to suppress, the trip up was without incident. We knew we had a game ahead of us and we wanted to win it. It was a beautiful night on the river with a fine moon, but we were all in bed by midnight without a beer—thinking about the game and the trip home. We were royally received. The Stockton boy had many friends and a lovely home and parents. The game was a riot but we won it after a long afternoon of rough-and-tumble playing. I caught the ball on the opening kickoff and was running down the side lines headed probably for a touchdown when a Stockton substitute jumped off his bench and tackled me. Protests were of no avail. The referee said he hadn't seen it so the game went on to a rough but for us satisfactory conclusion. After the game we were given a reception at the Stockton home of our fellow player. It was a gala affair but most of us were rather badly shaken up and tired and couldn't liven up. We were anxious to get on the boat which was supposed to sail at eight P.M. We had said good-bye and were all on board by seven or so but it was after midnight before we left the pier. That meant we would not be in San Francisco until late afternoon on Sunday, there would be no trains to Irvington at that time, and the commandant would have to arrange for us to stay over night in the big city. Everyone except the commandant was happy at the prospect. A little boyish beer-drinking began, with a night and a day to look forward to. There wasn't anything successful about the day but the night was fairly so and rather noisy. The commandant couldn't subdue us but something finally did and we could be called a very subdued lot as we appeared at the academy Monday morning. The commandant was fired, our games for the balance of the season were canceled, and the players held in bounds for two weeks. Being a day scholar, I could come and go and bring my fellow playmates news of the outside world. Except for the score, the Stockton trip was not a success. Those of us who are left talk about it occasionally with much laughter and slapping of knees, but only when our sons are not around.

From the time we moved from Colusa to Irvington until I entered

Stanford, I went every summer with my grandparents, my mother, and my relatives to Santa Cruz. The occasion was the annual state meeting of the Christian Church. A large and imposing tabernacle had been built in 1890 in an addition to Santa Cruz known as Garfield Park. This was named after President Garfield who had been an active member of the Church. Surrounding the tabernacle in circular form were streets named after pioneers of the Church and enough lots had been sold at the outset to make a well-populated settlement. The Durham cottage faced the tabernacle on Errett Circle and when I last visited Santa Cruz it was still there. The meeting was always of two weeks' duration, very well attended, and with fine speakers from out of the state as well as the outstanding preachers of California. The tabernacle was most commodious, with a large auditorium and gallery and was filled at all of the principal occasions, day and night. Unusually good music was provided by a well-trained chorus with selections well prepared in advance. My mother and Aunt Mary were the principal organists and on proper occasions I played cornet solos. I doubt there was a year in any of the ten or twelve I attended that I did not play "The Holy City." It came to be accepted as a tradition and I can state modestly that I put my soul into it with each succeeding year. One day under the spell of an evangelistic meeting in the tabernacle, I arose and pledged a dollar for some cause being expounded by the evangelist. I was about eleven years old at the time and when I sat down I began to wonder where the dollar would come from. I arose again and inquired "How soon do I have to pay the dollar?" And the preacher replied: "We will want you to pay it as soon as possible." That was all right with me and I said with satisfaction: "I can do that all right." Everybody laughed and I never hear the expression without thinking of the incident and how indefinite and unsatisfactory "as soon as possible" is in a business transaction.

The Santa Cruz interlude is still fresh in my memory. We drove from Irvington to Santa Cruz, a distance of seventy-five miles. Preparation for a stay of two weeks was quite a chore and a good many people were involved. Some two or three would go by train and check as many trunks and bags as the rules allowed. At times one or two wagons were used and always one with two horses. The roads over the Santa Cruz Mountains in those days were steep and narrow and very dusty. As I grew older I did the driving. The great advantage was that in the mountains all but the driver had to walk when we went up hill and there were twelve miles of road to the summit. Once or twice the trip was made in a day. We called it that, but we would then be on the road at three in the morning and not reach Santa Cruz until late at night. Most of the time we took two days and camped out overnight. I particularly enjoyed those nights. Also, there were several different routes with different scenery and we never took the same one two years in succession or on the return trip. I don't know what the roads are called now or whether they exist but then we knew them as the "Mountain Charley Road," "Bear Creek Road," "Soquel Road," "Boulder Creek Road," and so on. I always plan to explore them all again by automobile and see if any of my boyhood memories can be revived. I never go to Santa Cruz without a nostalgic tang from the salt grass approaching Garfield Park. Of course, there isn't any salt grass any more but the fragrance lingers.

It is still a wonder to me how all the Durhams and Cutlers and relatives and visitors crowded into the Durham cottage during state meeting time. For the first year or two the inside plastering had not been completed and curtains were hung between the rooms. Family groups were divided up for sleeping purposes and cots were used in the kitchen. We had a "sitting room" of course and I drew the sofa there for my repose and that article of furniture had been in the family for a generation or two. It was not too comfortable but I preferred it to the cot my uncle used in the same room. We had to be the first ones up and our paraphernalia stored so that the others could circulate. Also, it was my job to get the fire started in the kitchen stove and rout out the kitchen sleepers. As testimony to the fun we had, I have no recollection of being crowded or of anyone being in the way. Instead of dreading the stay in the Durham cottage, I looked forward to it and it is a pleasant memory.

My grandfather told me that in the earlier days, state meetings were held at different places each year—first at Stockton, then Vacaville, and so on. Campgrounds were provided by Church members of the neighborhood and everything was free, hay and wood for all campers and free meals for the delegates, beef, lamb, and pork being provided by the ranchers. I remember one such at Irvington. My grandfather provided a hog and we killed and dressed it on the farm. As a I remember it my grandfather showed me a resolution of the Church Authorities that "we have future State encampments with free table and entertainment for all who desire it." My grandfather's stories on those state meetings always interested me. Several acres were necessary. Church members brought their whole families, and camping equipment and coops of chickens were brought along and a fat cow or ox tied to a wagon as a donation to the general meeting. Contributions of money were voluntary and probably not very great in total but most of the aid was in provender—beef, sheep, hogs, flour, potatoes, and vegetables. Bake ovens and roasting pits were set up as though for a Fourth of July celebration. These meetings, according to my grandfather, were always near a stream where baptisms could be held and sometimes there were as many as a hundred baptisms on the Sundays of the meetings. Localities throughout the state vied for these state meetings as cities do now for conventions. Only a few votes at times would decide the next location.

The free-table custom in the later years of state meetings, according to my grandfather, became sorely taxed. He told me with a twinkle in his eye that a great number of tramps seemed to "catch a vision" and gather about mealtime. When Santa Cruz was decided upon as the permanent home of the state meeting the free table was abolished but only after much debate and misgiving on the part of the brethren. It was felt that attendance would be cut down materially. Accordingly for the first few years at Santa Cruz, meals were provided in the campground area for a trifling sum and much food still donated to the cause. Many tents were still in evidence. Those who had cottages would have their meat dishes furnished by the camp kitchen. I was frequently sent over with twenty-five cents and a bucket and brought back enough stew or roast to feed our multitude. Our younger set always looked forward to the hominy man who drove around in a little wagon ringing a bell. He served it hot with plenty of butter and I have often wished I could find that man again.

I got away from meetings and to the beach on every possible occasion. Afternoons were always given over to the beach and the plunge. A trolley car ran from the Casa Del Rey Beach through the city to Garfield Park to View de Leu where the cliffs were and where the ocean crashed ceaselessly. There were short cuts to the beach which we used for walking and I can recall only once or twice when any of us rode. The car ride was five cents! Also, all of the boys used the big pier under the railroad bridge for getting in and out of their swimming suits. This was a hollow caisson over the San Lorenzo River where it emptied into the ocean. It had a ladder on the outside and inside and wasn't too dry inside, but like the well and the barn door, it served.

The Santa Cruz beach was always a gay attractive place. I was fascinated by it. A band played every afternoon. The boardwalk was always crowded and I seemed to know many people, young and old. I liked swimming in the plunge better than the surf but it was ritual to take them both, with the plunge first. Santa Cruz is one of the bright spots in my life. My first job on graduation from Stanford was there and it continued the memories I had as a boy on the beach and at the state Church meetings. Some of the great friends of my later life were made there, with influences that I cherish and never want to shake off.

Dr. Rufus Lee Rigdon was one of the outstanding medical men of San Francisco and a great citizen. As a boy I knew him first at the state meeting at Santa Cruz. When he died in 1936, Mrs. Rigdon asked me to deliver his eulogy. This I did at the West Side Christian Church in San Francisco on January 21, 1936.

I offer words about a friend. As we grow older year by year, we search our memories for the starting place of our own lives—the first objects we recall; the strange fair scent of fields which make us homesick still for something we cannot quite explain, the first consciousness of play and people—boys and girls and men and women.

And as I look back on all of these, save for my own kin, my memory and my heart can find no earlier man I knew than Doctor Rigdon.

I knew Doctor Rigdon all my life and, next to my kin, he helped me most to believe in God.

I was a boy not yet in my teens when I first went to the State Meeting of the Christian Church at Santa Cruz.

And in those days the sturdy pioneers of the Church knew what Alexander Campbell stood for and how this Christian Church was born, and because I was a boy, I was sometimes awed, as I remember it, by the older men who preached, sometimes a little ponderously.

46

And I never will forget a man who did not preach at all, but sat and listened and touched reverently to his lips, communion with his Christ.

And that same man, Doctor Rigdon, smiled and understood when children ran up and down the tabernacle aisle, impatient of pulpits and yearning only for the sunshine and the surf.

Boys remember men most of all for kindliness, and Doctor Rigdon was very kind to me. One morning, still at Santa Cruz, very early, there was of the Church a sunrise prayer meeting on the cliffs beside the sea, and as I straggled out reluctantly to go, Doctor Rigdon put his arm about me and walked the way with me. And to this day I have within my heart the tempering of his tread to my youthful pace; his silent prayer while others spoke aloud; and then the walk back home the while he talked of things a boy would like. And so I was helped to believe in God by a churchman who made no pretense to the cloth, but who was ordained of God to translate religion into life, where all of us, whether we will or no, must walk together.

Doctor Rigdon was a churchman and did as much as any man in our City's generation to keep the Church alive. He knew the meaning of the word Salvation and that this great country of ours would be pagan first and then would die without churches. He knew the forms of faith and the discipline of belief as well as any cleric—but he wanted his Church, the one he knew from boyhood, to be an open home for boys and girls and where worship might be entwined with song and comradeship for old and young alike.

Doctor Rigdon fitted his daily conduct to the needs of other men, and in this community of ours took leadership with his courage and his understanding and his smile, in the making of this City a better place in which to live, not only for himself, but for the countless thousands he could never know.

And yet, as much as San Francisco needed Doctor Rigdon, I think God needs him more to help God carry out His plans.

And Doctor Rigdon leaves to you and me his courage and his understanding and his smile, for God has given him a greater thing than all—Peace.

In 1901, which was the beginning of my second and final year at Anderson, my sister Georgia was ready for college and my mother and she moved to Palo Alto. My sister always had her mind on Stanford, while I was a University of California enthusiast. That will be hard for my friends of today to believe. Most of the boys and girls of Washington Township had gone to California or were planning to go. The principal magnet for me was the California football team captained by James Whipple of the Centerville High School, and several of my fellow but older players were also on the team. My Uncle Haley, too, had graduated from U.C. Dental College and the McCollough boys on the adjoining farm were already enrolled. I had no thought but that I would go to California and could already see myself coming to Irvington on week ends with a Golden "C" on my blue turtle-neck sweater and my thick bushy hair parted in the middle. Incidentally, my nickname in those days was "Curly."

I realized later how courageous it was of my mother to take my sister and start a new life in Palo Alto. All she had was her talent and her great character. She had friends there, of course, but not particularly close ones. Many of them she had known over the years at Santa Cruz. She had to make her own way and her own place, from the start. I hauled such household goods as they would need in a lumber wagon via the same Alviso road that my mother had used to finish her trek from Colusa. They did not take too many things for they were setting up housekeeping in rented rooms. My mother immediately began to organize painting and music classes, which, as can be understood, was not too easy in a college town. It was natural that she should be the organist for the Christian Church. Later she alternated at the Los Gatos Church where they had a pipe organ, and stayed over an extra day or two for painting classes there. She had studied china painting and fired her own kiln. The pupils she had were in the main fine stimulating people and my mother was enthusiastic in her work and with her friends. Despite the long hours she put in and the hard work and uncertainty of it all, she was always cheerful and eager and made new friends every day of her life.

My sister majored in English at Stanford and in off hours was society reporter on the *Palo Alto Times*. Happy in Irvington on the farm with my grandparents and enjoying school at Anderson I didn't realize the rather grim day-to-day planning that my mother and sister had to do. I was only sixteen, with shelter and plenty to eat provided by others and a happy daily school life with gay companions. I visited my mother and sister when I could but it wasn't often. Palo Alto was thirty miles or so from Irvington and longer by train by way of San Jose. None of us spent much money for railroad travel in those days. Horseback was out of the question because of the time element and hay and oats on the Palo Alto end. Buggy or a bicycle was not conducive

48

to frequent visits. My mother told me later that, outside of my father's death, that one year at Palo Alto, with me at Irvington and apparently unmindful of her or my sister, was the saddest and hardest of her life. When I have flashes now and then of hunger for outward evidence of affection or companionship, I think of my mother's lonely year in Palo Alto and inwardly revel in the family I have about me.

Graduation from Anderson Academy came in May 1902. I had "risen" to be a corporal and for the second time a valedictorian. I have forgotten the subject but I am sure it was not as pretentious as my grammar-school one, for I was learning. For the second time in my young life, I was given a long, rolled diploma tied with red ribbon. This was a real one, however, and theoretically entitled me to admission to college. All of the Durhams and Cutlers and Ingrams were there to see me, for it was the site of the old Washington College, of which my Grandfather Durham had been president, and of Curtner Seminary which Mr. Ingram headed. My mother and Aunt Mary had taught in both and the early home of all of them had been there.

I still could think of nothing but the University of California. All of the 1902 Anderson graduates were going there. One or two of the previous class had gone to Stanford but California was my choice and the school's affiliation. The original family plan was that my sister would go to Stanford for one year and then transfer to California when I was ready. That time had come. My sister was enamored of Stanford and my mother was becoming established in the Palo Alto community. My only claim to fame was that I was a nonenity without portfolio. The only practical conclusion therefore was that I must go to Stanford.

My mother bought a house at the corner of Cowper and Hamilton in Palo Alto and I spent the summer in hauling furniture and belongings in the same old lumber wagon from Irvington to our new home. My grandfather, who was very handy with tools, went with me on the first trip and stayed to remodel and repair the house under my mother's direction. A large and well-lighted studio was developed on the ground floor and my mother continued her painting classes almost without interruption. Also a kiln house was built outside for china burning and my mother fired china for her pupils and for her own painting two or three times a week. Between trips to Irvington I painted the house and served as carpenter's helper to my grandfather. I also remember trying to paper the house inside, but the ceilings defeated me and it took my mother and grandfather with their steady patience and acceptance of hard work to accomplish it. After I had delivered the household penates and proved not too helpful at all-round carpentry, it was decided that my grandfather would stay on at Palo Alto and I would return to prune picking and the hayfields.

In September I made one final trip with the lumber wagon, which my grandfather drove back, and I was ready for Stanford. At least I thought I was but it did not quite turn out that way. I had done my preparatory schoolwork in three years and naturally there were several subjects ascribed to the fourth year which I had not explored. Stanford then admitted applicants conditionally and added five extra units for each deficiency in entrance credits. There was a minimum of recommended entrance credits required. This I overlooked. My sister told me it would not be necessary to get a recommendation in English composition because an entrance examination in that subject was required regardless of recommendation. This was known as "bonehead" English and was mandatory for all entrants. I took the examination in a large room with many others. I started out using a fountain pen and when the ink ran out finished in pencil. I was never much of a penman and the scrawly appearance of the composition must have been pretty terrible. Undoubtedly the content was not so good either for I flunked the examination. I learned later that many did. Legend has it that Mr. Hoover tried it eight times. I doubt that one. I also doubt the legend that the examining professor made spitballs of the composition papers and passed only those which stuck to the wall. The examination, however, could be taken twice a year and had to be passed before graduation. My difficulty was that I had not taken the trouble to get a recommendation from Anderson Academy, taking it for granted that I would pass. Next morning the bulletin board outside the registrar's office contained the terse announcement: "L. W. Cutler—Admission denied." It was a gloomy day in the Cutler household. I remember now the words I used in telling my mother and sister, but they can't be printed here. I had read in the Stanford announcement that recommendations would be considered at any time. I still don't know just what that meant but I took heart and telephoned Professor Anderson, explaining my predicament. It was the first time I had ever used the long-distance telephone and I made the most of it. I urged Mr. Anderson to send immediately to the registrar by special delivery an extra-strong recommendation of me as a writer of English and impressed upon him that it was my only chance. The next day I haunted the registrar's office waiting to see Dr. O. L. Elliott, the registrar. John Ezra McDowell was assistant registrar but freshman gossip was that he was tough and to be avoided. He later became one of my close friends and wasn't tough at all, but I waited all day for Dr. Elliott. Mr. McDowell asked me several times what it was all about but my Stanford life was at stake and I held to my purpose. Toward the close of the day McDowell interceded for me and ushered me into Dr. Elliott's office. He was a soft-spoken kindly man with eyes that twinkled behind his glasses. Dr. Jordan had brought him to Stanford from Cornell and he was one of the stalwart old guard of Stanford. I saw on his desk the letter from Anderson Academy. I pretended not to see it and asked if he had received a recommendation for me in English composition. Dr. Elliott replied that he had and asked me how I had fared in the examination. When I told him I had flunked he smiled and said "What kind of class in English did you have at Anderson; this letter says you were head and shoulders above everyone else in the class." He bantered with me a bit and then said he would accept the recommendation, and I was in.

III

STANFORD UNIVERSITY

ONLY those who have been on the anxious seat over admission to college can know the great relief and joy I felt. This was shared by my mother and sister to some extent but not to the full. My mother just naturally took it for granted, I think, that her son would be admitted somehow. To this day I share the anxiety of parents and boys and girls trying for the difficult entrance to our present-day universities because the memory of my own is still so vivid. I can't help them much but I talk to scores of them every year and give all the information and advice I can. It is strange, however, how little the average parent understands the fairness of admission rules to our universities. Many of them seem to feel that influence of big names is the deciding factor. To emphasize the fairness, I patiently explain that when I was President of the Board of Trustees of Stanford, my son graduated from Palo Alto High School but could not get into Stanford at the time. He had to go to coaching school for a year and was then admitted and graduated. Most parents listen carefully and when I am done remark, "Yes, but our boy is bright!"

I was now a Stanford freshman but the penalty of only three years of preparatory work was upon me. Instead of 120 units of work for graduation I had 153 to make. This was spread over four years of two semesters each and did not prove difficult. I took special examinations in some subjects, passed the composition examination easily on the second attempt and reached the last semester of my senior year with only twelve units to go. It is not generally known but I made up nine units by attending summer school at the University of California. I took physiology, botany, and agriculture. The botany course was under the great botanist Hugo De Vries of Amsterdam, and agriculture was given by Dean Wixson, the head of that department at Berkeley. Both courses were intensely interesting to me. My Grandfather Durham had been quite a botanist and had instilled enough of the elementary things in me so that I followed De Vries easily. Professor Wixson was a lovable man and very understanding of young people. I had plenty of first-hand knowledge of agriculture, and as this particular course was an elementary one, it was not at all difficult. As was the habit in those days—which I don't recommend to my grandchildren—all of us did not attend classes at the same time. Three of us in particular arranged that one of us would go every third day and look out for the others' interests. Something misfired and when I appeared one morning I was told before class that the day before at roll call three voices in different parts of the room answered "Here" in response to my name and amidst great laughter. I entered the classroom in fear and trembling but when Professor Wixson called the roll and came to my name, he looked over his spectacles and remarked dryly, "You were very much in evidence yesterday, Cutler." I stayed after class to explain but he just laughed me off and took me to lunch two days later. We became good friends and met many times and on many occasions during the remainder of his life.

President David Starr Jordan was a firm believer in the elective system of education which permitted students to choose their own major subject of study and the professors they wanted. He felt it was also a great boon to real teachers to be rid of what he called "reluctant students." I heard him say once that "Men and women draw mental nutriment from what their minds assimilate" and he was certain that the change from prescribed courses to the elective system led to an enormous increase in university attendance. Certain fields of study were of course required as a balance and supplement to a chosen major, but in the main a major subject and a major professor were the order of the day. I chose English as my major. I liked everything about it, even the grammar. I liked particularly the derivation of words in which Latin and Greek played such a part. I continued these subjects and also took up French. History always fascinated me, and for many years in later life I would take a volume of grammar-school or high-school history with me on my travels east to New England or through the Civil War territory. Those particular books were simple but they told the history of our country from the beginning as it was impressed upon me in my youth. It meant much to me to go over the same ground and read of the men and women who started our United States of America and fought to preserve it. Also on later trips with our children, we would read American history together and it made the great figures and places real to us.

Unconsciously as a boy I had been taught the comfort to be found in good reading, both prose and poetry. I particularly liked poetry—and still do—and prose passages with a poetic turn. Having a retentive memory I easily remember passages I like. I have such a respect for authors that in the main I remember them accurately.

At Stanford the cost of books, however small, was an item to be considered, so I used the library books whenever possible. This frequently meant that I did not stop with prescribed reading but kept on with what I liked and with other works of authors I liked. Frequently too this led to other writers entirely outside a given course. I really had a field day where the library was concerned, and if I had it to do over again and had my way I would just roam the library and read as I willed.

When I look back, the great joy of my four years at Stanford was with the teachers I had. Those few who are living now are my close, understanding friends. They remind me frequently that I was no scholar, but admit that I was not "reluctant" to learn and that I at least listened. I took Evolution I under David Starr Jordan and Geology I under John Casper Branner, who succeeded Dr. Jordan as President. The impress of countless other teachers is still upon me and led me as a Trustee to fight for the preservation of the Lower Division so that boys and girls in their teens might have a taste of the best the University could offer.

On Dr. Jordan's death, as President of the Board of Trustees of Stanford University, I delivered his eulogy at Memorial Services in the Stanford Church on January 19, 1932:

DAVID STARR JORDAN

Countless times have I heard David Starr Jordan say the words he loved: "Let the winds of freedom blow." And because of him, countless Stanford men and women walk the wide ways of the world with those words graven in their hearts.

Doctor Jordan wanted the winds of freedom to blow. He knew that science

54

from the stars and sea and earth could partly form the rules of life, but he knew, too, that rules would make of life an empty thing unless those rules were tempered with an understanding heart. And so he put his mighty arm about youth's shoulder and while he pointed to the sky and searched the sea, he held youth close and talked of human things, as a father talks to children of the years ahead. And just as children who are trained at home remember in their later years their father's kindly words and love, so Stanford men and women everywhere, though they may fully understand the things of science that he said, remember most the warmth of his great heart, the nodding of his sage and shaggy head, the twinkle and the humor in his eyes.

He wanted the winds of freedom to blow because he knew that youth would, day by day, grow up and change its mind, its wisdom and its plans, and because he knew that freedom in education would mean the life of youth and banish age.

And so he caught the winds of freedom in his hands and threw them to the world. He drew the winds of freedom to his mind and gave them back to men, but best of all, he warmed the winds of freedom in his heart for young men and women, so that what they learned from him might help them walk a tempered path throughout their days.

Doctor Jordan believed in youth and held sacred his great trust that came from youth, that day a man and woman, in memory of a boy, gave into his care and keeping their love and dreams of youth and their prayers and vision of the things that youth might do. And amid a great beauty of stone and of green fields in spring and burned pastures in the summertime, Doctor Jordan translated their love, their vision and their dreams into an understanding for young men and women of the difference between right and wrong in daily conduct, in thinking and in the work of life.

You and I remember how boys and girls, still in their teens, could take his courses and smile with him because he smiled with them, although then he probably knew more about the scientific facts of life than any other living man.

Neither you nor I can say what science meant to David Starr Jordan, but we know well he wanted youth first to face life with courage and with twinkling eyes and then to lift their eyes to science, if they could, as to a star.

Of course he knew that youngsters, if they were taught aright, would first have memory of a kindly arm and from that memory be reminded of their obligation to the discipline of classrooms and of books, and from that discipline and love, would somehow make the world a better place in which to live, not only for themselves, but also for the countless thousands they could never see nor know.

I can't appraise that wise and kindly man, but I think to the day he died, youth was greatest in his heart. In his later weary days, I used to see him in his garden stroking flowers as they grew and telling those who sat with him, that flowers were like men: If they were planted right and nourished well, they would give fragrance to the world. The stalks, he said, would only live a little while but there would be fragrance to the end.

And in those days, he used to gather wise men and women 'round a fire in his own home, and while he talked of the life the scholar knew, he also talked of youth, their blunders and their enthusiasms and how learned and older men must keep close to youth because some day youth would walk ahead. And a quarter of a century before he died, he talked to my graduating class about Life's Enthusiasms and he pretended to quote from an Ancient Philosopher, the words I think were his own: "My son, lay up a stock of absurd enthusiasms in your youth, else you will lose a great many of them by the way and reach the end of your journey with an empty heart." Doctor Jordan wanted Stanford men and women to reach the end of their journeys without empty hearts and to give their absurd enthusiasms to the world.

Forty years ago on his inaugural day as President, he said that he looked upon our young University, as heir to the wisdom of all the ages and where the long corridors, with their stately arches and their circle of waving palms, would have their part in student training as surely as the chemical laboratory or the seminar room, and where each stone in the quadrangle would teach its lesson of grace and genuineness and occupy a warm place in every student's heart; and where pictures of our fair region would cling to memory and where boys and girls would not forget the fine waves of two mountain ranges over-arched by a blue Grecian sky, nor forget ancient oak trees nor sloping gentle fields. All these, and a thousand more, would fill the student mind with bright pictures, never to be rubbed out in the wear of life.

Those words were his own, and he said them because he knew that a long time before, God and Youth had made up their minds to live together and that God had asked a lad He knew and loved to leave life in his boyhood and sit with Him; and God asked, too, a man to stay on earth for four score years and make amends to the two lonely hearts which gave the lad away. And that man, David Starr Jordan, lived a life that made God proud, for unto the day he went away he kept faith with those two lonely hearts and so much believed in Youth that he was Youth itself—and that is why I know he is God's good friend now.

Within a few days after my admittance to Stanford, I began looking for a job. I had my mind on football and didn't want anything that would take up my Saturdays. Due to my undoubted skill as a church janitor in Irvington, I acquired a few churches at $5 per month each. The work of course was not hard and consisted mostly of sweeping and dusting. The latter was not difficult because I didn't do it. One

56

day I was walking in Palo Alto with two of the campus heroes, one of whom had attended Anderson Academy with me a year earlier. I wasn't advertising to anybody that I was a janitor and was content to have that as the skeleton in my own personal closet. We passed a drugstore, the owner of which was clerk of one of my churches: "Leland Cutler," he said in a loud voice, "Ain't you able for to keep that church clean?" "Yes, Sir," I mumbled. "Then," said he, "why don't you aim for to do it?" Thus my shame was bared to the world, and becoming suddenly brave I asked for my monthly wages which were slightly overdue. He beckoned me into the store and the two aristocratic students followed. The drugstore owner paid me with ten silver half-dollars and my old Anderson friend said, "I'd like to borrow two of those until Monday." Overcome by several emotions—my own shame as a janitor and pride that I was able to help out a campus big shot—the transfer was quickly made and my friends departed. As of now, the dollar has not been repaid. The man is one of the influential and respected citizens of the community and I see him frequently, never however without thinking of the dollar that he borrowed from a church janitor and has owed for nearly fifty years. Some Monday I may ask him for its return with compound interest!

Jasper Paulson had a fine livery stable in Palo Alto and I had become acquainted with him and his establishment on my various trips from Irvington with the lumber wagon. I always left our horses with him for hay and oats and parked the wagon behind his corral. Leland Green was a fellow freshman with whom I had become quickly acquainted. We had a mutual love of horses and experience with them, so we braced Paulson for a job. We didn't want janitor work this time, but riding. Paulson frequently brought horses from Halls Valley in the Mount Hamilton country which needed taming for trading purposes and he agreed to try us at that. It was just to our liking. The animals were not vicious and were mostly cayuses which had to be gentled but we liked to think of ourselves as horsebreakers. We always had a horse to ride and some months made $10 or $15. Also at times I would have a horse and buggy for a ride to the neighboring Kings Mountain—but that is another story.

All of my classmates were not as fond of horses as I. In my senior year I was riding one of Jasper Paulson's skittish cayuses when my sombrero blew off. We were opposite the chemistry building, and having an audience and a chance to show off, I came up in a gallop to lean over cowboy-fashion and pick up my hat on the run. As I swept the sombrero up, the horse tossed its head and, in my leaning position, cut me rather badly over the eye. I swung off, holding the rearing horse with one hand and my eye with the other. I called to Dennison Clift to hold the horse for me. He paled and said he didn't know anything about a horse. I explained between gasps that he did not have to know anything about a horse to hold him but he shook his head and refused to come any nearer. Denny Clift later wrote many of Two Gun Hart's wild West scenarios!

I earned money in various ways. Roller skating was in vogue and I had a steady engagement playing the cornet in the skating rink which had been opened in Mullins Hall. After football season I worked in a furniture store on Saturdays from seven to seven, for $1.50, and at odd hours during the week when I could get off. After a time I was local correspondent for the *San Jose Mercury*, for which I was paid $30 a month. I took an English composition course known as English Eight. There I learned the trick of writing stories which might be acceptable to various Sunday supplements of newspapers. I had quite a run with the Sunday supplement of the *Los Angeles Times* and, as I remember, received $3 a column, with the average story amounting to about $12. Out of a course on prosody I evolved a sonnet which I sold to *McClure's* magazine for $12.50. I sold a few stories to *Sunset* magazine, which was then controlled by the Southern Pacific Railroad. My pay was in scrip, however, and didn't buy groceries. Once I sold a story to the *Smart Set* magazine for which I was paid the very large sum of $50. Like all aspiring writers, I made several attempts at the big magazines and received enough rejection slips to paper my bedroom.

One money-making incident stands out in my memory. A small circus had its winter quarters outside of San Jose about fifteen miles from Stanford. I noticed a band of monkeys one day sunning themselves and picking up little stones and objects of various kinds. That gave me an idea which I explained to a fellow Stanfordite with a camera. He took several pictures of the monkeys picking up things and looking intently at the ground. I then wrote a story of a farmer in the Santa Clara Valley, who, owing to the shortage of labor, was training monkeys to pick his prunes. I gave the farmer a fictitious name, and as the Santa Clara Valley covers a lot of territory, I had no trouble in placing him where he could not be easily located. We had good pictures to prove it and syndicated the story through San Francisco to the East. As I recall, we had about $60 apiece for our discovery of the labor-saving experiment.

I signed up for freshman football as a candidate for quarterback. My grandparents and uncles were still hovering over me and wrote strong letters objecting. The letters of course disturbed my mother greatly and I took care of the situation for two or three games by having my name spelled backward in the line-up. Reltuc wasn't a name that anyone had ever heard of but it kept my people quiet. As it began to look as though I might get on the team, no one took the alias seriously, and I was brazenly out to make it.

At this time I was taking a course in English history under Professor E. D. Adams. It was rather a large class for Stanford and was held in the old Chapel on the inner quadrangle. At the close of class one day, a week before the California game, Professor Adams asked: "Is Leland Cutler present?" Replying in the affirmative, I was told to stay after class. "Are you," asked Adams, "the Cutler who is trying out for quarterback on the freshman team?" "Yes, Sir," said I. And then— "Are you going to make it?" "I don't know but I'm trying awfully hard." "Well," said Adams, "I've been teaching history for a long time and you are just about the poorest history student I have ever had; in fact, you haven't shown any evidence of being a student, so your mind must be on football. Anyhow, it isn't on history. I'll make you a proposition; forget about history, make the team, and I'll give you two weeks after the California game to catch up with your class. Otherwise you're out." And then he added, with a pat on the back, "Good luck at both." I made the team, caught up on my history work, and took every course Adams gave for the next four years. We formed a friendship which ripened with the years and ended only with his death.

To me the great event of my first semester at Stanford was the freshman football game with California. I made the team at quarterback and played the full game of two thirty-five-minute halves without substitution. The game was played at Berkeley, and several selections including my own were not made until the last minute. My Uncle Haley Durham, who had objected always to my playing, came up from Irvington to see the game, and I doubt that he really rooted for his alma mater, California, as he always claimed.

We had one outstanding fullback and punter, Jack Magee, probably the best on the Coast at the time. As we came on the field for the opening kickoff, I overheard a California trainer tell one of his men whom I later learned to be a substitute center to "get" Magee on the the kickoff. I warned Magee, and this center dodged everyone and made straight for our man and swung on him. Magee covered up and took it because it would have been fatal for us to have him thrown out of the game. California's center wouldn't have been missed. California rather quickly made a touchdown and I reported the matter to Everett W. Brown, linesman whom I knew. Brown was an ardent California man and later judge of Alameda County and a sterling citizen. On the next kickoff the center repeated the performance, with Magee merely protecting himself. Judge Brown grabbed the California man, led him to the referee, and he was expelled from the game. California's regular center then came in. I will never forget that incident or Judge Brown's part in it. He always took a great interest in California student and alumni matters and was the center of many a controversy between the two universities, but my respect and admiration for him were firm and were shared by all the Stanford people I knew. All of this—even though Judge Brown in his early collegiate days at California stole the Stanford Axe.

One incident of the game is Stanford-California history. It has happened since in other games, though sparingly. For the first time in football to my knowledge a player ran the wrong way. On third down we had California backed up against the goal posts, and their punter prepared to kick from behind the goal posts. I played dual safety man with one of our halfbacks who shall be nameless, although his name was known to everyone in college at the time. The kick was high and came out not more than ten yards into the playing field. The halfback caught it and I turned to give him interference. He was headed the other direction at full speed with a clear field before him. Billy Middleton, captain of the California team—whom I see almost daily—together with Bosbyshell and Gillis was following our man. I set out after him and tackled him from the rear just short of our goal line. I always felt pretty good about that because he had come to Stanford as a track man with a reputation as a sprinter. I must have made something of a record myself that day. The unfortunate halfback was so lampooned that he left college shortly thereafter. I lost track of him until a few years ago when I was in Seattle on the eve of a Stanford-Washington game. In the lobby of the Olympic Hotel I saw him from a distance and went over and spoke to him. He went through the formula of my face looking familiar, because it had been about forty years since I chased him. When I told him who I was, he said, "Oh, my God, don't tell on me. I am making a speech at the Stanford dinner tonight and nobody up here knows about that one." Of course I didn't tell, and we both made speeches. As of now he is a successful attorney.

On the very last play of the game I tackled halfback Bosbyshell of California, who was headed for a touchdown, and broke a couple of ribs in the process. The game was over and the California band marched over me, playing "Palms of Victory." That is one band piece that I have never liked since nor even like to think about. I didn't know my ribs were broken. I just knew that I felt badly bruised and had been "out" for a moment. A few days later I was sitting in an easy chair when my mother called me to dinner. I had for the moment forgotten about my side and jumped out of the chair. I let out a yell that could be heard for blocks. It was of course a good thing, for I had a doctor in who strapped me up and pronounced my football days over for the balance of the year. This gave me the chance of real importance to make up my history work and catch up with my classes generally. I must have applied myself rather diligently, for my work came easily to me and I had no trouble in making good progress. This applied to the things I liked. It did me no particular good to avoid the things I didn't like, but that is what I did, and under the elective system there was a minimum of prescribed courses.

Some of the lasting friendships of my life, which are green to me and which I cherish dearly, were made with the professors whose courses

I took. They had me in their homes and they visited me in mine. With others we had long evenings of discussion on a great range of subjects—almost everything. We read prose and poetry aloud and I learned early that prose doesn't have to rhyme to be poetry. Dr. A. T. Murray of the Greek department was a fine friend of mine and a great gentleman. I have the impress of some wonderful evenings with him and an association over the years that means much to me. Dr. Murray understood young men as well as any man I know. He was a fine athlete himself and believed thoroughly in all forms of athletics. His sons participated in many contests for Stanford and are as well known as any Stanford men. Lindley Murray was national tennis champion at one time. Feg Murray was an outstanding hurdler, and is now a noted cartoonist; and Babe Murray in his own right was an outstanding athlete. I played many a game of tennis with Dr. Murray and on several occasions almost beat him. When President Wilbur formed the Board of Athletic Control, Dr. Murray and I were on it and disagreed firmly and pleasantly at almost every meeting on the procedure to be followed in setting up American football, after a long siege at Rugby—but that too is another story. Dr. Murray had been one of Mr. Hoover's teachers and was of the Quaker faith. When Mr. Hoover became President, he arranged for Dr. Murray to have a leave of absence from the University and become pastor of the Friends' Church in Washington where President and Mrs. Hoover worshipped. I saw Dr. and Mrs. Murray there frequently.

Professor Samuel Swayze Seward was one of my English professors and at that time a bachelor. He had a Vandyke beard, the soul of a poet, and a great sense of humor. I spent many an evening with him. A poet who was working for his Master's degree did Seward's cooking and was particularly good with corned beef and cabbage. We had wonderful discussions over plates of it. Professor Seward was a mild-mannered man whose appearance belied his great heart and character. He enlisted in an ambulance unit of the First World War and came back with the *Croix de guerre* with palms and a lot of other real medals. I took him to lunch at the Olympic Club the day after his return and tried to draw him out on some of his war experiences. I had no luck at all. In response to my question as to what about the war impressed him most, he answered that it was the sound of horses galloping—in iambic pentameter. He declined to go to a baseball game with me and I left him in the club library reading a volume on the *Private Life and Letters of the Romans.*

I cannot attempt to name all of the teachers who entered into my life at Stanford because there were many of them. Fine, human, understanding men whom I remember with a glow of satisfaction and comfort. Those men convinced me of the great work that can be done in the lower division of a university when boys and girls are in their teens and in the formative period of their lives. Those years are the important ones and call for the impress of the best teachers we have. The great minds of the faculty of the Stanford of my day as an undergraduate come close to me in friendliness and are still vivid to me. I make no pretense of having grasped their learning or their knowledge, but I want the Lower Division at Stanford to be preserved so that boys and girls and great minds and characters can meet.

My four years at Stanford were productive of fine friendships and heartening memories. I kept up with my classes, worked for necessary money at various things on the outside, and participated in many phases of college life. I led the band and at times the orchestra, and that meant at least two nights of practicing a week. I was a member of Sword and Sandals, which was the dramatic club, and took part in quite a few of the college plays. These ranged from farces and student-written pieces to Old English productions and Shakespeare. Between music and the drama and library work, my nights were pretty well occupied on the campus. We lived in Palo Alto, and three round trips on foot were generally the order of the day. There were no automobiles, and even when they came in vogue none were allowed on the campus. Occasionally, I had a bicycle, but Bracchi's bus at five or ten cents a ride was too expensive for my blood. I went out for track as a broad jumper and in borrowed spikes managed to jump twenty-one feet, three inches, the first day out. That wasn't very far, but in those days a little more stretching would have given me a place in a Stanford-California meet. Dad Moulton, the track coach, didn't like my form and started making me over. Before that could be accomplished, I tore a ligament in my leg and took to crutches. I probably wasn't varsity athletic material, but I did get into all of the class events. I was catcher on my class baseball team and essayed a varsity contest or two. Waseda University sent a baseball team from Japan and Stanford played them a five-game series, as I remember. I caught one of the games. In the ninth inning the score was 3 to 1 in our favor, two outs, two strikes, and two balls on the batter, and three Japanese on base. Naturally the runner off third made a pretense of running for the home plate. With great presence of mind, I pegged the ball toward third base. When the left fielder finally retrieved the ball all three runners were in and we were beaten 4 to 3. It took me quite a while to live that lapse down and I still am ribbed for it occasionally by some of the old-timers.

I was a member of the English Club and had wonderful evenings with our various guests of honor. Henry Van Dyke was particularly outstanding; Joaquin Miller was with us on several occasions—a most interesting personage but something of a problem. I was delegated to look out for him on arrival and "ride herd" until his departure. He was unorthodox, to say the least, but he read his own verse in most compelling style and was always welcome at the English Club gatherings. Paul Edwards, my classmate, and now President of the Stanford Board of Trustees, was president of the English Club and I have his signature on my membership certificate and also on the Sword and Sandals scroll.

At Thanksgiving and Christmas various friends of my sister and myself would go to Irvington with us for the holidays. I remember particularly that Merle Thorpe went with me on two or three occasions. Merle and I were particular friends, and are to this day. We were both working our way through college and both played the cornet, which meant band and orchestra work. It never was quite clear during the first year which one of us was the band leader. We used to divide the band into two parts for political rallies occurring the same night at different places. I remember particularly when one segment played for the Republicans at Mayfield, with Cutler conducting, while Thorpe played his boys for the Democrats at Redwood, and each group collected the going wage of $25. The advantage of such co-operation can be readily seen.

On Merle's first Thanksgiving with me at Irvington, we had a family dinner of at least thirty relatives. My Grandfather Durham, as was his custom, called on Merle to say grace. He did it without a tremor and

64

as though he was used to it. During his stay of three or four days with us, he captivated everyone, particularly my grandfather and grandmother, and their older relations. Merle told some stories too at which the elder people laughed—none of them by any stretch of the imagination risqué, but I know I couldn't have gotten away with them. At my suggestion Merle had brought his cornet along, and at the Thanksgiving services in the Irvington Church we played a duet. We also had a great deal of music and family singing around the fireplace at night. Merle Thorpe is one of the outstanding writers and speakers in America today and an expert on public relations. He was for many years editor and publisher of *Nation's Business*, a contributor to leading magazines, and has written many books. He is now a director of Cities Service and in charge of public relations. I revel in his friendship which has covered half a century.

Mrs. Stanford, while she traveled a great deal, was much on the campus during my time in the University. She drove about in a barouche behind two sleek horses and always with the same coachman. Frequently she had Dr. Jordan with her, and she apparently enjoyed picking up students and asking them to ride with her. Many times was I the fortunate one. Sometimes Dr. Jordan was along and sometimes not. Mrs. Stanford would ply me with all manner of questions which I answered to the best of my ability. She seemed yearningly eager to find out just what the University was doing for us, and sometimes she would refer to particular members of the faculty and want to know if they were teaching us as they should. Some of her questioning was almost embarrassing, particularly when Dr. Jordan was with her. No one who had the rare privilege of being with her could question her earnestness of purpose or her constant prayer that her boys and girls would not ever fail her. All of the students held Mrs. Stanford in the greatest affection and respect. There were stories of her turning to spiritualism on the death of Leland, Jr., and of little eccentricities that might bring smiles to the unthinking, but her students saw nothing but perfection in her and worshipped her as the great lady she was. Mrs. Stanford used to go to the Memorial Church, where the Florentine workers, whom she had brought with her from Florence, were fashioning mosaics into pictures. Students would flock there too and it was a rare treat to observe her directing these men in their white smocks high up on a scaffolding. Undoubtedly she cramped their style, but they showed her every reverence and did nothing but nod assent as long as she stayed in the Church. There was the time, too, when Stanford won a California football game played on the Stanford campus. I took the band over to her home to serenade her after the game. She had her servants pass out cookies and lemonade and then she came out on the front porch to address us. A football victory was in the air, but at a signal every sound was hushed. Mrs. Stanford said, "I am so glad you boys won that baseball game today." And it was her great tribute that nobody in the crowd laughed or groaned, but all applauded vociferously.

Having seen Senator Stanford when I was a small boy and knowing Mrs. Stanford at the University, I was particularly thrilled in the summer of 1937 by meeting in New York with Mrs. Gordon S. Rentschler and her sister. Gordon Rentschler was president of the National City Bank of New York, and later chairman of the board; he died only a few years ago. Mrs. Rentschler was Mary Coolidge of Boston. She told me that her father, Charles A. Coolidge, was one of the original architects for the University. She and her sister said that the entire family had urged their father to write his reminiscences and he had barely started them when he died. Mrs. Rentschler sent me what Mr. Coolidge called "Random Jottings," together with a number of photographs of the early beginnings of Stanford University which had been found among the family pictures. I turned these over to President Wilbur, who had the notes and photographs incorporated in a portfolio and they are now in the Stanford Library. Mr. Coolidge's account follows:

After Mr. Richardson died, I made a deal with the firm we formed (Shepley, Rutan and Coolidge). I had never traveled much around the United States, and I wanted to do so—to go to every State in the Union, and to every capital city in the States; and if in this way I got any work, they, of course, could pay my expenses; if not, I could pay them myself. The result of this was that I got a good deal of work. To come back to the University of Palo Alto: On that trip I met Governor and Mrs. Stanford. The Governor spoke of his plan to build a university; and it was decided in the course of the conversations that they see the various universities in the country. They came East to see Harvard, and I took them out and introduced them to President Eliot; that is the time the

66

famous interview occurred between the Governor and President Eliot. After looking at each other for a while, he said "Mr. Eliot, how much is your whole plant worth?" President Eliot explained to him it was not a question of dollars and cents, it was a question much greater than that; it was a question of education, getting men together, etc. In fact he gave him a long talk about what he should do to found a university; because the Governor, at that time, had the one idea to found a college where men when they graduated could immediately go out and go to work; and he did not think very much of the graduates of Harvard College, because, he said, he had them employed on a cable road in San Francisco, and they did not know enough to make change correctly! *His* college was to be a practical one. The result of this was that he gave me the job of making sketches of his college. I made some sketches, and I went out there; and I asked him if I could consult with Frederick Law Olmsted (the landscape architect); and later Mr. Olmsted and I went out there together. I brought out some preliminary sketches to see whether the Governor would approve the plan or not. He said "Fine!—and we shall begin work next Monday." As a matter of fact I should have had a year or so to prepare for this; but I didn't say so to him, but went up to San Francisco and engaged a band and ordered a silver spade. The Governor dug the first sods of earth, and we started in. I sat up nights to make these drawings in a little office with the engineers out there, and 2,500 coolies came down to make the excavations. I made the drawings during the night, and they dug the foundations in the daytime; and that is the way the thing started.

The layout of Stanford University was interesting, because I had seen all these Spanish buildings that had been in California for a long time. I made a design for the buildings in the Mission Style, which was the first time that this was done for modern buildings. Others took it up, and that was the beginning of the Mission Style in California. That was one of the things that really counted.

The layout of the University was that the educational buildings were in six parallelograms, and all the dwellings, streets, etc., radiated from that, so that all these streets led up to the educational buildings. At that time there was a great deal of vacant land around, but now Palo Alto is a large, prosperous place. The buildings were made low with the idea of safety in case of earthquakes; and as a matter of fact those first buildings which I built out there were not destroyed by the earthquakes which have occurred since then.

There was considerable criticism of some of the buildings which did not stand up, and I know that Mr. Lathrop and Charles Edward Hodges, the resident architect, did not agree on many things. My impression is that Mr. Hodges died shortly after the earthquake. Most of the construction following the earthquake had to do with restoration and repair. The University was without funds for any buildings and money was not available for anything except the most necessary repairs. Architect Clarence Ward, I know, was retained for restoration of the Church.

There was no Buildings and Grounds Committee of the Trustees until 1914 but there was a Ranch Committee. Mr. Hoover came back from Europe in 1913 and that is when Bakewell and Brown were retained on the Thomas Welton Stanford Art Gallery, really the first new construction following the earthquake. Dr. Wilbur and Mr. Hoover, principally Mr. Hoover, made the decision as to Bakewell and Brown. Parenthetically, I believe that Mr. Hoover's home had been started by Mrs. Hoover under the direction of Mr. Clark, and I believe Mr. Hoover was not too well pleased with it. Similarly, the President's house had for its architect Mr. Mullgardt, who I believe was chosen by Mrs. Wilbur.

The Buildings and Grounds Committee, as I said, came into existence about 1914 and undoubtedly was the result of the thinking of Mr. Hoover and Dr. Wilbur along the lines of their architectural plans. Dr. Jordan by this time was Chancellor and Dr. Branner was President. There was still a Ranch Committee, and the first Grounds Committee was Messrs. Newhall, Leon Sloss, and Vanderlynn Stow. These men would frankly go along on any building plans or architectural selections that might be suggested by Mr. Hoover or Dr. Wilbur, and that is what subsequent building and grounds committees did. I can say this because I became a Trustee in 1920 and was continuously on the committee or its chairman for a great many years, although the bylaws stated that the Campus Committee "shall have general charge of the Campus and its housing quarters." We did not, to my recollection, ever initiate anything or do very much in the way of independent action. The membership of the committee was generally Mr. Hoover, Judge Nourse, and myself. Buildings would be decided upon at the campus and Comptroller Roth would sometimes call attention to the fact that the plans would first have to be approved by the Campus Committee.

When I first went on the Board, Judge Nourse and I were on the committee, and a sharp difference of opinion arose in connection with the matter of tuition. The Judge and I understood Dr. Wilbur and Mr. Hoover to indicate that the money would go for professors' salaries.

68

However, a building program for new professors' houses was launched. The Judge and I made a fight of it in principle and, needless to say, came out second best. We really had quite a session over this one, with night meetings on the campus with Dr. Wilbur and others, and I had several meetings with Mr. Hoover on the subject. This committee was in no sense a really live active committee until Mr. Morell became chairman fairly recently.

From the time of Mr. Hoover's return from Belgium in 1913, at which time Bakewell and Brown were employed until seven or eight years ago, there was never any question about Bakewell and Brown being accepted as the University architects. At the first suggestion of a change, made in Board meeting and having to do with some preliminary plans to be drawn, as I recall for the Law Building, Mr. Hoover made a particularly strong battle for Bakewell and Brown. It was not until Dr. Tresidder became President of the University that Mr. Spencer came into the picture. He had been the architect for Don on the Hotel Ahwahnee at Yosemite.

I recall that for a long time there were in the museum the original sketches of competitive plans for the building of Stanford University, and included was a large bird's-eye view of the accepted plan of Shepley, Rutan, and Coolidge. The circumstances of the competition I do not know but I am sure it was guided by Senator Stanford and may have accounted for Mr. Coolidge's expressed surprise that he had been chosen.

When Don Tresidder became President, without the Trustees paying much attention to it he presented Lewis Mumford's memorandum on planning. Really without the Trustees' knowledge this was incorporated as our architectural "bible." We were saddled with it, and the new style of architecture without the tile roofs was the result. Herman Phleger, a Trustee, referred to some of it as an example of "Early Marinship Architecture." From that time on the Trustees have watched the situation very carefully and are trying in every way to correct it. Personally, the so-called modern architecture does not appeal to me nor does it to many of our Trustees. We still like the stone buildings or appearance of them and red tile roofs.

In 1905 Mrs. Stanford died suddenly in Hawaii. This was my junior year at the University and I was president of the Junior Class. Alfred

Trowbridge, my good friend who after University days lived with me for a number of years, was president of the Senior Class. We originated the custom of the Senior Class of the University placing flowers at the Stanford mausoleum. In a simple ceremony in the old Chapel, Al declared the establishment of the custom as a trust, and I accepted it in behalf of all graduating classes to come. The custom has been carried out for forty-eight years and is now a Stanford tradition.

It had long been a custom for "Junior Day" to be a University holiday ending with the Junior Prom. Naturally all University festivities were curtailed until after the funeral services, and with the distance involved, considerable time elapsed. Dr. Jordan wrote me a letter at the time asking that Junior Day be held in abeyance and stating that it would be possible to have the day "later in April." No member of the class or others of the University community allowed me to forget the promised holiday. I called a class meeting, which was largely attended and not limited to juniors. The holiday was voted unanimously for the following Friday. I went to Dr. Jordan's office, reminded him of his promise, and told him what the class had done. He smiled assent and, in view of the great amount of classwork that had been lost, suggested we compromise on a half-holiday. I suggested Friday morning and he suggested Friday afternoon. Not knowing what to do then I went home. A student reporter for the *Stanford Daily* had gone directly from the class meeting and inserted in the *Daily* over my signature an announcement of the holiday. Dr. Jordan had a very prominent notice in the same issue that my notice was to be disregarded and there would be a half-holiday Friday afternoon. W. H. B. Fowler, for many years Business Manager of the *San Francisco Chronicle* and at that time editor of the *Daily*, wrote an article captioned: "President vs. President," with myself on the receiving end. The general tenor was that President Jordan was delighted to find that I had left him desk room, but even so a half-holiday would prevail. In later years Dr. Jordan chuckled over the incident frequently and the story grew considerably in his telling.

I cannot think of Dr. Jordan without recalling his marvelous sense of humor and the many delightful occasions over the years that I encountered it. In my freshman year he spoke at a football rally on the

70

campus the night before a Stanford-California game. The games then were played in San Francisco at the old Sixteenth and Harrison Street grounds. President Jordan told us that we were going to the big city and that the honor of the University was in our hands. "I want you," he said, "to behave like gentlemen. Stay out of saloons for saloons are evil." Then he paused and added forcefully: "If you must go in a saloon, however, be sure and give the California yell."

Several years after my graduation, I was on a train from Visalia to San Francisco. Aboard also were Dr. Jordan, Hazel Pedlar, and Mary Ashe Miller, Stanford newspaperwomen. They had attended a state women's club convention at Visalia, where Dr. Jordan spoke. At Goshen Junction, the Doctor got off to walk around and the ladies asked him to bring the morning papers. The four of us were seated facing each other as Dr. Jordan handed out the papers. I noticed they were dated as of the day before. The ladies, not wanting to hurt his feelings, read them carefully through. When they had finished, Dr. Jordan produced two fresh ones and said "How would you like to read today's papers?"

I can never forget a bit of philosophical advice that Dr. Jordan gave me early in my university career. Charles Lathrop, Mrs. Stanford's brother, was Business Manager and Treasurer of the University. As manager and promoter of various student activities, Paul Edwards and I found Mr. Lathrop rather difficult at times and so we complained to President Jordan. The President undoubtedly had his difficulties too, for he smiled and said: "There are three ways of dealing with an accepted fact. If you don't like it, do away with it entirely. If you can't do that, mold it to your liking. If you can't do that—make the best of it. Now boys, what are you going to do?" We made the best of it, and his advice is still good.

It was my great privilege to be very close to Dr. Jordan and see a great deal of him. He had a great influence on my life, as I am sure he did on the lives of countless others. It seems to me now that he always talked of human things and made no attempt to display his great knowledge of science or impose it upon you. As I look back I realize that the art of conversation was one of his strongest points and he brought young men and women along in that art. He may not have been much of an administrator, but he gave Stanford its indelible character and he had fine and inspiring men around him. There was no affectation about him. He produced the effect of simplicity and always made me feel comfortable.

Shortly before he closed out his twenty-five years as President, Mr. Hoover and Dr. Wilbur asked me to head up a Jordan Portrait Committee, as they wanted a good likeness of him preserved. Xavier Martinez, who was an excellent artist but very much of a Bohemian and one of the rollicking members of the Bohemian Club, was chosen to paint the portrait. Dr. Jordan and Martinez did not hit it off at all. Dr. Jordan did not like Xavier and Xavier had no use for the President of the University. Dr. Jordan was then working on his *Days of a Man* and would not sit as Martinez wanted him to sit but was so engrossed in his writing that he at times was undoubtedly oblivious of Martinez' presence. Martinez was never punctual and they just did not hit it off. Finally Martinez exploded and said he was through, and as a matter of fact he never came back to Stanford. I knew he had a portrait, however, and was asked by the committee to run him down and try to get it. We had started out with an original price of $2,500 but I was authorized to go as high as $250 if we could buy Martinez off, even if we did not get the portrait. The artist lived in the Berkeley hills, and I traipsed over the fields one afternoon trying to find his little house. I finally did and the door was opened by a beautiful lady who I thought was Mrs. Martinez and who I later found out was one of his models. I then started to work on Xavier, whom I knew quite well, to have a look at the portrait. The model would call him into another room and I could hear her whispering to him to look out for me, that I was trying to trick him. Martinez knew me well enough, and finally brought out the portrait, which he apologized for just before he unveiled it. The likeness was excellent—better than any I have ever seen of Dr. Jordan, but Martinez, probably under the influence of red wine, had paid tribute to Dr. Jordan as an ichthyologist and painted little minnows for vest buttons and for a collar had a big carp around Dr. Jordan's neck looking soulfully into his eyes. I used all of my arts in trying to get the portrait, but Martinez, I think regretting his playfulness, would not let it go. He did settle, however, for the $250, which he seemed very happy to get, although the model gave me quite a tongue-lashing for taking advantage of him. We later commissioned another artist and paid out our $2,500.

In 1916 I was elected president of the Stanford Alumni Association and served for two terms. In the spring of that year we had an alumni luncheon of about four hundred in the Memorial Court, at which I presided. Dr. Wilbur, tall and immaculate, in a frock coat and a very high collar, stood in sharp contrast to Chancellor Jordan, whom he was succeeding. Dr. Jordan's clothes were baggy and his hair was shaggy and he lumbered in his walk, but he had a twinkle in his eye and gave one of the finest talks I ever heard him deliver. He gave an account of his stewardship of the first twenty-five years of the University. He spoke of the "six dark years, illuminated and saved by the devoted loyalty of Mrs. Stanford," and I remember a phrase of his to the effect that he "wanted to bring the education of tomorrow straight to the youth of today." He stressed that Stanford in its founding had no history to fall back upon and that in its progress it was hampered by none, but that traditions and associations were ours to make. All we had was all the experience of the world to search out and use as we pleased.

Dr. Jordan was to me one of the greatest speakers I have ever listened to. He spoke in a monotone but with an appealing inflection. All of his life he had been a tremendous reader, and he had command of a great many subjects. He could always draw on the wisdom of the ages. Great scientist that he was, he was a poet at heart, and many of his poems were published. None of them were heavy, but were humorous or light and tender. His verse to his beloved young daughter, Barbara, and his "Castles in Spain" will, in my opinion, always live. His many tributes to Mrs. Jordan, who died in late 1952 and whom he always called "Miss Jessie" are monuments of their kind and showed clearly his great humanness.

Dr. Branner, who had been interim President between Dr. Jordan and Dr. Wilbur, was presented by me at the alumni lunch and took full advantage of his title of "Emeritus" to poke fun at himself and renew the deep affection all Stanford men and women had for that wise and kindly man.

As my senior year approached its close, I was busy preparing for final examinations and in rounding out the various courses I had undertaken. Commencement was set for May, and in addition to the degree I was after, I was taking work to qualify me for a high-school teacher's certificate. I probably did not seriously contemplate teaching, but my relationship with the faculty had been so inspiring that I sometimes thought of a university professorship as my ultimate goal. Professors Lee Emerson Bassett and Melville Best Anderson, my major professor, talked to me about going to Harvard for my Master's and further degrees, and assured me of an instructorship in English at Stanford thereafter. It was attractive to think about and I was trying for a high school certificate as a preliminary. I was seeking this in English, Latin, French, and history—a rather ambitious program. Professor Anderson, who was a scholar of many facets, conducted an oral examination of each student personally, in every subject on which the candidate desired a recommendation. This took an hour or two and had acquired the reputation of a grueling ordeal. I got along all right until it came to French. After the Professor had tried to converse with me in the language and had me read some passages, he looked considerably puzzled. "Do you intend to teach French?" he asked. I thought I was supposed to reply affirmatively so I said, "Yes, Sir." "Well," said the Professor, "I'll tell you what I'll do, I'll pass you if you give me your word that before you attempt to teach it, you'll get a job in a French laundry and keep it for a year."

On the afternoon of April 17 I appeared before three examining professors in an advanced course in literature, which required two hours of oral presentation on my part. The subject was Beaumont and Fletcher's *Isle of Man* and I had to talk without notes. I wasn't called on until late in the afternoon and was getting along unusually well. I saw by the clock that there were not two hours before adjournment and it occurred to me that if I gave everything I had before adjournment I would not be called on to resume the next day. I had my audience laughing and could see that my plan had worked. Professor Anderson stopped me and said, "Mr. Cutler will resume tomorrow and we will look forward to another hour of him."

Next morning, which was Wednesday, April 18, I wakened at 4:00 A.M., propped myself up in bed, and started studying Beaumont and Fletcher all over again. By trying to be cute the day before, I had ex-

74

hausted my repertoire and had an hour's recitation of new material ahead of me. Above my head was an old-fashioned set of bookshelves suspended from the molding. At thirteen minutes after five, the bookshelves and books fell on me, and the great earthquake of 1906 was in process.

According to the official record, the earthquake lasted only forty-seven seconds, but that is a long time for an earthquake, and the havoc wrought is history. To the north the glow and smoke from burning San Francisco were plainly visible. I dressed and hurried to the campus, where ruins were all about. Two men had been killed: Junius Hanna, a student from Pennsylvania, whom I knew well, and Otto Gerdes, a fireman in the powerhouse. Three or four students living in Encina Hall were injured but not badly. The Memorial Church, the unfinished library, and numerous arches in the Quadrangle were completely wrecked and practically no building escaped some considerable damage. Although the first estimate of damage of $4,000,000 was exaggerated, the loss was nevertheless a heavy one.

Several bulletins were issued by Dr. Jordan and almost immediately he announced that all University activities would be suspended until August. A meeting of the Academic Council was called and degrees voted to all seniors who were up in their studies at the time of the earthquake. One English professor by bulletin called his class together on the post-office steps and announced that we would have to write a final term paper before he would recommend us for graduation in his course. Without library facilities this was quite a task and proved really difficult as practical problems of immediate relief work in San Francisco developed. We remonstrated with him to no avail, and I went to work on the paper as best I could and mailed it to him about a month later from San Francisco. In August when the University reopened, the papers we had written were still in the professor's post-office box unclaimed and unread. He had left the University a few days after issuing his weird order to us and never returned. I think none of us ever forgave him.

On the afternoon of April 18 I was certified as a relief worker by Dr. Jordan, and with James Lanagan, our football coach and a great Stanford man, reported to Mayor Eugene Schmitz in San Francisco. I was put in charge of a bread and milk station at Twenty-fifth and Valencia Streets in the old Southern Pacific depot. I dealt out bread and milk all day long and slept in the depot on a bench at night. Two of us operated this station for more than a month and did special work at times and of different kinds. My cousin, W. F. Barnes, who lived at Clay and Scott Streets, had a White Steamer, which I drove on special missions and always with a soldier guard armed with a rifle. The credentials I carried were honored by the railroad for free passage and I went back and forth to Palo Alto frequently. A big gap had been torn in the railroad embankment at San Mateo, which for a considerable time necessitated a long walk between trains.

When conditions settled down to routine and there was no emergency need for student relief, I returned to Palo Alto to the various jobs I had and a few new ones. I was still Palo Alto correspondent for the *San Jose Mercury*, and the skating rink had reopened for my night cornet playing. Guards were required at the University, for the buildings were still wide open to prowlers. Dr. Jordan decreed that no student was worth more than $1.50 for a twelve-hour day and $1.75 for a twelve-hour night. That might have been debatable, but the University paid no more. Frank Havenner, now congressman, and I became two of Stanford's most stalwart guards, sometimes by day, sometimes at night. We augmented our pay considerably by cleaning brick at so much per brick. It wasn't pretty work and it was hard on the hands, but it was remunerative, and all in all we had a profitable summer.

The 1906 Commencement, which ordinarily would have been in May, was set for September 15. I did not want to establish myself in a permanent job until I had actually graduated. Early in the spring I began thinking about the position of graduate manager of athletics, then an elective job. My close friend, Richard Barrett, had been manager for two years, but after the earthquake he decided not to run again but to take up the practice of law. During the summer I definitely decided to run and started my campaign as soon as the semester opened in August. Election was to be shortly after Commencement. Graduation exercises were held in the old Assembly Hall. Dr. Jordan and President Benjamin Ide Wheeler of the University of California both addressed us. With the majority of my relatives present as witnesses, I became a Stanford alumnus. Two weeks later the student-body election was to take place. Dudley Sales, varsity pitcher and a very popular figure in campus life, and I were the two candidates for graduate manager, and the job paid $100 a month. The campaign was a vigorous one and had one amusing side. *Two Gentlemen of Verona* was in the process of preparation, with Sales and me cast as the "Gentlemen"—he as Valentine and I as Proteus. The night before election, one of the opposition, deep in his cups, confided to me that two hundred extra votes would be stuffed into the ballot box and that I was a sure loser. Such turned out to be the case. There were in fact more votes cast than were registered in college and I lost by 175 votes. This meant, of course, that I actually won by 25 votes. Being the loser, I would not recount this if all of the men involved had not admitted it to me over the years. Sales was not a party to it and knew nothing about it. Other motives were involved. A committee of the faculty investigated the matter, and even though Sales was re-elected a second year, he was not allowed to continue. Although it was the best thing for me that I was defeated, it was quite a blow.

IV

SANTA CRUZ, CALIFORNIA

T HE NIGHT of my defeat for manager I stayed with Karl Bickel, who took many courses with me and was a good friend. He was later president of the United Press. He knew a good deal about the election maneuverings and the students involved, so we talked most of the night and pretty well reconstructed the entire plot. Karl's fraternity house boasted a telephone, a box affair attached to the wall. Before we were up it rang noisily and was for Karl. I heard him say: "Thank you for saying that; I enjoyed my experience with you too but I have a job and can't take yours." At the word "job," I let out a yell, and without knowing what it was all about or to whom Karl was talking, I said, "If it's a job—I'll take it!" Bickel put his hand over the old-fashioned mouthpiece of the telephone and said: "It's Duncan McPherson of the *Santa Cruz Sentinel* telephoning and he wants a city editor. I had the job last summer and he wants me back, but I've got another job. If you want it, hurry up and say so because McPherson's paying for the call and he won't wait long." I had never been in a newspaper office but I shouted, "I'll take it!" Karl relayed it: "I have an experienced man who will be down on the afternoon train leaving here at three o'clock!" He added that Cutler could handle everything just the way he had done the year before, and then the words, "Yes, to-night"—the telephone clicked and I was a city editor!

Bickel spent most of the day briefing and advising me. He told me to be friendly and everybody in the office would help me, particularly the linotype operator and the printer's devil, who would work together and teach me how to write heads.

And so I went to my first job as a college graduate. I walked into the *Sentinel* office just before dinner time and met Duncan McPherson and his business partner, Charles Waldron. The two of them told me to have some cards printed with "City Editor" on them and go to work. My pay would be $16 a week and Bert Spencer, the linotype operator,

78

would show me over the plant. Bert did more than that. He told me all the things I would have to do, because I told him first that I had never been in a newspaper office and I didn't know how to begin. It was a good thing I did, because Spencer took me in charge and was my fast friend and tutor as long as I was with the *Sentinel*. He was more than a linotype operator. The Associated Press correspondency was one of the prerequisites of the paper and was in Spencer's name. Similarly, the printer's devil was the correspondent for the *San Francisco Call*, then a morning paper. I thought it best to make no inquiries about previous deals, but I soon learned that the city editor did most of the work as correspondent and that a division of the receipts was in order. A very satisfactory arrangement was soon made amongst us and proved fairly remunerative to all parties. Being city editor meant that I first had to rustle the news, write it, compose the headlines, and read the proof. This meant, of course, that I put the paper to bed and didn't go home until it was safely on its way. I earned my $16 a week, and this was given me in silver every Monday by Duncan McPherson out of a leather sack as we stood in line by his desk.

"Home" was the Durham cottage at Garfield Park, which was unused except at Church State Meeting time in the summer. There I lived alone and didn't like it. I did my own cooking except on payday when I celebrated with a restaurant meal and an extra piece of pie. I sent $50 a month home, and my extra earnings from the metropolitan press became increasingly important. The famous Colton will contest was on in Judge Smith's court, and the well-known Delphine M. Delmas, later Harry Thaw's attorney in the Stanford White murder trial, was one of the attorneys with Judge Slack on the other side. I came to know all parties quite well and the case provided many columns of good reading in San Francisco papers as well as in Santa Cruz County. The Republican State Convention was held in Santa Cruz shortly after my arrival. I was accredited not only from the *Sentinel* but from the Associated Press, as I had in the meantime been substituted in fact for Bert Spencer as its correspondent. There was no direct primary in those days and candidates were chosen by the old political processes. A large tent was erected on the boardwalk at the beach for general meeting purposes but the actual work and behind-the-scene trading was at the luxurious and spectacular Sea Beach Hotel overlooking Monterey Bay. All of the top newspapermen from California were in attendance and many from the the East, and I started some of the most interesting friendships of my life. Many magazine writers and newsmen had gravitated to California, attracted by San Francisco's great disaster, by rumblings of scandal in its city administration, and by business rebuilding. All of them were in Santa Cruz and all were probing for something they could not quite reach. It was in the air and newspapermen talked more than usual about motives and "blowoffs."

George C. Pardee of Oakland was the Republican Governor whose term was about to expire. He was by far the most popular candidate, and from all I could learn his administration had been a good one. It was common knowledge, however, that the big corporations, notably the Southern Pacific, would oppose him. Governor Pardee had openly attacked the Standard Oil Company and he was not one of that corporation's favorites. Pardee had built up a strong personal following, however, and seemed the logical choice. Two candidates were in the running against him: J. O. Hayes of San Jose, who owned the *San Jose Mercury* with his brother, E. A. Hayes, a congressman, and James N. Gillett of Humboldt County, a lawyer and also a congressman. Abe Ruef, the acknowledged political boss of San Francisco, was being very much talked about in connection with graft in that city, but the talk had not been serious enough to discredit him and he was a mighty factor at the Santa Cruz convention.

In the opening days Pardee seemed certain to gain the nomination. Ruef one day had a meeting with the newspapermen under a pledge of secrecy and told us that he would support Gillett. It was common knowledge later that he had introduced Hayes merely as a stalking horse and that money was involved somewhere in his switch. Pardee's strength began to wane and everything possible was done to belittle him. The day before nominations, Governor Pardee was addressing the convention when Charley Shortridge entered the tent auditorium. Charley was a brother of Sam, later United States Senator from California, and the two of them at one time owned the *San Francisco Call*, when it was a morning paper. Charley Shortridge was a state Senator from Santa Clara County and owned a newspaper there. He was unusually bright and personable, but an "outlaw" and very much of a character. He imbibed convivially at times and habitually wore a Prince Albert coat and high hat, carried a gold-headed cane, and usually had a rose in the buttonhole of his lapel. As he came in the auditorium, the crowd began yelling "Speech, speech!" Governor Pardee was forced to retire; Shortridge was hoisted to the platform and held up his hand for silence. When he had it, he used the preamble for which he was noted: "Will someone name a subject, please?" A cry, "The price of prunes in the Santa Clara Valley!" started him off and he continued hilariously until the sergeant at arms dragged him off stage. It was an entertaining but disgraceful episode and there were others which made it clear that Pardee was doomed.

The night before nominations Ruef gave us the slate under pledge that it would not be published until after they were made. Gillett, of course, was to be Governor. On Ruef's program was Hyatt for State Superintendent of Public Instruction, a fine man in every way, and to Ruef's credit that he was chosen. As an illustration of the devious way in which Ruef worked, however, the next day in a beautiful speech on womanhood and woman's influence in education he placed Miss Kate Ames of Napa in nomination and affected surprise when all of his henchmen to a man voted for Hyatt.

The night after the nomination I attended a dinner at the palatial home of Major Frank McLaughlin in Santa Cruz. The Major, according to legend, had acquired his wealth by a large bet on Fitzsimmons in his fight with Corbett at Carson City. The Major was then chairman of the Republican State Central Committee and the dinner was a love feast for all factions. Unknowingly, one picture was taken showing Abe Ruef's arm about the shoulder of a Supreme Court Justice who later rocked the state with scandal. The picture was published once, I believe, then suppressed, and I doubt is now in existence.

To digress—the name of Major McLaughlin's estate was Golden Gate Villa. He called me one day at the *Sentinel* office and told me that his Japanese gardener who had laid out Golden Gate Villa was dead. I misunderstood him and, not knowing my San Francisco history very well, had quite a story and a big headline to the effect that the Japanese gardener who had laid out Golden Gate Park was dead. Years later, when I was a San Francisco Park Commissioner, I was to be reminded of that frequently by John McLaren, as I was immediately by E. K. Taylor, editor of the rival Santa Cruz paper *The Surf*.

Major McLaughlin was a suave and courteous gentleman with all the graces. One morning after giving an excellently appointed dinner the night before to friends, the Major's body and that of his unmarried daughter, always his hostess, were found dead by the Major's hand. His money was all gone and that was his way out.

Right after the Santa Cruz convention, Charley Shortridge rented the Garden Theatre in San Jose and invited all San Jose to attend. The theater overflowed and Shortridge addressed the crowd and accused the Hayes brothers, J. O. and E. A., of burning down their home for the insurance money. There were no more highly respected citizens in all California than J. O. and E. A. Hayes, and their contribution to the progress of Santa Clara Valley can never be measured. The peculiarities of Charley Shortridge were so well known that no one could take him seriously. It was just an entertaining evening. The Messrs. Hayes, however, had Shortridge before the court on a charge of criminal libel. I attended part of the trial. Shortridge was his own attorney and he would say: "Mr. Shortridge—I beg your pardon, Senator Shortridge, did you on the blank day of April make a speech in the Garden Theatre?" "I did" was his reply, "and a mighty fine speech it was." J. O. Hayes had black hair and black whiskers, while E. A. Hayes had red hair and a red goatee. Shortridge in court referred to them as "Black" Hayes and "Red" Hayes. Their attorney quite naturally objected, whereupon Shortridge commented, "Well, as 'Black' and 'Red' are objected to, I will hereafter refer to them collectively as the 'Roulette Brothers.'"

Shortridge was found guilty and ordered immediately to stand up for sentence. The Judge excoriated him mercilessly for libeling fellow townsmen of unquestionable reputation. "Because of your well-known idiosyncracies," said the Judge, "you are assessed a fine of $500 with no alternative of jail imprisonment." Shortridge adjusted his frock coat, picked up his high hat and gloves and cane, and said with wonder in his voice, "Do I understand, Your Honor, that I am fined $500 and that if I do not pay I do not have to go to jail?" "You understand correctly,"

82

replied the Judge sternly; "it is left to your honor as a man to pay." "That will be all right, Your Honor. Good day, Your Honor; good day, everybody." And Charley walked out with a fine unpaid and never paid.

About this time Shortridge offered me the job of city editor on his San Jose paper. He said, "The job is worth $50 a week. I don't know whether I can pay it to you or not, or whether you are worth it, but let's try it together for a while." I declined the adventure.

I decided, in fact, that I had had about enough of the newspaper business. My stay in Santa Cruz had been crowded with excitement. The Colton will case and the Republican convention with its aftermath, the campaign, kept my days and nights occupied. The letdown of ordinary humdrum days with winter coming on, however, wasn't so good. My father's cousin, Frank Barnes, whose White Steamer I had driven during earthquake days, lived in San Francisco and was starting a brick and clay manufacturing plant at Antioch. He had been a very successful lumberman and was semiretired. He offered me a place in his Antioch operations and in fact urged me to go with him. His only son had been killed in one of his lumber mills and his wife and daughter were like our own family. My mother and sister were still in Palo Alto and I decided to have a look at the Bay Area for a little while until I could make up my mind what to do permanently.

It was good to be home again. My mother's cooking was still better than mine. I commuted to San Francisco where I had a job on the *Call*. All eyes were on San Francisco and its scandal. A new Grand Jury had been impaneled late in 1906 and it marked the beginning of the graft prosecution. Prior to that Francis J. Heney and William J. Burns had been retained by Fremont Older, fighting publisher of the *San Francisco Bulletin*, and Rudolph Spreckels, to investigate everything about Abe Ruef, the boss, and Eugene Schmitz, the Mayor. Heney was a crusading attorney who had successfully prosecuted timberland frauds in Oregon, and William J. Burns resigned from the United States Secret Service to devote his attention to San Francisco. Spreckels' friendship with President Theodore Roosevelt had made this possible. The graft prosecution is now history. Ruef and Schmitz were indicted. Ruef was found guilty and sent to San Quentin prison. Schmitz was found

83

guilty too, but the verdict was reversed by the Supreme Court because he had been indicted as Eugene Schmitz, an individual, and not as Mayor of San Francisco. Many of San Francisco's most prominent citizens were involved, and the city was really divided into two factions—those who were indicted and those who were not.

Nothing in San Francisco's history rocked the city as did the graft prosecution, for with the exception of a comparative few, all of the men involved in one way or another were sterling citizens. Heney was shot in a crowded courtroom by a witness whom he exposed as an ex-convict, Chief of Police Biggy was drowned, and a Supreme Court justice was found to be involved with a large sum of money. All in all it was dramatic and mysterious, and is still talked about.

ANTIOCH, CALIFORNIA

ALL of this took several years and was most fascinating to a young reporter. However, I left it and went to Antioch, for my cousin had persuaded me that my future lay in a manufacturing career. I stayed in Antioch two years. I started as timekeeper and was manager at the end. I bossed a hundred fifty men of all nationalities, slept in a bunkhouse, and worked long hours. Most of the time we were on a day and night shift, and even when nominally a timekeeper, my work was everything and everywhere. I picked up a patois of all languages, and even though the men laughed at some of my pronunciations, they understood me.

I enjoyed my two years at Antioch. The town itself was wide awake and progressive and had some fine citizens. It was in 1907 that I first met Roy Folger of San Francisco. He was then a special agent for the Royal Insurance Company and for many years has been one of the leading insurance brokers of California. He is, in my opinion—and so considered by many others—the greatest amateur comedian in the United States and only naïvely and slyly conscious of it. He and I teamed together and put on some amateur shows in the opera house for various benefits.

I had my boxing gloves at the pottery and boxed frequently with the employees. A Fourth of July bout was arranged at neighboring Cornwall, once called Black Diamond and now Pittsburg, between one Battling Ortega and Jack McCarthy. Someone in San Francisco interested in McCarthy arranged a job for him with us. He was a pottery worker and trained two or three weeks before the fight. I boxed with him daily. A preliminary bout as curtain raiser to the main event was arranged between Kid Scotty, a local telephone lineman, and myself. Six rounds with a purse of $10—$7.50 to the winner and $2.50 to the loser. I came off with $7.50, and no damage was done to either party. I am still referred to occasionally by my children as a professional.

CHICAGO

ARLY in 1908 I began to plan in earnest on my life's work. I had been out of college about a year and a half, had interesting jobs, and enjoyed myself. At no time, however, did I figure that I was settled for the long pull. My uncle, W. W. Durham, always called "Uncle W.," my mother's brother, was still in Chicago and making a success of the insurance business. Primarily he specialized in surety bonds and was Chicago city manager of the Illinois Surety Company. Uncle W. had been at my Stanford graduation and talked to me then about insurance as my life's work. He wrote me frequently and urged it on every visit to California.

Following an exchange of letters, he asked me to go to Chicago and work with him for a while until I learned something about the business. I could live with him and my cousins Anne and Frank, of whom I was very fond. Not having done much train traveling, I took the long route and saw the country. I went by Portland and Seattle with a side trip to British Columbia, then Northern Pacific to Chicago. I rode in a tourist upper berth, carried a history book for reading, and had the time of my life. It is a trite observation but there is no thrill like the first glimpse of this great country of ours.

I arrived in Chicago on the first day of July, wearing a derby hat. Where I acquired the habit I don't know, but I have always liked them and wore one for many years in season. I had to give them up when people figuratively started throwing rocks at me on Montgomery Street in San Francisco, which is distinctly not a derby hat town. Chicago wasn't either on July first. Probably no city in America observes its hat seasons as does Chicago—and July is for straws. My train arrived early from Minneapolis, about 5:00 A.M., at the old Wells Street Station. I asked the way to LaSalle Street and was told that it was just a few blocks over and parallel. I started to walk on the first street, which was South Water and part of the commission district. Trucks were lined up to warehouses on both sides and I took to the middle of the street. I had only walked a few feet when vegetables and fruit of every description sailed through the air and onto my derby hat. Neither my Stanford degree nor my worldly training as a newspaperman could save me, and I fled precipitately. I have forgotten what time the hat stores opened but it was a long time and I waited in the station. It was with a brand new straw hat that I appeared at my uncle's office.

My stay in Chicago of about six months is more than an outstanding memory. It was a milestone in my life. My Uncle W. may not have known much about underwriting, but he knew how to sell insurance and particularly surety bonds. He had some fine clients, especially among the contractors and bankers, and had built up a fine business. That was over forty years ago, and his great tribute is that those same clients or their successors give their business to W. W. Durham and Company today, of which his son, Frank, is now the head.

Uncle W. kept relentlessly at me along insurance lines and he wasn't very patient, but I learned and I did it his way. I went with him on his calls and he made many of them every day. He hired a two-wheeled trap and a driver and made the rounds of the Loop and occasionally the outlying districts. Watching him work was a revelation. Like all good salesmen, he sometimes in his enthusiasm promised more than his company could deliver, and I learned many a good lesson in observing him admit it or replace an item with something else and leave everybody happy. Uncle W. didn't let me relax a minute of the day. He allowed me $10 a week for spending money and of course bought most of my lunches. Our home life at night was natural and ideal. Aunt Nellie was dead and my cousin, Anne, took her place as the head of the home. Both Anne and Frank today are as my own sister and brother. All of them liked good things and had good things, and Uncle W. was an excellent provider. He had an explosive temper, as sudden as any I have ever seen. Dinner had to be ready the minute he was home and the hour of his arrival was always uncertain. He would break off from an outburst and say grace hurriedly and be all smiles and give forth with interesting stimulating conversation. At the office he was an aggressive, dominating driver, but at home he was a happy father and uncle and a companion whom you enjoyed. He constantly arranged little excursions and shows and entertainment for my cousins and myself. He insisted on our going to church and he went too, but I doubt from the notes he frequently made in his little business book that his mind was ever on the sermon. He told me once that some of his best thinking and planning was done during a long sermon.

Fred Blount, a former banker, was president of the Illinois Surety Company and gave me a lesson in taking financial statements which I have never forgotten. I went into his office one time with the statement of a contractor which we had been after for a long time. The contractor was a big operator and the statement was a good one. Blount, who was a little man with a puckered face, sharp eyes, and a very strong voice, looked over the statement for a while, then tore it to little pieces and threw them in the waste basket. "Bring me a true statement," he bellowed, "and I'll consider it." I stammered and asked him what he meant. He said, "Young man, never forget that a true statement is never in round numbers. No man has exactly $26,000 in the bank or $12,000 in accounts receivable. He might have $26,014.29 and $11,983.02, and his debts too would total in odd cents. Get such a statement from him and we can probably do business."

I could not have been under a better teacher than my uncle or in better insurance surroundings. Chicago is one of the mighty business cities of the world and I was in the give-and-take of it every day. Nowadays insurance companies have schools where young men are trained in the theory of insurance. The students are chosen with great care from the graduating classes of colleges and the companies have quite an investment in the boys before they are of any practical use to their employers. These young men of today are paid a living wage of say $200 per month while the companies try to teach them the business. It is very much of a gamble for both sides, especially the companies. Forty years ago there was no such arrangement and I was thrown the first day into the firing line of rough-and-ready solicitation of insurance. My uncle taught me as I went along. My principal job was to get the business. Others would take care of its acceptance and the underwriting. Bad business was easy to get, and I soon learned what bad business was and not to waste my time going after it. My uncle gave me leads, of course, and I suppose he got an overriding on business I brought in. He

88

didn't make any money at that, for he had to help me financially all of the time I was with him. I learned there that the insurance business is really a profession and that there is no short cut to the mastery of it and that it is a long hard pull before a young man can earn enough at it to support himself, let alone a wife and family. Most insurance companies today will not take young men into their training schools if they are married and yet they pay them a minimum of $200 per month. Young lawyers and doctors have the same hard row when they start. The insurance business of today is infinitely more complicated than it was forty or more years ago but it is fundamentally and basically the same. It is a fine, dignified, useful, and helpful industry, and I am proud to have had a part in it.

Uncle W. was a firm believer in working on a commission basis and without salary or subsidy. He strongly believed that was the only way to get ahead. If you couldn't produce, you weren't going to eat. He used to say that if a young man wanted to learn by starting out on salary, he might as well be selling ribbons in a department store or behind a desk copying figures from a pink slip onto a blue slip. His religion was that selling was the most important part of insurance. Years later the president of my company, Charles R. Miller, referring to my long association with Guy LeRoy Stevick in the West and the results, would say, "You two do all right, and don't change your style because you first have to get the business before Stevick can underwrite it. It takes just as long to build up an insurance business as it does a law business or a medical practice or any of the professional clientele. I am a firm subscriber to the restrictions and regulations that have been placed around the conduct of insurance by insurance commissioners and companies and legislative bodies. In the older days, however, lawyers learned their law on horseback and learned it well. Some outstanding doctors started practice after very little study. So it is with insurance, and the people's interest has been well taken care of by those who learned the principles and practices of insurance the hard way.

There is no finer business or profession in the world than that of insurance; it is operated and administered by men and women of the highest character and without superiors in any other walk of life. It is a sound and constructive business, which has benefited untold millions of people, and in one way or another has been the greatest contributing factor to the construction of our nation: cities destroyed by fire and wind and earthquake have been rebuilt strong and proud and beautiful, with insurance money; the spirits of fire-swept citizens in metropolis and hamlet and lonesome fields have been kept bright by the knowledge that they carried insurance; great industries have been saved by insurance; families have been kept together when the wage earner was injured or taken away. Men have died with nothing but insurance money to leave behind, happy in the knowledge that great insurance companies could be trusted with the responsibility of caring for their families. In peacetime the surety companies so planned the mantle of their protection for worthy contractors that in America's hour of need, construction forces of our country were able to accomplish impossible upon impossible tasks in preparing America for war and in the winning of the war. There is no brighter page in our nation's industrial history than that written by our country's contractors, and all of them will testify to the guidance of their surety companies in earlier contracting days. The great dams of the country—stemming, as they do, devastating floods and creating millions of acres of fertile soil—are monuments to the partnership existing between contractors and surety companies. So it is with the great bridges across our bays and rivers, great buildings, and tremendous projects of all kinds which have been made possible by surety companies joining forces with the builders and by the complete understanding between them. There isn't a spot in America that hasn't been brightened and bettered by insurance and there isn't anybody in America who would want to visualize what our country would be if there had been no insurance companies and if the operations of insurance companies had not been so soundly administered.

Insurance companies constitute one of the great bulwarks of America. There is hardly a man, woman, or child in the United States who has not benefited by the impregnable structure of insurance finances and the human translation of its documents into the common humdrum of life. We often hear men in business say that they do not want their sons to follow in their footsteps. I believe in insurance and am proud and happy that my son decided to make insurance his career.

I formed friendships during my short while in Chicago that meant much to me as the years went on. William H. Hansmann, director and vice-president of our company, in charge of the Illinois territory, was an office boy with John McGillan of the United Surety Company, and we hit it off from the start and have kept it up for over forty years. The same with William B. Joyce, later president of the National Surety Company, who had a general agency there; Andrew R. Sexton, with whom I later associated in the Aetna companies; W. Herbert Stewart; John McKeever of the Maryland Casualty; "Honey" Stuart; and many other outstanding insurance men of today. They all learned about insurance the hard way too and are great producers of insurance individually and through their organizations.

My time in Chicago was not all devoted to work. I have indicated that my home life with Uncle W. and Frank and Anne Durham was pleasant and stimulating. Uncle W. saw that we went to theaters and concerts, and one night he paid $10 a seat for us to hear Dr. Cook lecture on how he discovered the North Pole. I never will forget the lantern slide showing the Pole as a big pile of snow with the American flag on top. That convinced everybody in the audience and a mighty cheer shook the ceiling. I think we still believe it was the real thing! We were all baseball fans and particular supporters of the Chicago Cubs. Frank Chance, the "Peerless Leader," had gone to school to my Grandfather Durham at Washington College, as had his brothers, all from Fresno, California. As a boy I played croquet with Frank. The office of the Cubs was in the Corn Exchange Bank Building, where Uncle W.'s office was, and I saw Chance and the other officials and players frequently. Ovie Overall, a great athlete at the University of California whom I knew at Stanford, was pitcher for the Cubs. He had been raised at Lemon Cove, a few miles from Chance's home in Fresno. About the only time we didn't have passes would be for the Saturday and Sunday games with the New York Giants. Despite our strict religious upbringing, Uncle W. always had a Sunday box on the third-base line. We had this same box all through one World Series with Detroit. There were many weekday afternoons when "Honey" Stuart and I took in a game when we were ostensibly seeing some good client about insurance. That probably had been done by others before and might possibly be practiced in some circles today!

The famous or infamous Lorimer-Hopkins deadlock for United States Senator was on in the Illinois Legislature at Springfield. Senator Hopkins was one of the founders of the Illinois Surety Company, heavily interested in it financially, and vice-president. His battle with Lorimer was a long-drawn-out struggle ending in a big scandal. There were many ramifications and many special jobs to do. I had met the Senator frequently, and he asked me one day if I would do some outside work for him. He had arranged the appointment of my cousin Frank as a page in the United States Senate and he and my uncle were good friends and worked together politically. One of my first assignments was upstate at Rockford where I was to meet one of Senator Hopkins' lieutenants and work with one of the newspapers. I had practically no money with me because the Senator told me his man would supply me with whatever I needed and "take care of me." I didn't know as much about politics then as I do now or I would not have arrived in Rockford with only fifty cents in my pocket. I went to the main hotel where I was to meet the Senator's man. He was not there and the room clerk had never heard of him. I did not even have a return ticket to Chicago and it was night and I was hungry. I couldn't even register because the hotel was filled. I sat in the lobby for a while, hoping my man would show up, and got hungrier by the minute. I took a walk to think things over and spotted a vaudeville theater advertising "Maud the Bucking Mule." Posters in the lobby offered $5 to anyone in the audience who could stay on Maud's back for a full minute and the admission to the theater was ten, twenty, and thirty cents. That was my opportunity, because when I was in Irvington Fay Chadbourne and I used to follow the circus around and ride the bucking mule for just that reward. We had gotten away with it so often that the circus hands came to know us and shoved us away with the growl that we were too big. So certain was I that I could get the $5 that I spent ten cents for bananas and top price for a seat and had ten cents left. Maud was a wicked-looking, fawn-colored little mule in charge of a big Negro. When volunteers were called for I held back so that I might be last on the stage. There were five or six of us and two were undoubtedly "ringers." They were thrown quickly and the other three, who were real aspirants, didn't fare much better. I was the only one left and I was hoping the little mule was tired because it had been a long time since I had tried one of the beasts. I knew no one in the audience, of course, and had no embarrassment and I wanted that $5. I took off my coat and climbed aboard. The Negro stood at Maud's head (her hoofs were padded) and she was docility itself until he stepped away. Such bucking and gyrations I had never encountered. The mules trained to buck are entirely different from a bucking horse and the trick is to sit way back and wrap your legs around the flanks. You have nothing to hold onto and such mules are quiet for their trainer only. It seemed to me that I had been on the mule forever and couldn't stay another second when she got her feet tangled up in a rope that was protecting the backdrop and began kicking holes and daylight out the scenery. The big Negro grabbed her, and with a stop watch in his hand, motioned me off the stage, shaking his head. I had been on less than fifty seconds. The crowd was on my side and began yelling: "Give him the money." I stood my ground and didn't even put on my coat for I wanted the money too. The audience kept on shouting and a sour-faced man came out of the wings and handed me the five bucks. I went out, had a steak and went to bed in a lodginghouse. Next morning I met Senator Hopkins' man, did my work in two or three days, and went back to Chicago.

I spent Christmas in Chicago, my first one away from home, and I was homesick because Christmas had always meant much to me and still does. It was my first white Christmas. There was something about the snow and the white trees and the sleigh bells that almost made up for my loneliness. Snow has many drawbacks and I don't like it much, but I wish San Francisco might know the great joy of snow for Christmas Eve and Christmas Day—without the attendant hazard of our hills.

Just before the holidays, Anne and Frank and I went to visit our relatives at Cameron, Illinois. My mother had been born there, as had my grandmother, and we made their old home our headquarters while we went to near-by Galesburg and Monmouth and Eureka. There my grandfather had gone to school and taught and it seemed that everybody in that part of the state was related to us. It was very cold, with a great deal of snow on the ground. We had bobsled parties which were a real treat to a Californian. One sled held twenty-seven and all of us were cousins of various degrees. The houses did not have heat in the bedrooms but did have plenty of covers. We had gooseberry pie for breakfast and that meal was an early and a hearty one. Earlier still was the milking. Anxious to be accepted and not to be known as a city boy, I had volunteered the night before to help with the cows. The look of unbelief on my cousin Whitman's face strengthened my resolve and I was up at four-thirty. I shaved in the kitchen in hot water and was in the milking barn by five. It was bitter cold and well below zero. Although somewhat out of practice, I milked two cows satisfactorily, except probably to the cow. My face, fresh from the hot water and lather, was frostbitten, and ever since to this day I have shaved in cold water. As a declaration of independence, I set forth that I still shave with the old-fashioned straight-edged razor. My favorite set contains seven razors —one for each day in the week, and was given me many years ago by Merle Thorpe. When I want a real reminiscent shave, I get out the razor which gave me my first shave as a boy of fourteen; it was given me for Christmas by my Uncle W. and it is still in excellent condition although the blade is very thin.

I had never intended staying permanently in Chicago nor trying to qualify for a place in my uncle's business. I wanted to learn all I could about insurance in as short a time as possible and then return to California. My ties were there and that is where I wanted to start. Uncle W. had given me a very intensive and valuable training, particularly on the selling end. I had a general smattering knowledge of the various forms of insurance and I had my uncle's oft-repeated admonition to stay on a commission basis.

Early in January I started for California. I went the long way, for I had of course been no farther east than Chicago and wanted to see the country. I went to New York still carrying my favorite history book and this time my derby hat was in order. New York was everything I had dreamed it to be and so big I couldn't grasp it. Marion Scheitlin, one of my numerous cousins who had spent summers with us at Santa Cruz and had covered the San Francisco earthquake for his New York paper, was feature editor on the *New York Sun*. Scheitlin arranged for me to see everything that could be crowded into a week. He finished with the *Sun* about 2:00 A.M. and personally conducted me after that. One morning about two-thirty, we ate hot cakes at a lunch counter near

94

the *Sun* building and he introduced me to Samuel G. Blythe. We became fast friends over the years and remained so until Sam's death at his Pebble Beach home forty years later.

It always amuses me to see a sailor on horseback, and I see many of them in my canters through Golden Gate Park. I can understand it in reverse, because when I was a boy and rode daily, I always dreamed of the sea and longed for a ship. When I was taken to San Francisco, I would spend as much time as I could wangle on the docks watching the great ships coming in and sailing for unknown parts. Everything about a ship and the sea fascinated me and still does. It was natural therefore that I should take a ship from New York to New Orleans. It was the SS *Proteus* of the Morgan Line and was sunk in World War I. Being in the dead of winter, the trip was stormy, but I enjoyed every minute of it and was not seasick. Off Cape Hatteras it was so rough that we had to stay in our cabins and as we passed Key West the masts of a wrecked schooner were pointing up out of the water. On that trip of six days, my reading matter was *The Oxford Book of English Verse* and my American history. It meant much to read of the Carolinas and Virginia as we sailed by their shores and on to Florida. Going up the Mississippi to New Orleans from the Gulf is always associated in my mind with Andrew Jackson and his Florida campaign and the battle for New Orleans. The history was real in those surroundings.

The impress of my first visit to New Orleans has never left me and has been repeated countless times. It is one of my favorite cities.

I stayed at the Gruenwald, now the Roosevelt, and instead of inquiring about an eating place, looked through a restaurant guide. Still under the spell of Andrew Jackson, I chose the "Old Hickory Restaurant." I had not heard of it before, nor have I since, but I still count my dinner as one of the best I ever had. I remember the cost particularly as being seventy-five cents and that included a bottle of good red wine.

The train ride from New Orleans to San Francisco on the old Sunset Limited was a long one and impressed me greatly with the vast stretches of land in this country of ours. I had my faithful history book with me, and a long stop at San Antonio gave me a chance to reconstruct the drama of the Alamo.

SAN FRANCISCO

IT WAS good to see my mother and sister again and feel that I was home. They still lived at Palo Alto in the home they started when they moved from Irvington. I wandered all over the Stanford campus and renewed memories and friendships as though I had been away for years instead of months. I doubt that anyone knew I had been away, but I liked to think they did. I was eager to get to work, however, and in a few days was in San Francisco looking for a start. I had several strong letters of recommendation from company executives in Chicago. I knew many people in San Francisco, and I was well acquainted with conditions locally. As I was determined to work on a commission basis and did not want a salary, I assumed I would have no difficulty making a connection. My first approach brought me a shocking surprise, which puzzles me still.

One of my letters was from the Chicago office of the United States Fidelity and Guaranty Company, one of the great insurance companies of America. I had met their executives frequently during my stay with my uncle and the letter was a good one. I called at the office of Borland and Johns, San Francisco general agents for the company, and had no difficulty in seeing Mr. Borland. I presented my letter and at the start explained that I wanted no salary but wished to work on a commission basis and that all I would need would be a desk and some application blanks. Any insurance executive in America will tell you that such an offer will be received with open arms, particularly with the local background which I had sketched for Mr. Borland. He was very cordial and receptive and sent for his partner. Mr. Johns came in, and when he heard my story he shook his head and said, "No, our organization is complete." Borland looked as dazed and incredulous as I did, but the interview was over and the U.S.F.&G. and Cutler had lost a great opportunity.

I went out on the sidewalk and stood for a moment wondering what to do next. Harold Cruzan, a Stanford friend, came along and remarked that I looked worried. I recounted my experience. Cruzan refused to take it seriously and said: "Try John Robertson of the Pacific Surety Company across the street. The firm of Robertson, Spengler and Lloyd have just taken over the general agency of the company and I'm sure Robertson will be interested." The Pacific Surety Company was a conservative California company founded in 1885 and had suddenly become aggressive under the new general agents. John Robertson was seated behind an imposing desk and I remember a rich green-carpeted floor. I introduced myself and gave him a letter from John McGillan, who represented the United Surety Company in Chicago. I did not know it then but Robertson had at one time been general agent or manager for the United Surety in California. McGillan's letter was rather personal and flattering and Robertson warmed up immediately. I explained that I was a Stanford graduate, had been briefly in newspaper work, then in terra-cotta manufacturing, where I had met many contractors, and had gone to Chicago deliberately to learn something about the insurance business. Also that I was on my home grounds again and eager to get started. Robertson asked, "What starting salary do you want?" I replied, "I don't want any salary; I want to work on a commission basis." Robertson frowned as though he misunderstood but there was a twinkle in his Scotch eyes: "Will you please repeat that?" I did and then he got up and made me a bow and with a wave of his hand said: "Take my chair. You're the first of your kind I ever met." He then called in his secretary and dictated a letter which I still have, to the effect that "We will allow you a drawing account of $50 a month until we become better acquainted."

Robertson called in the main people of his office and introduced me as "one of my new boys." He then chatted with me awhile about various men and conditions in San Francisco and the insurance business generally. I realized that I really was undergoing an examination but I enjoyed it. Later he took me down the hall to the "brokers' room" and assigned me to a desk. There were nine of them in a rather small room. The desks were small too, roll top, and the only place the desks didn't touch each other was where the windows were.

John Robertson was one of the finest and most interesting men I have ever known. He was an individualist with a host of friends and there were plenty of people whom he didn't like and with whom he would have nothing to do. He had a long experience in the insurance business and over the years represented some of the biggest companies in America. He was nationally respected even though it was conceded that his underwriting was frequently prejudiced by his blind belief in his friends. He and I warmed to each other and over the years did business with each other whenever we could. His advice and philosophy in the early days of my insurance career were invaluable and we had many a chuckle later on when I was the executive and John Robertson was the broker, for we understood each other. The firm of Robertson, Spengler and Lloyd was one of the most aggressive in California. Ed Spengler was widely respected and a fine citizen. He died only a few years ago. Will Lloyd was a brother of Fred Lloyd, who had taken over the presidency of the Pacific Surety Company and who had a rather checkered career. Will was a fine producer and a fine singer and entertainer. For a number of years he sang in the famous Knicker-bocker Quartette and quite a bit of of our extracurricular activities after hours were devoted to harmonizing.

One of my fellow tenants in the brokers' room was John P. Jackson, Jr., of the famous California Jackson Napa Soda ownership. One Christmas Eve very late in our office, Will Lloyd, Jackson, a few others, and I were singing Christmas carols. Jackson suddenly decided to go home and we taunted him with the thought that he was afraid to go home at that hour and with frivolity on his breath to Mrs. Jackson. John stood up against the wall in great dignity and said: "If I would go down the street and rob a blind man of his pennies, and if I would go further down the street and take schoolbooks away from a little child and go further down the street and shoot a minister of the gospel in the eye, killing him utterly, my wife on hearing it would say, 'I know John had some good reason for doing it.' Gentlemen, I bid you good night." Whereupon Will Lloyd sang solo, "I Love You Truly."

Play, however, was only occasional and was an interlude to the grim, hard struggle of getting an independent start in the insurance business.

Forty years ago insurance was not so tightly controlled or as complex a business as it is today. I plunged into a great deal of door-to-door

98

"cold" solicitation, not literally ringing strange doorbells of residences, but making office calls on men and corporations I did not know. Of course, I tried out all my friends, as any beginner in insurance or any other calling will do, but I pride myself that I have not ever unduly bothered my friends, and the treatment and consideration they have accorded me over the years is proof enough that I did not pressure them. All of them, however, know pretty well the nature of my business and have done excellently by me in their insurance matters.

Although I had a drawing account of $50 per month, I was occasionally allowed to keep particular commissions. John Robertson and Ed Spengler were very understanding and knew that the first year on a commission basis was tough. My first sale was a personal accident policy with a $12 premium and my second a $138 general liability premium. Not much involved in commissions but encouraging, and I still have as my client the man who signed up for the $138.

One experience in that first year made a profound impression on me and later influenced most of my dealings with young men trying to start in business or seeking any sort of advice. Stanford University carried a great deal of insurance and I naturally thought about getting some of it. Vanderlynn Stow was a Trustee of Stanford and its Treasurer. I did not know him but had heard him speak at Stanford gatherings and decided to call on him. I wasn't too sure of myself and like all beginners looked up at his window for a day or two, telling myself that he probably wasn't in. One day I gathered my courage together and lay in wait for him outside the Nevada Bank Building where he had his offices. I went up in the elevator with him and followed him into his office, a technique which I do not recommend to any salesman. He looked amazed and very formidable as I explained that I was a Stanford man, starting in the insurance business, and would like some of the Stanford insurance. Nor is that approach recommended, but it was unfortunately mine on that occasion. Mr. Stow had very bushy eyebrows and a black walrus moustache. He gave me the full treatment and glowered at me. "You went to Stanford, young man?" "Yes, Sir," said I. "You went there four years?" "Yes, Sir." "Stanford gave you a degree?" "Yes, Sir," again I stammered. "I think," said Mr. Stow, "Stanford has done enough for you, young man. Good day."

Of course that was a good thing for me, but I didn't know it then, and I left his office talking to myself. I vowed first of all that I would never throw a young man out of my office or deny him a chance to tell his story and I never have. I also vowed that someday I would see to it that Stanford men would handle Stanford insurance. I had no idea how it would be brought about but later on it was, and I did have something to do with it.

I worked very hard that first year and did not give up, but it was pretty discouraging. I did a great deal of walking and many a time decided between five cents for carfare or a bag of cookies for lunch, which I ate at my desk. I had bought a secondhand typewriter and had stationery labeling me as being in "General Insurance." From my news-paper days I had learned to type in satisfactory style with two fingers and always had a notation at the bottom of the letter, "LWC/SE." The "SE" was for "Self," to whom I dictated, and provided, I thought, con-siderable class. There were periods when I put false bottoms in my shoes to save half soles because every penny counted. Will Lloyd kept me supplied with expiration cards of risks that undoubtedly had been combed over by others, but occasionally one would pay off. My desk mate in the brokerage room, John T. Costello, had a Cadillac car when there were very few in San Francisco. One day I walked to Twenty-third and Valencia after a machine-shop risk outlined on a card handed me by Lloyd. The premium was only $25 but the commission would be $6.25. My heart sank when I met Costello coming out of the shop. Not knowing anything about my purpose he offered me a ride back to town. He told me as we rode along that he had just increased a $25 premium to $100 and was so pleased he took me to lunch at the Olympic Club. Neither one of us had any idea that we would one day be partners.

At the end of the first year I had an accounting with Ed Spengler, who was also treasurer of the Pacific Surety Company. With the com-missions I had been allowed to retain and which did not really amount to much in money, and with the $50 per month drawing account charged against me, I owed the company $135. I had some few accounts which promised well for the future, and the three members of Robertson, Spengler and Lloyd expressed every confidence in me and said that they would see me through. I had worked hard and been frugal to the penny and yet in dollars I had accomplished very little. The knowledge and experience of my own beginning on a commission basis are still vivid and I know better than most what the young men of today are up against when they start out in insurance even with the $200 or so the companies pay them. Also I know what a real investment the companies must make for years in these young men on the chance that they will retain their enthusiasm and go ahead to be self-sustaining and real producers.

I started my second year with $135 against me but with a few good contractor clients and plenty of encouragement from John Robertson and Ed Spengler. We are apt to forget as we get older that encouragement and calm advice mean much to younger men. The memory of the help I had along those lines is still with me and I know I could not have gone on without it. When my second year was completed I had paid back the $135 and averaged $185 per month in addition. These figures are indelibly stamped in my memory and I almost unconsciously use them in talking to young men about their future in insurance. I have yet, however, to find one who takes my figures seriously, particularly on the first year. They all invariably know they can do better and undoubtedly feel a trifle superior in that certain knowledge.

A combination of fortunate incidents and good luck led to my progress in the second year, however. The Pacific Coast Casualty Company was a California company rival to the Pacific Surety Company. It started writing contractors' bonds at a quarter of one percent against the established rate for all companies of a half of one percent. One noon when I was eating my cookies in the brokers' room, Will Lloyd came in asking for Jack Costello. Jack had a large contractor clientele and handled the business of most of the members of the powerful and important Builders' Exchange. Lloyd was very much perturbed when I explained that Costello had gone to Alaska on a vacation and stalked out of the room obviously angry. He came back in a few minutes and asked if I knew any of the contractors in the city and particularly on the Builders' Exchange. I stretched the truth considerably when I replied that I knew them all and intimately. Lloyd looked very doubtful but explained that a rate war was on and that the Pacific Surety was prepared to offer a three-year contract to contractors to write their bonds during that period for a quarter of one percent. He said he had counted heavily on Costello annexing the cream of the business, that the agreements had all been printed, and that the immediate solicitation was imperative. He had a large supply of the agreements in his hands which he gave me and said definitely that any contractor signed by me would be considered my client and that for the life of the contract all commissions would be mine. I didn't wait to finish my cookies but took the agreements and started out. For the balance of the week I did nothing but work with contractors and was amazingly successful in signing many of them to the cut-rate contract. Quite a few of Costello's best clients were included. I explained to them that if the procedure did not meet with Jack's full approval on his return, I would step out of the picture and leave it to them to work out but in the meantime the contractors would have the protection of the agreement. I had come to know Costello very well and we had a mutual liking for each other. I was certain that he would be fair with me. He was an older man with quite a few years of experience under his belt and was a shrewd and successful broker. I was just a beginner, with everything to gain and nothing to lose by agreeing to work it out with him on his return. When he did return, I had the majority of his contractor clients signed to an agreement that I would in effect have their business for three years ahead. Costello was of course chagrined because his relationship to his clients was a particularly close one. A meeting with all three of the firm—Robertson, Spengler, and Lloyd—and Costello and myself was stormy at first but when the circumstances were fully understood by Jack, everything went smoothly and we had no difficulty reaching an agreement. Within a month or two we formed a partnership and for a short time took in a third man who had a brokerage desk with us, Percy Webster. The firm name was at the beginning Costello, Cutler and Webster. This lasted only a short time; Webster dropped out and the firm of Costello and Cutler continued until Costello's death in an automobile accident a few years later. Costello frequently jested about my signing up his clients and forcing him into the partnership, but day in and day out we had a most satisfactory relationship and we became fast friends. He was a fine, aggressive, and sensitive man with a great sense of humor and I still think of him with a warm sense of satisfaction over our few years together. The Panama Pacific Exposition was being planned and we were recognized as a successful brokerage firm and had no difficulty in making preferred arrangements with various companies.

The Pacific Surety Company after a time got into difficulties and we did much of our business with the Pacific Coast Casualty Company. Marshall Franck was its head, but the man who attracted us and lived minutely up to his agreements with us was Carl Brown. He is my friend to this day and has played a big part in the insurance world. Will Lloyd died and Robertson and Spengler joined forces with Frank Hall, later Robertson and Hall, in a general agency for the Massachusetts Bonding Company. T. J. Falvey, the founder of the Massachusetts and until his death a few years ago its president, came to San Francisco and made an agreement with Costello and Cutler which operated very satisfactorily for a while. Wallace Falvey, the son of T. J., is now president of the Massachusetts, a national leader in insurance, who has been my good friend for many years.

Our firm took full advantage of the rather liberal commission arrangements available from some of the companies in those days; also rental subsidies and clerical assistance could be had in exchange for a proper volume of business. Those things were all right for the usual run of business but when real problems arose we found more and more that we obtained needed help from the Aetna companies. Walter Chowen, western manager, now well in his vigorous eighties, retired from the Aetna to head the California Rating Bureau, and J. R. Molony came to the Coast to take his place. Molony was a graduate of the University of Nebraska, had been a star football player, and was a keen student of insurance. I will always consider him one of the soundest insurance men on the Pacific Coast. Our business had grown so rapidly that a connection with Molony and the Aetna was a natural one. Molony would not deviate from the rules in any particular and so we had no excess commission from him. There were no regulations against office space, however, and Costello and Cutler was fitted up in good style on the second floor of the building occupied by the Aetna, and our relationship was not only close but of great advantage to both parties and we produced a fine volume of business as a result.

When his automobile overturned and Costello was killed, his effects disclosed a letter asking that I administer his estate and look after his widow, who was an invalid. The executive end of insurance had always appealed to me and I saw no reason why I could not sell through an organization as well as through a brokerage firm. Accordingly, I worked out an arrangement where I sold Costello's business and exercised a protectorate over it so that Mrs. Costello had a reasonable income until she died. Also, I joined forces with Molony and was made head of the Fidelity and Surety Department of the Aetna Casualty and Surety Company's western branch. All of my personal business remained with the Aetna and my compensation was fixed accordingly. In addition I was given a profit-sharing contract.

At this time in my life I was changed from boyhood to manhood. Belle Jarvis, my first wife, died. I had gone to grammar school with her and carried her schoolbooks and loved her as a boy loves a girl. She was a dear, sweet woman when she went away, and we had only a few years together. Dr. Wilbur was then Dean of the Stanford Medical School and not practicing, but he came to Berkeley to help me and told me what other doctors had avoided telling—that I should know the truth and that Belle could not live for more than a week. He urged me to stay with her every minute and be cheerful if I could stand it, but if I felt like breaking down to get out and walk. "Those minutes," he said, "will be precious with your girl, as they are with mine." Dr. Wilbur and Mrs. Wilbur were boy and girl together, and he always called her by his childhood pet name. Is there any wonder about my affection for him? And I never will forget my Stanford friend now of fifty years, Carl Braun, a millionaire industrialist, who knew I might break and came and took me away to Sausalito and walked beside me and talked and kept me going and brought me home again just before services began.*

When your house burns down, you don't build the same house over again. You build a new house. I have built a new one with Ethel Jane. I wanted to change my life. I was empty and tired and had to start over again and forget everything.

In my loneliness I turned to my friend from childhood, Blondie Ingram, and with only a day to prepare, we set out to see our fascinat-

* Braun died suddenly in February 1954 as this book was being prepared for press.

ing country. With memories still fresh of boyhood reading of Mark Twain, we boarded a Mississippi River boat at St. Louis and floated our way to New Orleans. There were many stops en route and countless historic spots where the history book came in handy: Memphis, Vicksburg, Natchez Under the Hill. Blondie has always been a poet a heart and in his memory were an unbelievable number of verses. The great river gave him many chances, and as we rounded the bend at Natchez I will always remember his reciting under the moon John Hay's "Jim Bludso of the Prairie Belle." And today after sixty years of friendship "at Jedgement I'd run my chance with him." Those who were in college with Blondie will remember that he had a language all his own—a lingo which still permeates nooks and corners of the fraternity house where he lived. We used the lingo exclusively on the Mississippi River trip, and with the Negro roustabouts strange to us we had many unusual opportunities to try out new figures of speech. Today in reminiscence we use it still while strangers wonder. Those comparatively few days and nights upon the Mississippi are fresh and stirring still, and the many stories of the Mississippi have new-found meanings at every reading. Probably ours have too in the telling.

My days with the Aetna and Molony, which began in 1915, were most interesting and stimulating. I made two trips to the Hawaiian Islands during that time. One was on my own with Al Trowbridge, my old Stanford buddy, when we visited another Stanford friend, Doc Savage, on Maui. In 1915 I went to Honolulu for the Aetna to install Walter Dillingham's company as general agent for the Aetna companies. Many people from all over know Walter Dillingham as one of the good men of the world. For thirty-eight years my friendship for him has grown and my world will never know a finer contributor to the things that count.

San Francisco was an active stirring city in these days. The spirit of its citizens had won against all other cities in having itself declared the official site of a World Exposition to celebrate the opening of the Panama Canal. There could be no better illustration of the tenacity that is always required to make dreams come true.

An American canal had been recommended by President Grant and an American Interoceanic Commission appointed in 1872. M. de Les-

105

seps brought about an international conference in Paris on the subject in 1879, with America having no part of it. No one will ever know what part we would have played if the battleship *Oregon* had not been built in San Francisco. In April 1898 we were at war with Spain. The *Oregon* was on the West Coast fourteen thousand miles from Cuba in the Atlantic. The ship took over two months to reach the scene of action, and the eyes of the nation were on it every day of its historic voyage.

The peace treaty with Spain was signed in December 1898, and the following year Congress began an investigation to determine the best available route for an isthmian canal. President McKinley appointed a Canal Commission, and on his assassination in 1901 President Theodore Roosevelt carried on vigorously.

Reuben Hale, a member of Hale Brothers, merchants, was one of San Francisco's outstanding citizens and remained so until his death a few months ago. In January 1904, two years before San Francisco was to go through a devastating earthquake and fire, Hale wrote a letter, which, if only for the encouragement of practical dreams, is worth the printing. He wrote:

To the Directors of the Merchants' Association—Gentlemen: Numerous articles have been published recently on the subject of what should be done to beautify and improve San Francisco, and as all municipal improvements are proper subjects for consideration by this association, it occurred to me that in conjunction with the discussion of other important matters, it might be well for us to consider one, which to my mind, is of much greater importance to this community than any so far suggested.

There are many reasons for believing that San Francisco is on the verge of very great financial prosperity. The Panama Canal will probably be built; trade relations with the Orient are constantly improving; our steamship service has long been inadequate for the demands of shippers, and our foreign possessions have centered the eyes of the world upon San Francisco.

Is the time not ripe for us to consider a World's Exposition in San Francisco in 1915? This is looking far ahead, but it is better for us to build for the future than to repent the past. After long-continued agitation a convention finally assembled in St. Louis on January 10, 1899, at which convention an executive committee was appointed which decided on celebrating the event of the Louisiana Purchase by a great World's Exposition to be held in St. Louis. This was over five years before the date fixed for the exposition. Five years of active preparation would leave us six years to develop the interest in a proposition of immense magnitude. If St. Louis can give an exposition which will expend in that community approximately $50,000,000, why cannot San Francisco develop an exposition of even greater magnitude? St. Louis' population was, according to the census in 1900, 575,238. This is not very much greater than ours at the present time, and certainly not greater than ours will be ten years hence. Her bank deposits are much less than San Francisco's and her capital and surplus invested in banks was, in July, 1903, only about 20 per cent more. St. Louis raised $5,000,000 by private subscription, $5,000,000 by municipal bonds, and received $5,000,000 from the Government of the United States. San Francisco could do the same thing, and it might be possible that the State of California would appropriate $5,000,000.

This money could be raised easily, providing it seemed practical to divide the subscription into a ten-year proposition instead of raising it all at once. Five millions of dollars divided into ten-year payments would mean five hundred thousand dollars per year; but as this money could be placed at interest safely at 3 per cent during the ten-year period it would only be necessary for the city to pay about $423,450 per year. Ten yearly installments of $423,450 placed at 3 per cent interest, compounding as it comes in and the interest accrues, in the ten years would amount to five millions of dollars. This would mean about one-tenth of 1 per cent of our present assessed valuation per year. Surely San Francisco can afford to pay one-tenth of 1 per cent of its assessed valuation for advertisement purposes; and what greater advertisement could she have than to carry out the greatest World's Exposition ever attempted?

The next thing to consider is the site, and a plat of ground of twelve to fifteen hundred acres could be located between the ocean boulevard drive and the hills. What more delightful scenic ride could be pictured than one from the ocean around the Exposition grounds, up the terraced hills in the back, with a marine view of the Farallones and the panorama of San Francisco Bay as it would appear from the top of the hills in that vicinity? By starting early the terraces on these hills could be laid out under the supervision of the Park Commissioners and the immediate direction of Superintendent McLaren, and a very artistic effect could be obtained. A wharf could be run out into the ocean and bay steamers make the trip through the Golden Gate on to the Pacific Ocean. Tourists from the interior parts of the United States would value this trip highly in order to say that they had ridden upon the peaceful waters of our old ocean, and lovers of nature would be interested in the trip because of its scenic beauty. The entrance to the Exposition could be on a magnificent scale, such as it was as you entered from the lake at Chicago. The Golden Gate could be electric lighted and other protections instituted for the purpose of making it a safe and pleasant trip.

The occasion could be advertised as the opening of San Francisco as the center of trade for the Pacific Ocean, or in commemoration of the completion of the Panama Canal. Horace Greeley said: "Go West, young man"; but when he goes west from San Francisco he goes east. It is the beginning of the east, and the ending of the west. We are the center around which trade revolves between the United States and all European countries that are looking for trade with the Orient and other Pacific Ocean points . . .

This plan is respectfully submitted to you in its crudity with the suggestion that this matter be carefully considered, and if thought of sufficient importance that it be the subject for our next semi-annual dinner this spring and that we take such other action as seems advisable to further the promotion of this project. Respectfully submitted,

Yours truly,

R. B. Hale

All of the commercial and civic organizations of San Francisco joined. Mass meetings were held, and with San Francisco in ashes a corporation was formed "to inaugurate and hold a World's Fair in the City and County of San Francisco."

No task could be greater with the conditions that prevailed, but in 1915 the Panama Pacific International Exposition opened its doors. It was a thing of magnificent beauty; and its buildings, together with the reconstruction of San Francisco's earthquake town and fire-ridden city, produced an unbelievable activity, and a faith, living courage, and optimism which touched the humblest worker and carried San Francisco forward for many years to come. I had a humble part in this activity and building and was one of the countless beneficiaries of San Francisco's great spirit in those days. I can't ever forget the men who dreamed their dreams and by sheer courage, generously mixed with faith, helped their dreams come true.

VIII

SAN FRANCISCO AND STANFORD

I REMAINED with the Aetna and Molony for eight years. All of the Aetna people throughout the country and at the home office in Hartford were fine and outstanding. The head of the Fidelity and Surety Department at Hartford was Dan Gage and he and I became warm friends. He died too early and would undoubtedly have been the outstanding surety man of America had he lived. His son and daughter, who were babies when I first knew them, still call me "Uncle Cut" although they are married now with children of their own. I visit Hartford frequently when I am on the Atlantic seaboard and always find a warm welcome from the executives there.

This period from 1913 to 1921 was an eventful and busy one. I had early become a member of the Press Club, and when its location was transferred from the Commercial Building to the present building at Sutter and Powell Streets, Al Trowbridge and I took up quarters there, and the Press Club was my home until my mother and sister moved to San Francisco from Palo Alto. I had found a large flat on Alpine Street with a good view of the Bay and shipping. It was well arranged, and Al and I moved in and included "Honey" Stuart, who had been in my uncle's Chicago office and was now my assistant in the Aetna. All of this was fine too for my mother and sister and it was good to have a home again.

Late in 1915 Molony announced that he was to be married and asked me to be his best man. The wedding was to be in Los Angeles, the home of the bride-to-be. She was Edith Holder, a graduate of the University of California, whom I had never met. Neither had I met the bridesmaid, who had been Miss Holder's roommate at the Delta Gamma House at U.C. Her name was Ethel Jane Pierce and she was born in Fresno. It was too soon for me to go through a wedding with its memories, and I tried all one night to reach Molony and get out of it. Providence must have been with me, and happily I could not get hold of him. Without going into details, it is to be recorded that Ethel Jane and I became engaged that first day we met and are living happily "even" after, and have Jane Le, Leland, Jr., and Mary Ellen, and all eight grandchildren at this writing.

My days at Stanford had made such an impression on me that as an alumnus I took a deep interest in everything pertaining to Stanford. I served on the Alumni Advisory Council, was twice president of the Alumni Association, and was asked by President Wilbur to help him form the Stanford Board of Athletic Control. I was chosen as one of the first three alumni members and served for eleven years. During that period I was chairman of the committee which built the Stanford Stadium. I also went to Pittsburgh and negotiated with Glenn S. (Pop) Warner to come to Stanford as football coach and later with Andy Kerr and Tiny Thornhill to fill in for Pop until Pittsburgh would release him from his contract, which had two years to go. Pop had thought Pittsburgh was dissatisfied with him but found differently when he asked the authorities to release him to Stanford.

To go back a bit in football history, Presidents Jordan of Stanford and Benjamin Ide Wheeler of California decided in 1906 that the American game was too rough and directed that the Rugby game be substituted. James Lanagan, who was the Stanford coach and an unusually successful one, although he had never played the American game, went to Australia accompanied by George Presley to study Rugby. For eight years Stanford and California played Rugby, which made them misfits on the Pacific Coast and very much so in the national picture.

In the meantime the University of Washington, under Gil Dobie, developed a very strong American football team. In 1912 Johnny Stroud, graduate manager at California, who had been a brilliant Rugby star, advised me that California was going to return to the American game. President Wilbur had repeatedly been quoted as saying that Stanford would never play the American game again. "Never" is of course a long time and I always doubted that Wilbur made any such statement. We had many meetings with Stroud and others at California, but the best

President Wilbur would do at that time was to agree on an American football game in the spring if California would play us Rugby in the fall. This wasn't much of a concession, as any follower of sports knows, and so Stanford had to watch California play its Big Game with Washington (Washington 73—California 0), while Stanford had its big Rugby contest with the University of Santa Clara. This silly arrangement continued until 1916, when the Student Army Training Corps was under military jurisdiction at Stanford in preparation for the first war. The commandant in charge, without too great respect for President Wilbur's civilian authority or too great confidence in his own coaching ability, arranged an American game on his own with California and was trounced for his pains, 67-0. Stanford was in a pretty weak position on all sides. I discussed the matter with Dr. Wilbur at length and he finally agreed that we could resume relations with California on American football. His conditions, however, proved most embarrassing to Stanford. Dr. Wilbur insisted that we resume American football via the so-called gymnasium route. That meant our coaches could not be paid more or less than an average professor. We might as well have employed the professors to do the coaching, for the results were about as satisfactory as if they had been at the helm.

With all the hit and miss, Stanford nearly had a winner one year under Bob Evans whom we had obtained from Milligan College as a baseball coach. Some of us knew well that he was also a football coach. He had a great collection of stars, including Dink Templeton and Reg Caughey, just returned from Europe, where in the A.E.F. they had won everything at both football and Rugby. That team of 1920 missed defeating Andy Smith's Wonder Team by inches, with a score of 10-7 in California's favor.

I have generally been blamed (and wrongfully) for not renewing Evans' contract, for clearly he was a good coach. When the student body realized that he was not going to be rehired, a parade of indignant students, many of them my friends today, descended upon the Board of Athletic Control meeting, carrying a large banner. I found this a few months ago in my basement. The banner is somewhat tattered but its inscribed battle cry is very legible and bold—"For Evans and Justice— Down with Cutlerism."

While we were fumbling with changing football coaches every year, we did one very constructive thing in building the Stanford Stadium, and comparatively inexpensively. As Stanford's representative, I met with Chaffee Hall of California and negotiated a ten-year agreement between the two universities. Among other things, the construction of new stadia was recognized and ticket prices agreed upon in the first stadium to be built. It was generally taken for granted that this would happen at Berkeley. Preston Delano, just resigned United States Comptroller of the Currency, but then with Twohy Bros., Contractors, invited Dr. Tom Williams of the Stanford Athletic Board and me to lunch and pointed out how Stanford could build its stadium right away. This was in May—just as the universities were closing up for the summer. Delano was a Stanford man; he and I were old friends, and I had every confidence in him. His plan was to dig down twenty-five feet, bank up the earth thirty-five feet, and produce a stadium to hold 55,000 people and capable of later enlargement. He assured us that it could be completed in time for the Stanford-California game in November, and with the increase in admission charges it would very much help pay for itself. We had no money or any plan of raising it, but the idea was very tempting.

Through Chaffee Hall I arranged a meeting with California's Executive Committee, explained what we had in mind, and asked for some edge on the gate receipts over and above a sum which we would guarantee. None of us knew how much a large stadium would draw at the $5 charge which we expected, but it was certain in my mind that the net results would be far and away above the small returns we had received for so many years in small fields and with a top price of $2.50. California had plans for proceeding with its own magnificent stadium, and, in fairness, it must be admitted that it was not to California's interest to concede Stanford anything. California was proposing to the public to raise about a million dollars by actual advance sale of tickets, ensuring seats for a period of ten years. The answer to my proposition was "No," and Dean Probert added for good measure, "and there will be no knotholes in the California stadium." This remark decided me, and we made hurried plans for building. Bids were called for and opened in my San Francisco office because Stanford was closed for the summer. Despite the helpful idea of Preston Delano, his corporation was not low bidder. The firm of Silas Palmer and Douglas McBride was low, with a bid of $218,000, and they proposed to do the work with fresnos (scrapers) and mules and have the stadium ready by November if we could give immediate acceptance. It was a big gamble because we had no money and no campaign as yet. Palmer and McBride arranged a loan for us of $100,000 through the Bank of Palo Alto and I signed the contract for the Board of Athletic Control. Joseph R. Hickey was placed in charge of a campaign for funds. We did not sell our seats in advance but merely the right to buy them for a period of ten years at a discount of $1.00 over the regular price. In this way we still got revenue from future games whereas California was actually mortgaging its future. The two campaigns were going on at the same time and California's proposition was of course more appealing to the public. We did pretty well, however, and counted heavily on getting the final payment of 25 percent out of gate receipts of the Stanford-California game.

Palmer and McBride and their mules did a magnificent job, and it was finished on time. We even planted a lawn on the playing field so that it would look green on the opening kickoff. It did, but it was too light to last beyond a play or two. Our prices for the opening game were $5, $4, and $3, and with the exception of about 5,000 seats which California held back in trying to force sale of its own script, the stadium was packed. Chaffee Hall later took the initiative in getting his committee to make financial adjustment to us for the empty seats, which was a very fair thing to do and in line with all of the dealings I have had over the years with Chaffee. The graduated prices of $5, $4, and $3 did not work out, because somewhere of course the $4 and $3 people had to sit next to the higher-priced patrons who were disgruntled. With great wisdom we accordingly thereafter raised the price of all seats to $5, which it is today.

Long after the stadium was completed I asked Silas Palmer if he would like to know how much money we had in the bank when we signed the $218,000 contract with them. When I told him it was only $5,000 he turned pale and said, "And we were the ones who gave the bond to Stanford instead of the other way around."

In 1920 I was elected a Trustee of Stanford University for the usual ten-year term. I completed thirty years' service on the Board in July 1950 and at this writing have just been re-elected for my fourth ten-year term. I served twelve terms as President of the Board, from 1931 to 1942, and, on asking that I not be considered further, was elected Vice-President of the Board. I consider the Trusteeship of Stanford the greatest honor that has ever come to me and I never go to the Stanford campus without thinking about the first day I arrived there as a green and awkward freshman, and always I have in me the feeling I had as a boy when I went up high in a swing.

When I was officially notified by the Secretary of the Board that I had been elected a Trustee, the first thing I did was to get on a street car and go out to tell my mother. I thought of course that she would be overjoyed. She took it very much as a matter of course and her only remark was, "Certainly, my boy ought to be a Trustee." My mother's subsequent behavior, however, proved that she did not take it that calmly.

Originally the Stanford Trustees were chosen by the Founders for life. Later Mrs. Stanford decreed the ten-year terms for subsequent Trustees, the Board being a self-perpetuating body under the original founding grant. When a committee called on me to say they wanted me to take the Presidency of the Board, it was headed by Timothy Hopkins, a Life Trustee. Mr. Hopkins opened the interview by saying that he would like to ask me some questions, "if," he said, "you feel I have any right to question you." "Mr. Hopkins," I replied, "I never look in the Trustee's Manual without realizing that you became a Trustee the year I was born. You have the right to ask me anything."

IX

STILL SAN FRANCISCO

D R. RAY LYMAN WILBUR had succeeded Dr. Jordan as President of Stanford. He had been our family doctor in 1902 when I first went to Stanford. He was President for twenty-six years. Most of that time I was a Trustee and for twelve years President of the Board. I was very close to him and our ties grew stronger with the years. I had a preponderance of admiration for him and a great affection. This did not interfere with our having some sharp disagreements, notably over the question of the elimination of the Lower Division at Stanford. Dr. Wilbur had announced definitely that, as of a certain date, the Lower Division would be eliminated. His reasoning was that Stanford, privately endowed, could not afford to duplicate the educational system of the state of California and that the junior colleges could take care of the freshman and sophomore years. Further, that a Bachelor of Arts degree did not mean much any more and that in law, business, and the sciences a student would have at least a four-year course in pursuit of the higher degrees. I felt very strongly that one of Stanford's great contributions should be to boys and girls in their teens at the impressionable age. I remembered my own student days and believed that we should give these young people a taste of the best professors we had; that if we were going to give them instructors only, we should abolish the Lower Division, but that it was not necessary. Many of the Board believed as I did and that Stanford certainly could do a better job with these boys and girls than the junior colleges, however excellent.

Dr. Wilbur was not an easy man to brook. He disliked opposition and was unusually resourceful in meeting it. He at all times had the support of his great friend, Herbert Hoover, who had been a Trustee of Stanford since 1912. In 1928, when Mr. Hoover was elected President of the United States, Dr. Wilbur stated bluntly at a Trustee's meeting that if we wanted to be rid of him, here was our chance, because

President-elect Hoover had asked him to be in his cabinet. We very sincerely tried to impress on Dr. Wilbur that we did not want him to resign and unanimously adopted a resolution to that effect.

Shortly after Mr. Hoover became President I attended the Gridiron Dinner in Washington as the guest of General "Wild Bill" Donovan, for whom I had a great admiration. He and Mr. Hoover had had a misunderstanding over Donovan's appointment to a cabinet position, and as I heard both sides of the story from the principals, I will not repeat them here. While Donovan was lampooned in a sketch at the dinner as the soldier who had gotten all the decorations the War Department could give, he was given a new one by his Commander in Chief—"The Order of the Boot." Donovan was very popular; he was loudly applauded and seemed sincerely affected, while the President, who sat directly in front of us, was plainly uncomfortable. Mr. Hoover had his inning later, however. Mr. Roosevelt was the speaker of the evening. He had been Assistant Secretary of the Navy when Mr. Hoover was Food Administrator under President Wilson, and they knew each other well. Everyone knew the legend that Mr. Hoover didn't know whether he was a Republican or a Democrat, and Mr. Roosevelt took full advantage of it. Always a felicitous and happy speaker, he was after all the leader of the defeated party, he was a guest, and was speaking about the President of the United States. He said, "In the old days I used to see a great deal of Mr. Hoover when he and I belonged to the same—" Mr. Roosevelt paused dramatically and everyone laughed, but self-consciously, because he was speaking to the President. Becoming emboldened he added, "when Mr. Hoover and I were Democrats together." Again the audience laughed, but you could feel the sting, and the Republicans plainly cringed. Mr. Hoover arose and, using exactly the same preamble, said, "In the old days I saw a good deal of Mr. Roosevelt when I, like all other good Republicans, helped his Democratic President win a war." The cheers and applause were deafening. Then Chief Justice Taft arose and, in the way that he alone could do it, turned to the President and with a chuckle said, "You may not remember it, Mr. Hoover, but I was President myself once," and followed it with his deep belly laugh way down low. It was an evening I will not ever forget, nor Bill Donovan's tears at the lines of the dialogue between the

116

impersonator of Mr. Hoover and a bystander: "What is Bill Donovan doing now, Mr. President?" "Oh," said the bystander, "he is sitting in the window watching the parade go by"; and the rejoinder, "You had better look out, Mr. President, or he might start a parade of his own." Bill turned to me and said, "Le, would you join my parade?" And I said I would, for I admired him and still do. On a wall in my home is an inscribed picture of him as General of the O.S.S., and he isn't the carefree young tenor that he used to be in a quartet. Joyce Kilmer, who wrote "Trees," died in his arms in the Meuse-Argonne offensive in World War I. Bill is a soft-spoken, steel-fibered man and a great guy who has seen everything, and I am proud of his friendship.

In this brief reference to Stanford I have passed over many years and many things which I now go back to, with Stanford reappearing constantly as an integral part of my life.

Mrs. Cutler and I had our first home on a hill in San Francisco at 1240 Washington Street. We had a beautiful view of the Bay and surrounding area. In all of our living we have managed somehow to have a view of beautiful country and always to be able to glimpse the great outdoors. We had a Chinese schoolboy, Louis Chew Nong, for our first cook, and thirty-five years later he still corresponds with me. We paid him $3 a week until he wrote me a letter asking that I increase his wages by "one dollar up," which I did. Nong was a great letter writer and I have a scrapbook filled with his interesting communications. They have caused many a laugh but how infinitely better are they than anything we could do in Chinese. When our first daughter, Jane Le, was born, I explained to Nong that she was a beautiful baby girl and that in all his life he would never hear of one so beautiful. The next day Mrs. Cutler at the hospital received this letter from Nong: "Dear Cutler: I am very glad to hear that you have baby so well and so beauty and I had never heard on my life. So I know your daughter will be wise woman and had good education to do as well as nobody can do in this country and can do great work like Joan Arc did for his country. How's your health and have you a time to do anything. Respectfully."

This was in 1918. Three years later Leland, Jr., was born, and in 1924 Mary Ellen was with us. We moved to a home on Twenty-fifth Avenue between Lake and Sea Cliff and there had a beautiful view of the Golden Gate. Also when the foghorn sounded you would think it was right under the bed. We had some happy years in that home. Our children went to the Alamo School and had many fine little friends in the neighborhood. Jane went to Miss Burke's when she was old enough. As a nurse for Jane when she was little we had Mrs. Ellen Gibson, who was nurse for all our children and then later our cook and housekeeper. She was with us for over twenty years and then helped our children with their children. We inherited a delightful old Chinaman in our purchase of the Twenty-fifth Avenue home. Wah Wah was what Jane called him and that was the only name he had. He would carry her in his arms while he shopped in the neighborhood and for eight or nine years, until he gradually became too old, was a faithful and efficient servant. Many amusing episodes of his years with us are fresh in my memory and our friends of those days remember him with smiles. The time came when Wah Wah's step was appreciably slowing and his vision faltering. I doubt he knew his own age, but we thought he was close to ninety. One day he said to Mrs. Cutler, "I very tired, I go away. I want to sleep three months, maybe four months." We arranged for him to leave on a certain day. The night before he was to leave, Leland came down with pneumonia and was desperately ill. I woke up Wah Wah and explained it to him. He asked, "Nurse lady come?" I said "Yes." He said, "Daytime, nighttime?" I nodded and Wah Wah said, "Nurse lady very trouble lady. I no go; I stay, cook, make coffee all the time." The faithful old fellow stayed for another six weeks until Leland was convalescent and we could take him to the country. Wah Wah wrapped him up in blankets and carried him to the waiting car, then he said, "Good-bye, I go now."

We purchased a home just across the street from us for my mother and sister, where they lived until their deaths just a few years ago.

In 1927 we purchased some property in Woodside with the idea of building a summer cabin. Every Sunday and holiday we would drive to "the land," as the children called it. We had eighteen acres, countless oak trees, and a half-mile of running creek. We built our summer place on a knoll facing the beautifully wooded mountains and called it "Slope Oaks." It wasn't long before we decided to sell our San Francisco home and live at Slope Oaks the year round. We added

118

considerably to our country property and never seemed to finish building. When we wanted another room or sleeping porch, all we had to do was to knock down a wall and arrange it. We were not very imposing on the outside, but we were very comfortable inside.

We were surrounded by endless miles of riding trails and I took full advantage of them. I leased six acres of adjoining Stanford property, fenced it for pasture, and acquired two horses. One was a magnificent white animal seventeen hands high, which had been imported from Ireland. The horse and his previous owner had had a serious misunderstanding, which enabled me to purchase him very cheaply. I rode him eight or nine years and he was a most satisfactory horse.

Shortly after we started our home at Woodside, a Portuguese gardener, Rufino Faria, was recommended to us and he stayed with us as long as we owned Slope Oaks. He was an excellent man, with the Portuguese eye for garish color. With the exception of a large lawn, we had no formal garden, but we had a riot of color and almost every flower known. The Portuguese language came back to me quite readily and Rufus and I had many a tussle with its idioms. I was a park commissioner of San Francisco at this time, and John McLaren, the grand old man of Golden Gate Park, and Jules Girod, his assistant and now the head, came down to give us their ideas. Blondie Ingram planted a small family orchard, and Louis Stewart, who had done so much for the Lakeside Country Club, directed the planting of some magnificent trees. Louis loves trees as he does people and I revel in his friendship.

The children went first to the Woodside Grammar School, then to the Stanford Campus School. A little later the girls entered Castilleja and Leland the Palo Alto Public School. One of Mary's classmates in the first grade at the Campus School was Peggy Hoover—Herbert Hoover's granddaughter. Mary said one day to Peggy, "My daddy knows your grandfather," and Peggy said, "Oh, everybody knows my grandfather."

Woodside was a great place to raise the children. They had freedom and learned to be resourceful, and nothing could take the place of the outdoors, of which there was such a plenty. All three managed to get into Stanford, and on week ends we had literally scores of Stanford boys and girls about the place, as many overnight as we had beds; and there was a barbecue pit where they cooked their own. We had built a guest house but Leland quickly converted it into a poker house for his buddies, and our guests wanted to stay in the main house anyhow.

With Jane and Leland in Stanford, Mrs. Cutler and I took advantage of our apartment at the Fairmont, which we had for about fifteen years, to have Mary enter Miss Burke's. She graduated there and her chance of going to Stanford was limited to her entering summer school, three days later. Mary had lost a year with scarlet fever and a double mastoid, with complications; though a bright young lady, she had been handicapped by these ailments. Also Leland, when he graduated from Palo Alto High School, as I previously noted, could not get into Stanford but had to go to Bates Coaching School for a year. Anyhow, the three graduated with good marks, which they made themselves. Of course, in all of our great universities, the basis of admittance is the preparatory record. I frequently tell parents that admission to Stanford is like getting into heaven. When the time for admission arrives, your record is what counts—you've made it and it's too late to change it.

Le's graduation wasn't easy. I didn't bear down on him too hard. He was majoring in political economy, and I had in mind that he might go on into the Graduate School of Business and then into business with me. The war come along and he signed up for the Navy and was taken over into Navy V-7. This permitted him to stay in college and graduate, provided he took the courses the Navy laid down. All of a sudden, from rather easy subjects he had to take navigation, astronomy, calculus, mathematics, and what have you.

On my desk I had a contract with the Navy to continue at Stanford, when Secretary Forrestal called me from Washington and said the Navy would have to renege, as it had been decided the Army would take over Stanford the first of April and the Navy would have to be out by that time. This would take three months off the time Le would have to graduate. I didn't see how he could do it, and Pearce Mitchell, the Registrar, said he didn't either—in fact, Mitchell went further and said he didn't have a chance. I'll not complicate matters by telling how many honor points he was minus. I did sever his connection with the Deke House and got him a room with my old zoology professor, Daddy Price. Le graduated three months ahead of time, as he had to; then he went to Northwestern where he got his ensign's commission and asked for a destroyer. I asked him why he didn't ask for a battleship. His reply was that being an ensign on a battleship would be like a lone delegate at a Republican National Convention! Anyhow, he got his destroyer, which he joined in the South Pacific, and was off Okinawa when the war ended and had been sunk by suicide planes in the meantime.

I continued with the Aetna for five years after Mrs. Cutler and I were married. Shortly after I joined the Aetna, however, Guy LeRoy Stevick offered me a place with the Fidelity and Deposit Company of Maryland. Stevick had come to San Francisco from Denver as Pacific manager and attorney, while I was still a broker. He was an unusual man, an excellent lawyer, and became undoubtedly the outstanding field surety man in the United States. It was destined that our lives should be close together for many years, but although there was from the start a strong spark between us, neither one of us knew what was ahead. Stevick was twenty years older than I. He had graduated from Dickinson College at Carlisle, Pennsylvania, and from the University of Pennsylvania the year I was born. Mrs. Stevick was the daughter of General Pratt, the old Indian fighter who founded the Carlisle Indian School. She was always a great lady. The Stevicks had five sons and five daughters. One day I was complaining about expenses of our youngsters, aged about three, six, and nine. The Stevick children were graduating from college, getting jobs, and getting married—all at the same time, with some of them coming home to live—and Stevick said: "You think your children are expensive now, but just you wait till they all get to be 'self-supporting'!" Also, at a reception many years ago I overheard some admiring young lady say to Mr. Stevick, "You don't look as though you had had ten children," and Mrs. Stevick spoke up, remarking, "He didn't have them—I had them." Mrs. Stevick, a sweet and lovely lady, died in 1952 after they celebrated their sixty-fifth wedding anniversary. Mr. Stevick is now eighty-eight and going strong.

Although Stevick importuned me to join him, I did not feel that I had done the job for the Aetna which I set out to do and thought I should give that my whole consideration.

121

In 1920 Colonel Edgar A. Hamilton was brought into the Fidelity and Deposit Company by Van Lear Black, chairman of the board, at Baltimore, and made vice-chairman with full power to rejuvenate the company a bit. He made Stevick vice-president in charge of a Pacific Executive Office at San Francisco, with jurisdiction over the eleven states west of Kansas and Nebraska, plus Alaska and Hawaii.

Toward the end of 1920 Molony and I were becoming a little unhappy together and Stevick's overtures were not easy to resist. Molony became very ill, and when he recovered he and I went to Hartford together. Despite the personal regard and affection Dan Gage, of the Aetna, and I had for each other and the other Aetna executives as well, it seemed that in fairness to myself and my family I should make a change. Stevick and Hamilton were then at the Vanderbilt Hotel in New York, and when I had made my decision in Hartford and said good-bye I joined them. We had quite a celebration when I told them that I had made up my mind to join forces with the Fidelity and Deposit. Salary had never been mentioned. Stevick used to tell me that a piece of paper with three columns was always ready for me: one column for my name, one for my title, and the other for my compensation. Again in the Vanderbilt he referred to these columns. There was no hitch on the name or title, but Stevick was Pennsylvania Dutch and when I suggested a certain salary he made a slightly lower counter-suggestion, which of course I immediately accepted. Colonel Hamilton, however, made an unusual contingent arrangement with us. We were to get an overriding on all business done in our territory over a certain amount. My salary was to be half of Stevick's and my contingent one-half. We worked together for thirty years and Stevick brought me along until our compensation was exactly the same both in salary and contingent. He of course was the boss, although he always called me his partner. Our approach to everything was different but we were generally recognized as a formidable team by our home office and our competitors, and we made money for our company.

Stevick was a great underwriter and put cases together that no one else seemed to be able to handle. He had his mind always on the day that trouble might arise and he wanted to avoid it or be ready for it. He was progressive and seemed to have few thoughts outside of the surety business. He was pretty much of a dictator in the way he handled cases, but he was so nearly always right that he more and more had his way. We naturally had differences at times, but I am sure that he loved me as one of his own children and I know I feel toward him today as I would to my own father, had he lived.

I refer briefly to my attempt to leave the Fidelity and Deposit Company and go into the investment field. I was walking in high places of course and wanted to earn more money, as insurance companies are notorious for paying their executives comparatively small salaries. For years Mr. Stevick and I were paid more than the president of our company because we were in the field and produced. My company would not let me leave. They elected me vice-president and director, and when I left Baltimore where I had gone to talk things over, Mr. Miller, our president, walked to the train with me and handed me a letter written in his own hand, with a check enclosed for $5,000. He gave me carte blanche to join a brokerage firm and also to stay on with our company. I became a member of the firm of Brayton, Cutler and Cooke and divided my time between my company and the brokerage house. We paid a tremendous price for a seat on the San Francisco Stock Exchange a few months before the crash. I didn't have the money but borrowed it and our silent partner was negotiating for a seat on the New York Stock Exchange for $500,000. One day Brayton asked me if I would go to Europe with him and Mrs. Brayton if he made a certain X dollars for me. Knowing he couldn't do it I said yes. Shortly thereafter he telephoned that he had. Mr. Stevick was planning to go to Europe about the same time. Our children were small and Mrs. Cutler felt she couldn't leave them. I put all the blame on Mr. Stevick and said he would not let me go. Brayton had me repeat in the most minute detail Mr. Stevick's words and then told me that Mr. Stevick had phoned him he would fire me if I didn't go. We went on two days' notice and spent seven days in London and the beautiful English countryside. A little longer in Paris, where we met Joe Ghirardelli, and our morale broke down—we were gone all told about five weeks. I called it the tour of the flying squirrels.

Of course I lost all the money I did not have in the crash, but was determined to keep my chin up and not go to the wall. I didn't. My friends and the bankers of San Francisco saw me through, and I paid off dead horses for a long time. There is nothing worse, and all I needed to have kept out of it was to apply to my own personal affairs the same sternness I always used in my company's operations. I am not going to embarrass the friends who came to my rescue. They did not have to and they have all been paid back, and many of them are gone but I can never forget them. I can't pass over James K. Lochead, president of the American Trust, without always being grateful, for he wasn't my banker then and didn't have to do a thing. That goes too for Herbert Fleishhacker of the Anglo Bank and W. H. Thomson, his successor, and all of their associates, none of whom were my bankers either.

It was my long friendship for Harold Brayton that got me into the brokerage business, which I knew nothing about, and which caused all my financial troubles. I am not blaming him. I just liked him. I still do, and after many battles and years of grief and despair in my one great financial catastrophe Brayton is closer today to me than most, and I have known him for forty years. Such again is the compensation of enduring friendship.

At that time, with me in two businesses and doing quite a bit of work *pro bono publico*, Mr. Stevick talked Vernon Peirson, now the outstanding field surety man in America, into rejoining us. He had been with the Fidelity and Deposit Company at Syracuse, New York, before I joined the company but had left us temporarily because of differences with Colonel Hamilton, our vice-chairman—the same man who brought me to the company. Peirson is known far and wide by the contractors of our country, makes good and fair decisions promptly and firmly, and after an association of a quarter of a century I can say that I have never known a fairer man not only in business but in the personal intimate daily things that count so much.

Also, my connection with the Fidelity and Deposit Company brought me John W. Latham, whom I engaged in Denver over thirty years ago to head our Phoenix, Arizona, office. He was so effective that we promoted him to San Francisco and later to be Peirson's associate in heading up the Western territory. He has been my brother-in-law for quite a few years, having married Mrs. Cutler's sister. John is as my own brother, a sterling surety man, and with claim to golfing prowess. Anyhow, he was president of the California Golf Association and

124

outspokenly claims the reason I don't play is because I know I can't win and will not take the time nor have the patience to practice incessantly. My only reply is that I have played two games of golf in my life and won them both, so why should I fool with the game. Also I frequently remind him of the many times I have beaten him at tennis.

On Mr. Stevick's seventieth birthday, I arranged a party for him at the Bohemian Club and presented him with a scroll printed by John Henry Nash and signed by all present.

GUY LEROY STEVICK—THREE SCORE YEARS AND TEN

With most men, seventy years are many and things to sigh about. With Guy LeRoy Stevick, seventy years are few enough in which to learn the ways of youth and give to all the years ahead the wisdom which must temper eagerness and keep alive enthusiasm of purpose and achievement.

Guy Stevick is just starting now, and because he has taken full advantage of his years, knows more than you and I can ever know.

Please may we take advantage of his knowledge and his understanding and tell younger men the while they watch his frown to also glimpse the twinkle in his eye.

He sits at his desk as business men are supposed to do, but he does not care if desks are mahogany or oak or pine. He only asks that men, across the table, use words to say the things they mean and he writes his bond accordingly.

Throughout the land, men who build and plan have come to reverence him and give respect to his plain and simple statement of the truth. Well they know when trouble comes, his words stand stalwart toward the meaning of the men who sign their names. Always underneath his sternness does he disguise the smiling of his soul, and the only weakness that we know of him is his great faith that younger men will some day pack the load.

Every day we learn from him as do pupils from a master, not only of the rules and routine of a business but of honor and the ordered way of dealing with our fellow-men.

He teaches us to love the give and take of life, to treat men fairly and demand fair treatment in return, to apply the Golden Rule to daily conduct and not to sound it as an empty phrase and to be unafraid in the application of the Rule to our own selves.

Above all else, we love him for the human side of him, for his great and understanding heart and for his fair appraisal of the other fellow's point of view.

We love his humor and his kindliness and his philosophy of life—to do the thing you think is right as you understand the right to be. For all of these, we who work with him, in friendship and affection, inscribe this scroll.

My work with the Fidelity and Deposit Company permitted me to participate in many outside activities. The company was broadminded and believed in public service and civic work. At least President Miller did. Mr. Stevick didn't think it was productive of anything in particular, but if I wanted to do a lot of extra work it was all right with him. The result was that I did a great many things that were not concerned with my business at all. I suppose my participation in public affairs attracted business to my company and I was always on the lookout for it. I can't recall, however, of any civic work I did with the idea of getting business. I never gave it a thought. I liked people, I wanted to help my city and believed in progress generally. I still don't know how we can have any kind of progress if we leave it to "the other fellow." Once started on a project I'm like everybody else, I don't like to be beaten, and the result was that I was fairly successful in the civic work I undertook.

I was three times president of the Chamber of Commerce and headed the Community Chest campaign twice. I was on practically all of Mayor Rossi's commissions at one time or another: Park Commission for eight years, and president of the Library Commission, which under the charter automatically put me on the Art Commission. I attended one meeting. Herbert Fleishhacker and W. W. Chapin as a joke engineered me into the presidency. Benjamin Bufano, an unusual sculptor, whom everybody in San Francisco knows, had done a statue of St. Francis of Assisi in stainless steel. There were many expressions of admiration throughout the city, but neighborhood clubs protested its being placed in their vicinity. The Art Commission had to decide. I presided over the wrangling for a few hours and then asked Herbert Fleishhacker to take the chair while I slipped out for a moment. I walked down the hall to the Mayor's office, wrote out my resignation, and did not return. I have referred to this since as being president of the Art Commission for one consecutive day.

Mayor Rolph was the most colorful Mayor San Francisco ever had. Eventually he was elected Governor of California. C. C. Moore, president of the 1915 Panama Pacific Exposition, was in 1933 chairman of the California Commission to the Chicago Exposition, for which the California Legislature appropriated $100,000. Mr. Moore died and shortly thereafter Governor Rolph telephoned me from Sacramento: "Le," he asked, "have you a high hat and a frock coat?" "Yes, Governor, I have." "You," said Governor Rolph, "are just the man we're looking for; we want you to take Charley Moore's place and be chairman of the California Commission." Such were my qualifications. I accepted the chairmanship and the first thing I did was to examine the finances. I found that $40,000 of our $100,000 had been paid to Chicago for a California building. I had just been in Chicago and there wasn't a building on the site of the Exposition. I telephoned President Rufus Dawes whom I knew very well and he referred me to Major Lohr, general manager and later president of the National Broadcasting Company, and a fine gentleman. Both men were very evasive and I couldn't find out a thing about our $40,000. When the Exposition was over and a big success, they confided in me that they built it with our $40,000, as it was the first and only real cash they had. Later when I was president of the Golden Gate International Exposition on Treasure Island, I knew what they meant and wished that we had $40,000 of real money to start with. Incidentally, the California Building and Exhibit were outstanding and were considered by many to be the best at Chicago. They were instituted by the Los Angeles Chamber of Commerce at my insistence. I was president of the San Francisco Chamber and came close to being mobbed, but we had no one versed in that sort of thing, and Los Angeles, on investigation, was found to be fully equipped and exhibit-wise. I have always been grateful to the Los Angeles Chamber for the job it did and the pleasant relations we had. Also, I cannot criticize C. C. Moore for advancing the $40,000. It produced results and we had full value received during the two years the Exposition operated. President Rufus Dawes had the middle name of Cutler. We were not related, but came out of the same big book, and used to jest about being cousins. On the opening day of our Exposition on Treasure Island in San Francisco Bay, I had a wire from Rufus Cutler Dawes, reading as follows: "I offer you my cousinly sympathy and prayers." I soon found out what he meant.

Theodore Hardee was secretary to the California Commission to the Chicago Fair, and did a fine job, but was somewhat inclined to take people for granted and to spend a great deal of time on details. The very first day I took office he brought a young man to see me who was scarcely out of his teens and who wanted the orange-juice concession in the California Building on a percentage basis. His father was a restaurateur and an old friend of Hardee's. I was busy and impatiently said, "Do anything you like but don't bother me with these little things. I'm chairman of the Commission, which has the big matters to deal with. If I stop to handle every $500 deal that comes along, we won't have any exhibit," and I waved them out. Later Hardee told me he had made the deal and I thought no more about it.

One morning in the rotogravure section of the Sunday *Chronicle*, I saw a picture of Hardee and a young man who was his office assistant at Chicago, pointing to a beautiful lagoon at the fairgrounds. I recognized the assistant as an embezzler. My company had once bonded him and paid a loss. The man had been prosecuted, found guilty, and sentenced to five years in San Quentin, and then granted probation. I went to Chicago, and while the man denied everything, I brought him back with me and went to work on his case. I found that he started forging Hardee's name the day he was hired, had forged warrants on the state treasury, and all in all had gotten away with about $12,000. We had him arrested, and as far as I know he is still in San Quentin. All of the commissioners were bonded but he wasn't. To rub it in further, the notaries public who attested the forged signatures were all bonded by our company, and we also had a forgery bond on the bank that cashed the checks. Under the law we would have to get through the Legislature an act appropriating another $12,000 to make up the shortage, and that chance didn't look at all good. This was about the end of the first year of the Exposition, and the orange-juice-concession boy, who had been too petty an item for me to bother with, paid us as our share the good sum of $16,000. That squared accounts and enabled us to pay $4,000 into the Treasury of California over and above the appropriation of $100,000. I shook the young man's hand warmly, wrote him a letter, bought him a dinner, and have never felt like a "big shot" since!

Early in my surety career I began going to the California Legislature in behalf of insurance legislation in which the surety companies were interested. It was about 1918 that I began to help out. Although I was then with the Aetna, Mr. Stevick was the dominant surety man

128

in the West and he saw the need of much progressive legislation. I was made chairman of the Legislative Committee of the Surety Association and as such was recognized at Sacramento as the spokesman for the surety companies and throughout the state. I made many fine friends at the capitol and have gone to legislative sessions for over thirty years on one thing or another and have always been welcomed back. I haven't considered myself a lobbyist nor have the legislators looked upon me as one, and I have never been paid for any work I have done there. The surety business was my lifework, and when it needed attention at Sacramento, it was natural that I should go.

Our San Francisco–Oakland Bay Bridge required very complicated legislation (and many things were controversial), as did the Golden Gate Bridge and the Golden Gate International Exposition, of which I was president. I have never had any political ambitions; I could not afford to indulge them, for one thing, but I have political ideals and I like to watch the wheels go round. I have seen them revolve behind the scenes for a good many years locally and nationally. I have made many fine friends among men who are in politics, and they have helped me immeasurably in the comparatively little things I have had to do. Similarly, I have had no difficulty in knowing the ones to avoid, but make no protestation of always avoiding them. Politics is a fascinating game and our country would be better off if it were a career here as it is in England. I have been urged at times to run for office and, when I was younger, for a very high office with powerful people behind me and the necessary money. It was a temptation, for I felt that I could be elected, but I declined. Had I been independently wealthy, I might have succumbed, but my thought was, "What do you do after you quit being United States Senator or Governor or congressman?" You have to break your home ties and those with the friends you have made over the years. The more times you are re-elected the worse it is. Comes the inevitable day you are defeated and you come home again. You get handshakes and warm words and that is all. You are forgotten, with no chance whatever of taking up where you left off, and you start all over again, generally unsuccessfully and bitterly. I have seen many such men, broken in spirit by the long drop to common life, and they have been pitiful figures.

Even though I may not have considered myself a lobbyist at Sacramento, I certainly have done a great deal of it over the years and under present rules would undoubtedly have to register as one. This applies to my many activities in Washington, too, in behalf of public projects for California.

My first experience at Sacramento was in 1918 in connection with very desirable surety legislation. The surety companies bonded public officials, amongst them treasurers, tax collectors, and custodians of public moneys. The law required these officials to put their moneys in banks and take as security from the banks physical securties such as government bonds, municipal bonds, and the like, equal to the amount deposited, plus 10 percent. Banks, of course, were willing to do this for inactive accounts which would remain deposited for a specific term and a long one. They were not interested, however, in putting up securities for so-called "active" deposits subject to daily checking withdrawal. The result was a deplorable condition throughout California, where treasurers were forced to meet payrolls over the county and leave immense sums of cash in antiquated vaults where a self-respecting citizen wouldn't leave his best hat over Sunday. Many states had solved the problem by legislation permitting banks to give surety bonds to the treasurers. Several attempts to enact this sort of legislation in California had failed. Matters were further complicated by the fact that the governing procedure was in the state constitution where it did not belong. The surety companies put me in charge and we succeeded in getting a constitutional amendment on the ballot. I worked out a slogan, "Let your Public Funds Earn Interest." This did not mean much but it sounded good, and we were able to get endorsements from practically all state officials. I wrote the argument which went into the official pre-election literature and did quite a bit of work with my friends throughout the state. The amendment carried by an overwhelming vote. It was, however, only an enabling act; a bill still had to be prepared and wangled through the Legislature and passed by a two-thirds vote in both houses. It was a hard fight and I spent eleven weeks at Sacramento. One assemblyman promised me a vote "if he could be present." He wasn't present and we were one vote shy. The clock had been stopped for two days when our bill came up. A call of the House was had and the sergeant at arms was

130

instructed to find the missing assemblyman, who was known to be in town. He was found hiding in the Governor's bathroom, was escorted to the Assembly chamber, and, true to his promise, voted Aye, and we just made the two-thirds necessary. Strange to say, the vote in the Senate was unanimous.

After the Legislature adjourned, a hearing was had in the Governor's office. Stevick and I presented the arguments and did so well that Governor Stephens vetoed it. The following session we had as Governor Friend W. Richardson, who had been State Treasurer and who understood the problem thoroughly. Also Stevick and I knew him very well personally and had been on his bond as State Treasurer. With his help, our bill had no trouble and became law. With it we enacted a return of securities bond to ensure to the banks that their bonds deposited with the treasurers would be safe. All in all we fared pretty well and did a constructive thing.

My eleven weeks at the Legislature the first time and the necessary attendance during the next session were great experiences and gave me friendships I will never forget. I learned some of the ways of politics and particularly that the less attention you attract to your bills the better off you are.

I came to have a great respect for the rank and file of the legislators. There were certainly some bad ones, but many of them were honest, sincere, hard-working men, putting in long hours for small pay and receiving much abuse. Their own business at home had to be neglected while they did the best they could to serve their constituents. Even between sessions they were called upon hourly to do favors with a long string of callers at their door. Many of them were courageous in doing what they thought was the right thing and often suffered for it at the hands of the voters. Many of the lobbyists too were honest and very hard-working. I know men who have represented big corporations at the Legislature for a score of years who have the respect of everyone. Why shouldn't they? There isn't anything wrong in business looking out for its interests when laws affecting them are being formed.

All of course were not lily-white. I learned whom to avoid and whom to work with and that many matters are settled before they reach committees. In fact many committee meetings are rough-and-tumble affairs with no semblance of form or order to one attending them for the first time. The life of a legislator or a lobbyist or anyone looking after matters at the state capitol or in Washington is a hard one. I once told Harry Hopkins that I was going to write the story of my experiences in Washington and caption it "Capitol Punishment." Hopkins said if I didn't hurry up and copyright the title, he would use it himself.

During my presidency of the San Francisco Chamber of Commerce, many controversial matters arose. The outstanding ones were the Golden Gate Bridge and the San Francisco–Oakland Bay Bridge. A lesser one, but fraught with trouble and differences of opinion, was the Sunnyvale Dirigible Base, now Moffett Field. This is in Santa Clara County and yet was initiated and brought to successful conclusion by the San Francisco Chamber of Commerce.

I had a wonderful Board of Directors. Mrs. Cutler asked me one time who my directors were and when I told her she remarked, "That isn't a Board of Directors—that's a gang!" Of course she knew that for years many of them had been my close friends and that we thought alike, and at times played alike. I had persuaded my great Stanford friend, George Presley, to leave the practice of the law and come with me as executive vice-president of the Chamber. Two men could not be closer. With his wife, we spent nearly every week end together, and while we sat around the fire in our homes George and I would sing nearly every hymn known to a choirboy, which he had been. Emory Wishon, vice-president and general manager of Pacific Gas and Electric Company; Joe Saunders, vice-president of the Southern Pacific Company; later Felix McGinnis, vice-president of the same corporation; Louis Stewart, vice-president of Sudden and Christensen Company; Ward Mailliard; Arthur Fennimore—all were directors and, on or off duty, we were inseparable. It was natural that we were able to accomplish many things because we thought alike and did not bother with red tape. My opening counsel when I first took office was, "Let's take our job seriously but not ourselves."

George Presley as executive vice-president and general manager relentlessly kept the work of the Chamber going. He had the respect and affection not only of the staff but of the city, and he had a wide circle of friends who had started with him in his college days. He died

132

of a heart attack on a train coming back from a vacation in southern California. I wrote of him:

If George were here he would not let me say these words, for he did not ever want the countless friends he loved to speak in praise of him. Save for his great lady, I think I knew him better than anybody in this world. When people listened he would not say a kindly word to me nor I to him. We did not have to for in the silence of our hearts we knew that we were twin. . . .

It was a pastime with his friends when he was near to say in jest some slighting thing about a man whom we all loved and though George knew it was in fun, he could not stay the words of loyal anger which leapt from out his heart.

Friendship with him was a torrent which neither man nor thing could brook. He challenged anyone who tried to stop his giving to the helpless and the weak, and proud he was and justified within his heart when worthy friends would pay him back.

He saw good in almost everyone and though he would disclaim it, judged well the good and bad of life. He would not ask you of your wealth or place but only that you use words to say the things you mean. To him, men who spoke such words were good but even when with trick or guile some word would fail to meet a promise, George would say "He isn't really bad."

He led the way in battle for the people whom he loved and was always first to lift his voice for truth. He knew the common weary days of men, for he walked some bitter lonely roads himself . . . we found that we were raised the same—to believe in God—to sing instead of mourn and let no balance weigh between the rich and poor. . . .

Stanford was his University, and he loved his Alma Mater with a sacred passion. He played at every sport and later coached the Stanford teams. In younger days he flaunted fair and plain to other schools his intense belief that the college of his choice was the best of any in the land. His great tribute now is that undergraduate hatred turned later to respect and love of him.

In his business, that of law, he was stern and fair and cherished most the day the Stanford Board chose him above all others that they knew as counsel and attorney for the Trustees of the University.

One day I persuaded him to leave the law a little while and give himself to civic work. I thought then that I was doing it for him but looking back I know now it was I who needed help. We had great days together in the Chamber of Commerce of San Francisco, and always will his personality and his character shine above our city as does a star.

Outside of friends, his daughter and his son and his wife, Florence, were his life, and because in youth he was taught to know of God, his faith was sure that one day he would live with them forever.

The teaching that he had of God was entwined with song and he wanted children from the day that they were born, to sing—not slow and weary songs but lilting eager songs of comradeship and love, and simple songs of faith that Christ is real and somewhere holds a door wide open for friends to sit and sing together when the day is done.

He knew the half-forgotten songs as truly as the singing of today and the privileged ones who sang with him around a fire or to the sky, could always sense above his clear sweet voice the rhythmic tapping of his foot and the yearning pulse of his great heart.

Because I loved him so, I can not say of him the things I feel. I will always miss the banter of his burning friendship. I need so much the spur and challenge of his righteousness. There is no song that can be sung which will not make me think of him.

And I know that even there, when choir time comes, God's own angels will ask George to sit close by and sing the lead.

I was president of the San Francisco Chamber of Commerce for three terms. We had many things of interest at all times, and many things of consequence for the city were accomplished. San Francisco has no greater asset than its Chamber of Commerce. Its directors and staff have always been men of vision, with the city's interest at heart. The officers and directors serve without pay, and because they genuinely concern themselves with progress they can't always be on the popular side but are frequently the center of abuse and ridicule. Any city takes its Chamber of Commerce as a matter of course, and in the old vaudeville days no performance was complete without a gag at the expense of the Chamber of Commerce. The San Francisco Chamber is the finest in the country and is recognized as such, and many of the great happenings in San Francisco have been brought about by it. San Francisco Chamber is as old as the city itself—one hundred years—and has always been manned by unselfish citizens with nothing but the city's good in mind and without thought of where the credit may fall. Being president or director is a thankless job except in one's own conscience and except for the knowledge that the reward will come at a much later date and in an astral sphere.

San Francisco has a livestock pavilion known on the circuit as the Cow Palace; it is outstanding in every way and the joy of stockmen and sports fans. It is responsible for millions of dollars coming into our city. The late Bert Sooy as an individual should rightfully have credit for bringing it to conclusion and he did a magnificent job, but the San Francisco Chamber of Commerce started it and was responsible for the initial appropriation of $250,000.

The Chamber's directors had approved the report of its Livestock Committee and voted to give its backing to an appropriation bill in the Legislature. It was a lean year and a big deficit was prophesied. Mayor Rolph had just been elected Governor, so George Presley and I went to the Mayor's office to see him. I told him what we wanted and said, "Governor, unless you are for it and will sign the bill if we get it through, we won't even go to Sacramento and start. We're all busy and there's no use wasting the Legislature's time if at the end you are going to veto the bill." He explained that Rolland Vandegrift was his director of finance, whom he would have to consult, and he invited us to Sacramento after he had been installed as Governor. Rolph was an ardent and accomplished horseman, had been president of the Chamber earlier, and was clearly sympathetic to our idea. He was, however, a consummate politician and had no idea of letting two young men wangle him into a commitment before he was even inaugurated.

We followed the matter religiously and by appointment went to the Governor's office shortly after he began his term. I again told him what we were after, adding that if he would say he could not sign the bill for $250,000 if it came to his desk, we would turn around and go home without bothering anybody. The Governor repeated that Vandegrift was in charge of finances and that we should see him. I said, "No, Governor, we don't want to see him except with you, because you know San Francisco and its needs. Will you please send for him?" This the Governor did, and when I had restated my case, Vandegrift told us about the big deficit in the state's finances and added: "What is more— you fellows can't even get by the committees." I replied, "That is our business. If we do get by the committees and the Legislature, will you, as director of finance, advise the Governor to sign the bill, and will you keep away from the committees and not talk out of the corner of your mouth to them or even twinkle your eyes at any one of them while we are working on the bill?" Vandegrift said, "Well, if they ask me for an opinion I'll have to give it." I said, "I talked as plainly as I could;

you know what I mean by talking out of the corner of your mouth to the committee. Will you promise as Rolland Vandegrift to Le Cutler not to do it and advise the Governor to sign the bill if we are successful?" Vandegrift hesitated and then said, "Yes—but you won't get through the committee." I again said, "That's our business and we understand each other. Shake hands on it." We shook while the Governor commented, "Vandegrift, what are you trying to do—put me in the hole?" Vandegrift again said for good measure, "Don't worry, Governor; they'll never get by the committee."

It was a hard fight, but we did receive the approval of all committees and passed the Legislature without a cut in the appropriation. I was in the East when the bill came to Governor Rolph's desk and read in a San Francisco paper that Vandegrift had advised the Governor to veto the bill on account of the deficit in the state's finances. I wired Governor Rolph asking for a public hearing and said I would come home immediately. The hearing was held with an overflow attendance. Vandegrift, not knowing I was there, explained the state's position very fairly but with no reference to our meeting in the Governor's office before the bill was introduced. When Vandegrift had finished, Governor Rolph said, "I'll have to ask Le Cutler to answer Mr. Vandegrift." I did, recited our meeting and particularly told of shaking hands on our agreement that Vandegrift would not talk out of the corner of his mouth or twinkle his eyes at any member of the Legislature. I finished with the statement that we all recognized the condition of the state's finances as presented by Mr. Vandegrift but all I was going to do was to call on him to keep his promise to me which he had made as man to man. Governor Rolph arose and very forcefully recited the need for a livestock pavilion and the great good it would do for all California, emphasizing particularly how it would put us on a par with other states on the livestock circuit. His whole presentation was on the merits of the appropriation. "But," he finished, "regardless of the merits, I remember very well the discussion between Mr. Vandegrift and Le in my office and Le's expression about Vandegrift's not talking out of the corner of his mouth or twinkling his eyes at anyone. They shook hands on Mr. Vandegrift's promise that he would let the Legislature alone and advise me to sign the bill if it came to my desk. If Mr. Vandegrift knew as much about

136

politics as I do, he wouldn't have made that promise, but he did. The bill is before me and the honor of the State of California is at stake. I will sign the bill." This the Governor did with all the flourish and drama which he could so well muster. Cheers shook the ceiling of the Capitol. The Governor handed me the pen, which I still have, and the Cow Palace was on its way, through the initiative and efforts of the San Francisco Chamber of Commerce.

Vandegrift remained in state service until he died just a year or so ago. He was an unusually capable man. We never had any hard feelings over the incident and worked together over the years on many things.

One outstanding accomplishment of the San Francisco Chamber of Commerce was the building of Sunnyvale Dirigible Base, now Moffett Field. This was at Sunnyvale in Santa Clara County, two counties removed from San Francisco. The cost was $450,000 and the money had to be raised and the deed given to the Navy in advance. The Junior Chamber of Commerce initiated the idea and the Senior Chamber backed it up. Unfortunately there was no underwriting or money in hand when the Chamber made the promise in writing "of any 1,000 acres that the Navy might select." Shortly after this promise was made I came into office and fell heir to the raising of the $450,000 or of reneging. I went to Washington to try and talk the Navy out of it. A nine-man board of admirals greeted me, headed by Admiral Peoples, as I remember. They were very cordial and said that in all the history of the Navy no such offer had ever been made. They added that they did not know why we made it and of course did not know where we would get the money, but that was our problem and they would hold us to our promise. These admirals had a large map on the wall and pointed out the 1,000 acres they had decided upon. It was the most costly in the area because it contained high-tension lines of the Pacific Gas and Electric Company, which would have to be moved at great expense, and mentally I was counting on the PG&E as a contributor. I have always thought the deciding factor was a large clump of trees where the commandant would want his house. The balance of the acreage was bare.

I came back to San Francisco and went to work. Santa Clara County, which was the chief beneficiary of the project, contributed $100,000, and

San Mateo County, $50,000, which dragged out for a long time and had to be supplied in the interim by our Chamber. Fifty thousand was raised by individual and corporate subscription, following a lunch and explanation I made at the Bohemian Club with practically all of our outstanding citizens present. This left $250,000 to be raised. I went to Mayor Rossi, accompanied by W. H. Crocker, Phil Fay, and Fred Koster, and asked the Mayor for $50,000 per year for five years from his advertising and publicity fund. City Attorney John O'Toole was present and pointed out to Rossi that he couldn't do it. The Chamber's attorney, Allen G. Wright, agreed with him. Both were in agreement on the benefits financially to San Francisco in the purchase of supplies and money that would be spent by the city and county, but it seemed that neither San Francisco nor any other body politic could pledge money beyond a fiscal year. Jack Dunnigan was then clerk of the Board of Supervisors, and he prophesied all sorts of entanglements for the Mayor and actual disaster at election time. Mayor Rossi said, "I know it can be nothing but a gentleman's agreement and I may not be Mayor for five more years. If I am, I am going to see that $50,000 a year is given to the Chamber of Commerce because I believe in the benefits that will accrue to San Francisco and I believe in Le. I know him and he knows me and he will trust me."

We had to translate all of this into real money. The Clearing House banks came to our rescue after a struggle, and we could not have done it without them. Acting on the advice of James K. Lochead of the American Trust, I went first to Charles McIntosh of the Bank of California, president of the Clearing House. He advised me to see Fred Lipman, president of the Wells Fargo Bank and Trust Company. After I told my story, Lipman said, "Cutler, my business is telling people what they should not do. Yours is a fantastic scheme and you must not do it. Sure, the Chamber of Commerce will be set back for years and suffer if it repudiates its promise. It never should have made such a promise without an underwriting to back it up. It makes no difference that you didn't start it; the Chamber of Commerce is an institution, and while it will hurt all San Francisco, my bank will not go along and I advise you not to waste any time on it." I was in the depths and discouraged and walked around the block three or four times before I saw any more bankers. I called on W. H. Crocker, president of the Crocker National Bank. He said, "Le, did I ever fail to help out in any worthy cause? I went to see the Mayor with you; I'll do anything the other banks do and you can tell them so." That was very encouraging and cheered me considerably, but I didn't have any other banks. The Chamber had voted to give its note to the banks and to take my word for Rossi's word. The whole $450,000 was involved; it was quite an undertaking and took a great deal of time. I went back to see Fred Lipman of the Wells Fargo. He greeted me cordially and said, "I understand you are having a hard time with some of the banks. I wanted the Chamber of Commerce to learn a lesson and I think they have. Don't beg any bank. This bank will not only subscribe its share but take up any slack that remains and you can tell my fellow bankers that too."

I did not have any trouble after that, as can be imagined. We bought the base and delivered the deed to Admiral Cole at a big ceremony on the floor of the Merchant's Exchange. People have forgotten it, as people do. So have the Navy and the Army, who held it for a while; but there it is, and the San Francisco Chamber of Commerce and the banks and citizens of San Francisco made it possible. Mayor Rossi was re-elected and kept his word to the letter. When he ran for Mayor the last time, I advised him not to, because I told him Roger Lapham would beat him, but that if he did run I would be for him. Lapham was one of the finest citizens San Francisco ever produced and my good friend. Rossi's close friends knew he was in poor health and probably could not live out his term. The downtown group were all out for Lapham and one of my friends urged me not to get on Rossi's band wagon. I replied that Rossi didn't have any band wagon, for I had attended a meeting of his "Board of Strategy" and, while they were old men in years, they were infants in the ways of politics. Election day, while people were voting and of course before the votes were counted, Lapham picked me up in his automobile and we rode around the city. I told him why I had to be for Rossi, that he had stood with me for thirteen years, as he had the Chamber of Commerce, and that I had been on many of his commissions and part of his official family. I added that I knew from the start and knew now beyond doubt that Lapham would be elected, but I would not desert Rossi in his hour of certain defeat when he needed me. Lapham knew all this and he said: "Le, no one would have any respect for you if you had deserted Rossi. It will make no difference at all between us. The only thing I wish is that you had made the speech for me that you made for Rossi over the radio." Here I say that it did not make any difference. The only favor I asked of Mayor-elect Lapham was that he keep Doris Barrett in the City Hall. She was a lovely, efficient girl, the daughter of my old friend, Dick Barrett, and had been with Mayor Rossi for a long time. She is still there under Mayor Elmer Robinson.

I urged Mayor Lapham not to make the only mistake of his administration. He announced that he would serve one term only and had a calendar over his desk captioned "Days to go." It was religiously changed every day and the public could see for themselves how long he intended to stay in office. No one believed him at first, because all the politicians use the same gag one way or another. Roger meant it and when the politicians realized it they just didn't bother with him any more. He set in motion many reforms and people voted for his bond issues because they trusted him. He could, in my opinion, have done much more if he had kept his resolution to himself and let the politicians and hangers-on worry to the last.

For two years, 1929 and 1930, I was campaign chairman of the Community Chest of San Francisco. It was most interesting work but there was nothing easy about it. At that time outside drives for funds, such as now occur, were very few in number and amount. Practically every worthy cause was embraced in the Chest and the whole city joined in. Catholics, Jews, Protestants worked side by side and the finest men and women in San Francisco worked as though their own daily bread depended on attaining the goal. Report lunches during the last two weeks of the drive were held at the St. Francis Hotel, with everyone paying for his own. Rivalry between the teams of volunteer solicitors was very keen. Of course they had been well organized, with captains and lieutenants to whom they first had to report, and it was very carefully seen to that each stayed in his or her own district. This was very important, for everyone had a close friend in some other one's territory who over the years could be counted on for a substantial contribution. To avoid criticism I assigned Mrs. Cutler to one of the poorest districts, where she climbed stairs and rang doorbells for a fifty-cent contribution or a refusal. One of her good friends in another district insisted on giving $1,000, to be credited to her team. We had a bad time over that one and nearly lost the thousand, but Mrs. Cutler's team did not get it and a rival team reported it amidst great cheers. My sister Georgia had many such experiences. She was a director of the Good Will Mission and worked among the small givers. She was also president of the YWCA and had many friends who wanted to give her large contributions, which under the rules she couldn't take. I wasn't very popular in the Cutler family during the campaign. This applied even to my six-year-old daughter, Jane. One night she climbed on my knee and asked me to write her a Community Chest poem, explaining that the grammar schools were having a contest and would give a prize for the best one. Sipping a highball and being in a mellow mood, I wrote one from the kiddie's viewpoint. A few days later Jane came home from school all elated and said that the poem she wrote was one of three chosen by the judges throughout the school system as eligible for the prize, and the winner would be announced in a day or two. Then it was I realized that I had offered a prize for the best poem written by grammar-school children from our public schools. I immediately explained to Jane that she did not write it—I did, as she well knew—and as I was chairman of the campaign, the poem could not be entered. It would have to be withdrawn, and she would have to tell her teacher the circumstances. We had quite a family scene, with Jane crying and refusing to tell the teacher anything. However, she told me many things, and I finally picked her up bodily and carried her up the stairs to bed. This was before supper and she was quite an armful and kicked quite sturdily and yelled so that I am sure all the neighbors put me on their blacklist too. Two or three days later she came home from school all smiles. "Daddy," she said, "you don't have to worry any more about that Community Chest poem you wrote—a little five-year-old girl got the prize!" I always wondered if her father wrote it!

We kept the report lunches snappy and interesting. We always had a program of entertainers and had no trouble getting the best in the city. Actors who happened to be playing in San Francisco, such as Leo Carrillo, whom I had known when he was a cartoonist on the old *Bulletin,* Clarence Kolb of Kolb and Dill, and many others gave of their talents to keep things lively and the workers in a good humor. Our own Larry Harris, whom in introducing I dubbed the "Wit of Woodside and the sage of San Francisco," was a tower of strength to us and of course Roy Folger helped greatly whenever we needed him.

Rivalry between the police team and the firemen was particularly keen. At their semifinal report lunch the police were ahead and great were the cheers from their side of the table. After the lunch was over, a fireman, whom I recognized but couldn't quite place, came up to me and said: "I am Ed Lamb. You did me a favor one time in saving my job with Mayor Rolph; now I am going to do you one. Us firemen know where all the bootleggin' joints is, so do the coppers, but they can't go in. We can because the places have to be inspected. I knocked one of them over for the Chest and here it is." He handed me a greasy roll of bills which when counted totaled $900, and the firemen were over the top and ahead of the police.

The last day of the second campaign I was walking to the final report lunch and was pretty discouraged. We were after a big amount of money and it did not look as though we could make it. I had my head down and my hands behind my back and I was thinking hard. I guess my discouragement showed, for I felt an arm around my shoulder and it was my great friend, Alfred Esberg, who too was on his way to the luncheon. "Le," he asked, "are you going over the top today?" "No, Al I don't see how we can do it and I feel very badly about failing because it will disappoint so many fine people who have worked so hard." "Oh, don't worry Le," replied Al, "You and Parmer Fuller and Al Ghirardelli will figure out some way of doing it, and Le, you will always have this satisfaction: five years from now you can walk into any group of businessmen in San Francisco—any group—and not a blankety-blank one of them will know who you are!" That was all I needed to cheer me up, for it touched part of my philosophy of life which O. Henry so well stated: "The truest test of friendship is to touch a match to your friend's collar and see if it's celluloid."

Incidentally, we did go over the top, and in the two years raised $5,250,000. I always think of the people who worked with me and made this possible with a rewarding glow of affection and gratitude.

I made a "talkie" which was shown daily in all of San Francisco's theaters during the campaign. The making of talking movies was not in the casual state of perfection that it is today, but was somewhat of an ordeal. I remember being placed in a sort of tent with extremely brilliant lights focused on me and perspiring profusely and having to say the speech over several times until it was acceptable. It was:

THE COMMUNITY CHEST

Men and women of San Francisco, your Community Chest is founded on the friendliness of a great city and on the faith of the deserving and the helpless, that your hand will sometimes touch their own and lead them for a little way, until they can walk alone. Your Community Chest is founded on the faith of children that this wide world was only meant for play and though you know their world will last for just a day, you smooth a path for childhood's step to walk to manhood's streets where men are gentled by the memory of their play.

Your Community Chest is founded on the faith of old and tired men that they can find a place to sleep and on a woman's faith that God will understand.

Your Community Chest is founded on your faith that all of these, the deserving, the helpless, the men, the women and the kids, will find in San Francisco's heart a friend—and privileged as I am to answer for that friend, I answer that we will not fail your faith nor theirs.

One of the big controversial issues to come for settlement during my presidency of the Chamber was the Golden Gate Bridge. It had been talked about for a long time and in 1929 and 1930 had been kept relentlessly before the people. A Bridge District, extending from San Francisco to the Oregon line and excluding only one county, had been formed and Joseph B. Strauss from Chicago engaged as chief engineer. I had known Strauss when I was in Chicago twenty years before, as he was a client of my uncle, W. W. Durham. He was an extremely capable engineer with many outstanding achievements to his credit, a master promoter, but shy and retiring, and with the soul of a poet. He did in fact write quite a bit of good verse, some of which I have. While there was no doubt about his ability to design the massive bridge, he was ill-fitted for the battles that raged in San Francisco over its construction. As I talked with him almost daily, there is no doubt in my mind that his death was hastened by the bitter controversies that raged around him. Under the law governing the formation of the Bridge District, the City and County of San Francisco would have to make good 85 percent of any deficiency in bridge revenues. In other words, the Golden Gate Bridge is a tax-supported structure, with San Francisco responsible for most of the support. A bond issue of $35,000,000 was on the ballot, with the heavy taxpayers and big property owners lined up against it. Women's organizations were formed to preserve the beauty of the famed Golden Gate and not have it marred by an ugly mundane bridge. They were a powerful and annoying force. It was expected that the Chamber of Commerce would come out against the bond issue and side with the property owners, who were the biggest supporters of the Chamber. Also, many of our directors owned stock in the Golden Gate Ferries, with boats plying to Marin County—and a very profitable venture, owing to the automobile traffic. Herbert Fleishhacker was president of the Golden Gate Ferries and many of our directors did business and owed money to the Anglo Bank, of which he was also president. The Southern Pacific Company, of which my great friend Paul Shoup was president, and a director of the Anglo, was vitally interested in the ferries. The Southern Pacific Company held 120 memberships in the Chamber.

The directorate of the Chamber was largely representative of corporate interests and in our preliminary discussions we all felt that the Chamber would oppose the bridge. I felt that I would, and most of my friends were against it and would be adversely affected financially by its construction. I also was one who owed money to Herbert Fleishhacker's bank and was daily in friendly relationship with Samuel P. Eastman, former president of the Spring Valley Water Company and organizer of the Golden Gate Ferries. Eastman was a very able and attractive man and a good organizer. Mrs. Eastman and Mrs. Cutler were good friends and the Eastman sons, Ben and Sam, were outstanding Stanford athletes whom our children fraternized with daily.

W. H. Crocker, president of the Crocker Bank, whom I mentioned previously as helping me so materially on the Sunnyvale Dirigible Base, and a man I greatly admired, was a heavy taxpayer and was bitter against the bridge project. One night at the Bohemian Grove Encampment, as I was about to deliver the Old Guard Oration, W. H. came up and, with one arm around me and his fist shaking in my face, cried over and over, "Le, you kill that bridge; I'm depending on you—and all your friends

144

in this town are." Most of the poetry of the occasion was knocked out of my system and I went very falteringly to my oration. The Crocker interests employed Robert A. Kinzie, a consulting engineer with a great deal of successful underground mining experience to his credit, to prove that the foundation for the south pier of the bridge would have to be built on serpentine rock and would not stand up. "Serpentine" became the word of the day and was bandied about as a horrible treacherous thing by the unknowing as well as by competent engineers. Bailey Willis, head of the Geology Department of Stanford, and Charles Wing, dean of engineering there, appeared before the directors of the Chamber in protest. Willis prophesied flatly that an earthquake would destroy the south pier because serpentine rock would not hold it up. Wing said the bridge would cost $100,000,000. Director Louis Stewart facetiously asked, "Who's going to build it—Shreve, Treat and Eacret, the jewelers?"

I appointed a hardheaded committee from our directorate to study the matter and report to the Chamber. Without exception all were friendly to the corporations and property owners affected. The chairman was L. O. Head, president of the American Railway Express—which was then owned jointly, I believe, by the Southern Pacific and the Santa Fe. Silas Palmer, a large property owner and a director of the Bank of California, and Fred Meyer, the architect, were members. I have the report of the committee. Unanimously, but I am sure reluctantly, it recommended the voting of the bond issue and the construction of the bridge as of great "development value not measurable at this time" and as something which our Chamber of Commerce should in the very nature of things support. The report offered engineering statistics to prove that, with the exception of a slight tax subsidy at times, it could be paid for out of tolls and built for $35,000,000. The report was unanimously adopted by the Board of Directors on October 2, 1930. The Chamber's action was a shock to the business community. Eight former presidents of the Chamber formed a Taxpayers' League against the bond issue and enlisted many of San Francisco's finest citizens. The shipping interests, all sponsors of the Chamber, objected to the height of the bridge on the ground that there were certain ships afloat which could not pass underneath the span.

I went on the radio many times with Francis V. Keesling, chairman of the Bond Committee, and made a campaign for adoption of the bond issue. I presented in pamphlet form a statement of the Chamber's policy with respect to the bridge, giving the opinion of five outstanding and nationally known engineers that the bridge was buildable. To be fair, I also quoted from the opinion of engineer Kinzie that "a foundation south pier cannot be safely built." My statement concluded:

The San Francisco Chamber of Commerce has received permission from the Supreme Court of California to have Col. Allen G. Wright, its General Counsel, take the necessary legal steps to appear as a friend of the Court on behalf of the Golden Gate Bridge District in the hearings which are to be held next month to determine the validity of the Bridge Bonds. We are cognizant of the doubts that have been created concerning the construction of the South Pier of the Bridge but we have also studied the reports of able and experienced engineers pre-eminent in their profession, which state that the foundations of the Bridge are adequate to its support. However, we believe that this question can be settled and determined beyond reasonable doubt and the San Francisco Chamber of Commerce pledges itself to bring about the earliest clearance of all disputed points and as far as is humanly possible through the expenditure of effort and money, to safeguard this great project from unnecessary legal obstruction and against physical uncertainty. Legal and physical hazards being safeguarded, the Bridge *must be built*!

The bond issue was carried by a vote of 3 to 1. There the bridge is. It was built within the $35,000,000 voted and no tax subsidy has been required. No one can question its overwhelming value to San Francisco, and every citizen will shudder at the thought of what the government would have done without it during the war. The aftermath of friend against friend left no scars and was one of the finest examples of San Francisco citizenship I know. Paul Shoup and Herbert Fleishhacker congratulated me and said smilingly that I couldn't be blamed as president of the Chamber of Commerce for coming out for the bridge, but with a playful slap on the shoulder added, "Of course, you didn't have to make all those speeches and publish all those statements." I cannot recall that our action was ever held against us by anyone, and later when I was chosen president of the Golden Gate International Exposition, every one of the fine citizens who fought so hard against the bridge helped unstintingly with Exposition, and it could not have been built without them. This was particularly true of Herbert Fleishhacker, who was chairman of the Art Committee, and the man responsible for getting the magnificent exhibit of old masters from Italy. More than that, he encouraged and guided me at every turn and asked for nothing except a successful Exposition.

During these interesting times I kept steadily at my work for the Fidelity and Deposit Company, guaranteeing that employers would be reimbursed for misplaced faith and that contractors would fulfill their contracts and pay their labor and material bills. I was present when Secretary of the Interior Ickes tried to change the name of Hoover Dam to Boulder Dam, while the President of the United States, whom I knew, stood beside him. The great dam was not built in Boulder Canyon but in Black Canyon, many miles away. Stevick and I had quietly worked on the project from a bonding standpoint for at least a year before bids were called for its construction. We initiated the surety bonds and had much to do with getting combinations of contractors together, and Stevick was chosen as one of the directors of the corporation which built the dam. It is a matter of record that all of the governmental documents and specifications relating to that great structure were written in the name of Hoover Dam. Dr. Ray Lyman Wilbur, President of Stanford, on leave from the University, was Secretary of the Interior under President Hoover, and both pressed relentlessly for its construction at the earliest possible moment. It made no difference to President Hoover that the co-author of the legislation paving the way for the dam's building was the man in public life who probably hated him most, Senator Hiram Johnson of California. This legislation was known as the Swing-Johnson bill. Philip D. Swing was a lawyer and classmate of mine at Stanford and a congressman from El Centro, California, the county seat of Imperial County. He was attorney for the Imperial Irrigation District and knew thoroughly the history of the Colorado River and what its control meant to the safety and prosperity of his county. He is one of the fine citizens of California and continues always in making contributions to its progress. I boarded a train one evening at Sacramento, California's capital, following a Republican State Convention. Both Johnson and Swing were aboard, and the observation car with seats facing each other was crowded with prominent

Californians. Just before the train started, a newsboy came aboard crying out that Interior Secretary Wilbur had named the forthcoming dam the Hoover Dam. There was much laughter and ribbing of Johnson and Swing, because everyone on the train knew of the great pioneer work of the two men but had heard of Mr. Hoover and Dr. Wilbur not at all in its connection. Senator Johnson was plainly indignant. Swing refused to be ruffled and said, addressing the crowded car, "I'll promise to get sore too if any one person on this train, including my colleague, Senator Johnson, can now name the authors of the legislation that started the Panama Canal." No one could, of course, but there was no other topic of conversation on the ride to San Francisco.

It was inevitable that Hoover Dam would be built. The rich empire of the Imperial Valley had been despoiled and ravaged by the Colorado River for far too many years. Amateur gaps cut in the riverbanks for irrigation purposes were always getting out of hand at floodtime and innumerable sandbag dams were washed away. As early as 1905, twelve to fourteen thousand people were dependent on control of the river for irrigation, and there was no control. In that year the main irrigation canal became a raging torrent with the summer rise of the river. Its width in places was 150 feet, and it was nearly two years before the break could be closed. More than 300,000 acres of land were flooded, and it took the mighty Southern Pacific Railroad, in response to a plea from President Theodore Roosevelt, to save the situation. It also took the railroad many years to get its pay from the government. Quite aside from the tremendous cost of flood protection, it was estimated that the yearly cost of handling the enormous silt deposits was $1,500,000.

Agricultural products in Imperial County had grown to a value of $100,000,000 per year, provided the Colorado stayed in its channel. Phil Swing announced himself for Congress, campaigning on a solemn pledge to obtain national relief of the situation, and was easily elected. In 1928 California's Senator Hiram Johnson joined forces with him, and the Swing-Johnson bill was introduced. This bill authorized the expenditure of $165,000,000 for a dam and related structures to be built under the jurisdiction of the Bureau of Reclamation, functioning under the Department of the Interior. Two years of bickering followed among the seven states claiming water from the Colorado. Powerful lobbies

148

were maintained in Washington against the bill. Swing and Johnson were master strategists and President Hoover threw his weight in favor of an early passage. It was not until June 1930, however, that the bill passed both houses, when it was promptly signed by President Hoover. The Reclamation Bureau called for bids for the construction of Hoover Dam, and all papers involving the gigantic enterprise referred to Hoover Dam until it was completed. Then Secretary of the Interior Ickes appeared on the scene one day to call it Boulder Dam. Former President Hoover merely smiled and said, "What difference does it make—there it is." (Some years later, by federal legislation, the name "Hoover Dam" was permanently established.)

Plans and specifications were completed in an amazingly short time under Dr. Elwood Mead of the Reclamation Bureau, and bids were called for in December 1930. This was but six months after passage of the legislation making the dam possible.

March 4, 1931, was set for the submission of bids by competing contractors and the time limit for completion fixed at seven years from the date of bid acceptance. The work itself was divided into five parts with separate completion dates for each—river diversion, the dam itself, two immense spillways, two outlet systems, and the largest powerhouse ever built. Any one of these units was a tremendous contract in itself, and in its existence of a quarter of a century the Reclamation Bureau had not awarded more than the total of the over-all contract. The river diversion involved two 90-foot cofferdams and four tunnels of nearly a mile in length through solid rock and with a diameter of 56 feet. The dam was 730 feet high and 1,200 feet long. The spillways were as big as the world's largest dry docks and the outlet systems had to be driven through solid rock to the powerhouse.

Such a great undertaking fired the imagination of contractors all over America. One hundred seven sets of plans were taken out. But arrangements with banks and surety companies had to be made and it was soon apparent that no one contractor in the United States was big enough to undertake the work alone. Even though the government was to furnish all materials, with the exception of sand and gravel, it still remained the greatest single contract ever undertaken. Bankers accompanied their contracting clients to the site and came away awed and de-

149

pressed by the towering cliffs rising straight up from the narrow box canyon. Looking up from a tiny rowboat, they could not muster any enthusiasm for the work and many openly stated that such a dam could never be built. One eminent engineer who examined the site for a group of Eastern bankers recommended against financing any contractor, and closed on this solemn note:

The dam is about twice as high as any heretofore built; the location is remote; the temperature will range from 20 to 120 degrees and on the bare rock surrounding the dam site the heat will be so intense at times that men cannot work. The location is extremely hazardous regarding floods and the establishment of diversion dams. The tunnel work is difficult and uncertain and the dam itself will require so many refinements in the method of placing concrete, such as expansion joints and a circulating system to cool and contract after placement, that I consider it almost impossible to build. A ten-mile railroad must be operated by the contractor and another eight-mile railroad operated to bring in sand and gravel. Even the water used in mixing concrete must be stored long enough to allow the silt to settle. The job will run over seven years and possibly longer and will require a great deal of financing. The hazard is much greater than in any construction contract I have ever known. It is a super-project which calls for a super-organization having super-financial strength and I know of no super-organization that may bid on it. Even if one is formed and the contract obtained, it would be impossible to relet the job in case of default, except at exorbitant prices.

This was not an extreme viewpoint. Various contracting combinations were discussed in engineering and surety company circles, but contractors were chary about having any part in such a responsibility. Banks were cold to making engagements on such a hazardous undertaking and neither banks nor surety companies relished binding themselves for more than seven years. A clause in the specifications providing "In case such appropriation as may be necessary to carry out this contract is not made, the contractor hereby releases the government from all liability due to the failure of Congress to make such appropriation" did not help the situation, for who could tell what Congress would or would not do over a seven-year period and a probable change of administration?

Nothing testified more eloquently to the appalling nature of the enterprise than the fact that the 107 sets of plans taken out in December 1930 produced only three bidders in March 1931.

150

As soon as the Swing-Johnson bill became law, Stevick and I began working on the idea that someday we might handle the bond, and we felt that if we started soon enough and worked out a plan, we would be able to take the lead. The first announcement was that a $25,000,000 bond would be specified. Stevick and I knew that such a bond could not be written and that, regardless of its size, the participation of virtually every operating surety company would be required. It was not a question of which company would get the business but of getting enough companies interested in writing it. We conferred over a period of months with the Towner Rating Bureau, and R. H. Towner, its president, appeared with me before the Treasury Department, which governed the underwriting capacity of all surety companies. I had numerous meetings with Secretary Wilbur and all of the government officials, who were finally convinced that a $5,000,000 bond would serve the purpose, regardless of the size of the contract. When the bond was written, twenty-seven surety companies participated, some for only 1½ and 2 percent, so impressed were they with the hazards of the job.

A. C. Posey, now vice-president of the Hartford Companies on the Coast, and Edwin C. Porter, then head of the United States Fidelty and Guaranty Company, and only recently deceased, and myself, were chosen to go East and secure the necessary reinsurance. We virtually had to go from door to door and plead with our friends in the surety companies to give us an extra half of one percent participation. It takes a great many halves to make 100 percent, as we can all testify.

Among the contractors themselves, there never has been any time wasted in claiming credit for forming the Six Companies, Inc. The Wattis brothers of the Utah Construction Company and Harry Morrison of Morrison-Knudsen Company had talked about it for some time, as had W. A. Bechtel, and Henry Kaiser, and MacDonald and Kahn. W. H. Wattis at this time was in St. Francis Hospital in San Francisco with an incurable illness, but with his mind as alert as ever. His brother E. O., who had worked with him all of his life, was anxious to have the Utah Construction Company take a leading part in the Boulder Dam building. Marriner Eccles, son of David Eccles, who had financed the Wattis brothers in early days, was also pressing W. H. to form a group or join a group who would construct this great enterprise. Through all the hard pioneer days, W. H. and his wife, Marie, had been very close, and because of his illness Mrs. Wattis guarded him very tenderly. Eccles and E. O. Wattis appealed to Harry Morrison and told him that Mrs. Wattis had forbade them to discuss the dam in any fashion with W. H. No ban was put on their visiting him as often as they chose, but all business talk was taboo. They seemed to think that Morrison might have a chance to win over Mrs. Wattis. Because Morrison believed in the dam and the things which the Utah Construction Company could offer, he undertook the assignment. It took him the better part of three days, talking principally with Mrs. Wattis. It wasn't that she was stubborn; she thought only of her husband's health and she did not want him to undertake anything that would shorten his life by even a day. Money could not compensate in her heart for anything that might disturb her husband's peace of mind. Morrison did not argue against this because there could be no argument. However, he did point out insistently that the Utah Construction Company belonged in the picture; it would be made the crowning achievement of the Wattis brothers' career, and to all of this Mrs. Wattis seemed to agree but she wanted to talk it over with her husband in her own way. Time was pressing because substantial money had to be put up. Morrison took Stevick to meet with Wattis and his wife, and after that meeting I took Harry Morrison and introduced him to Felix Kahn and Alan MacDonald. W. H. Wattis asked for one more day while he made up his mind, and when the day was over Wattis gave Morrison a check for the Utah Construction Company's share. From then until the time of W. H.'s death, he was most enthusiastically interested in the project.

The Utah Construction Company and W. A. Bechtel Company had worked together on the Western Pacific work, and Kaiser and Bechtel already had effected a combination known as the Kaiser Bechtel Company. Charles Shea represented the family interests in the J. F. Shea Company, which had been founded by his father, who had died some years previously. The Shea home office was in Portland, as was Charles Swigert's Pacific Bridge Company, and the two had worked together on many projects. MacDonald and Kahn not only had an enviable reputation as successful contractors but they had a great deal of available money and practically unlimited credit.

Many meetings were held among the contractors themselves and with the surety companies, and in February 1931, Six Companies, Inc., was agreed upon and became a reality. It was a Delaware corporation with an authorized capital of 80,000 shares without par value but with agreement that these shares must be subscribed and paid for at $100 per share. Fifty thousand shares were paid for at once, making a paid-up capital of $5,000,000. The $5,000,000 in cash was promptly paid in and the first officers of the company were: W. H. Wattis, president; W. A. Bechtel, first vice-president; E. O. Wattis, second vice-president; Felix Kahn, treasurer; and Charles A. Shea, secretary. The Board of Directors consisted of ten persons, each representing a unit of $500,000 of subscription; that is, the Utah named two, Kaiser Paving and Bechtel three, MacDonald & Kahn two, Morrison-Knudsen one, Pacific Bridge one, and Shea one. Stevick by unanimous vote of the board was then added to the directorate. The agreement provided for an executive committee with full powers of the Board of Directors, which consisted of H. J. Kaiser, S. D. Bechtel, C. A. Shea, E. O. Wattis, and H. J. Lawlor.

Bids were opened at the Reclamation Bureau's Denver office on March 4, 1931. There were just three bidders: Woods Brothers Construction Company of Nebraska (associated with A. Guthrie and Company of Portland, Oregon), $58,653,107.50; the Arundel Corporation of Baltimore, Maryland (associated with Lynn Atkinson of Los Angeles), $53,893,878.70; and the Six Companies, Inc., of San Francisco, $48,890,995.50.

Seven days later Secretary Ray Lyman Wilbur of the Interior Department awarded the contract to the Six Companies, Inc. Although its bid was nearly $10,000,000 below the high bidder, with a difference of $1.50 per yard of concrete in comparison with the Arundel Company, the Six Companies had no misgivings. The men in the company had a combined record behind them of $500,000,000 in contracts completed, and they were certain of the adequacy of their figures. Each unit of the combination had estimated the job separately and the submitted bid represented the final judgment of all of them. At a preliminary meeting of the Six Companies directors, Kaiser had suggested that the selection of a construction manager be postponed until after the bidding.

Morrison replied that the participation of the Utah and himself was dependent on Frank Crowe being chosen and that he was authorized by E. O. Wattis to so state. If any other name was in the background it was not put up. Kaiser made no objection and so Crowe was agreed upon. There could not have been a better choice. For more than twenty years he had been with the Bureau of Reclamation and thoroughly understood its methods. He had supervised for the Bureau several large dams in Wyoming, Washington, and Idaho, and had resigned several years before to become superintendent of construction for the Utah Construction Company and the Morrison and Knudsen Company on their joint building of the Guernsey Dam and the Deadwood Dam—also Reclamation projects.

Crowe started to work within a few minutes after the results of the bidding were known. By the time the contract was signed the Six Companies under Crowe had spent well over a quarter of a million dollars. President Hoover had stressed the unemployment problems, and the eyes of the country were on the project from that standpoint alone. The unemployed were flocking by thousands to the site despite repeated public warnings by Secretary Wilbur. Railroads and wagon roads had to be built and materials shipped in from many thousands of miles distant; houses had to be built and food supplies arranged; a complete and intricate water system was to be laid out and temporary water instantly provided for.

I have a record of the amount of money put up by each member of the Six Companies, and it was not an easy task for some of them to arrange. There is no point in going into this except to indicate how all the individual contractors have grown since the completion of Hoover Dam and in fact how the individuals have grown since their own boyhood, because the "Six Companies" story began a long time ago with ordinary American boys who emerged as the greatest construction men our country has known. The mothers and fathers of these boys, sometimes together and sometimes singly, did the best they could, unconsciously training them for their later roles: to work unceasingly until their job was done and never think of quitting just because their job was hard; to know what money meant and to take none unless they earned it; to love the land of their birth and make it better for the people in it.

Because these boys grew into manhood honoring their fathers and their mothers, their days were many in the land and the name of the Six Companies is a name to reckon with.

The Wattis brothers began life on a dreary Utah farm, but later dominated the heavy contracting industry of the West as the Utah Construction Company; Felix Kahn was a newsboy in Detroit without thought of Alan MacDonald in Kentucky, who would be his partner for twenty-five years in the relentless progress of MacDonald & Kahn; Harry Morrison did not let his boyhood tenor voice or guitar strumming dull the tie that would bind him to M. H. Knudsen, his elder partner, only in the last few years deceased; W. A. (Dad) Bechtel, the father of S. D. and Kenneth and W. A. Bechtel, Jr., learned his the hard way and so fitted well into the role of conciliator and peace-keeper among the hardy men who formed the Six Companies; Charlie Swigert, as a boy, watched the turbulent Columbia River, and later, heading the Pacific Bridge Company, built most of the bridges now spanning its banks, and anyone who knows that stream knows that from his boyhood he was destined to be a natural member of any group building the Hoover Dam; Charlie Shea was earning his own living and looking after his brothers and sisters when he was thirteen years old. Because he promised his mother on the family Bible that he would never drink, he did not touch a drop of liquor as long as he lived, but he used to tell with a twinkle in his eye how glad he was that his mother did not ask him not to gamble, because he said it would have spoiled him as a contractor and made him totally unfit for the Six Companies; Henry Kaiser is one of the most talked-of men in America. As a boy in New York State, Henry was a dreamer. He still is—and probably his greatest contribution to the Six Companies group was "the stuff which dreams are made on." Twenty years ago on his birthday I said:

It is not easy to appraise the friends with whom we daily walk and deal, for often does the sternness of exacting hours disguise the hearts of men. The world would be a still and lifeless thing if all we did was wait with listless hope for the morrow's commonplace. There must be men, impatient men and restless, who yearn to make, with hand and brain, the world a better place in which to live, not only for themselves, their families and their friends, but also for the countless thousands they can never see nor know. Compared with all the millions of the earth, such men are few and to be counted on a plane apart, for they are builders and we but the beneficiaries of their building.

Henry Kaiser is a builder, strong-willed and eager for new ways of doing worthy things, and unrelenting in his scrutiny of accepted order and the orthodox.

Although commending all tried methods of past years, he frankly feels there must be found some day a better way. He is respectfully destructive because he knows that the first essential of progress is dissatisfaction, that doubt is the instigator of investigation and that investigation breaks clear the worthless chains of precedent. No catalogued machine has ever fitted his ideas. This gear or that must be adapted to the job in hand as he sees the job to be. Machinery to Henry Kaiser must be the proudest and most perfect workman on the job and must understand and love the work it has to do.

Henry Kaiser is a dreamer, and because he dreams, builds better than most men. I think he never looks upon a rough and tangled wildwood without dreaming of a clear and sunlit field. I think he never saw the plodding horses of a plowman in the spring that he did not dream of waving wheat at harvest time, and I know the stark and ugly strippings of a quarry bring him dreams of marbled temples worshipping the sky.

Great builder that he is, I think he has not ever crushed a flower half-hidden in the grass that he did not wish he might have walked some other way. He has not built upon the ruins or the wreckage of his fellowmen nor erected selfish slabs of structured stone to glorify himself. He builds because it is his life and because he must live his life to the full. And in so doing, he becomes his Country's good citizen and our good friend.

That the observation about dreams be not misunderstood, I state at the outset that I have a great affection and admiration for Henry Kaiser. I have known him a long time, just as I have known all of the men about whom I write. As an executive of a bonding company, I have for more than a score of years guaranteed that every one of them, singly or in a group with other men, would perform his contracts and pay his bills. Without exception, all of them have—there has not been a failure among them. In the process of judging group resources and the ability to perform, men learn to know each other, and so I knew all of these men and counted all of them as friends. The story of one friend to another over twenty or thirty years comes pretty close to being the true one. The impulse of judgment which causes your friend to do a certain thing in a certain way is clear to you even though you may question it, but you believe in him just the same.

156

These men in the Six Companies have done so much good in their lives and are so human, that the boys of today should know about them. These men were boys themselves once and lived bleaker lives in their childhood than almost anyone of your modern acquaintance. Their world-wide label of success was tinged with the bitter knowledge that they were too old to enlist in the war, and so they poured all of their hardy boyhood efficient judgment and money into practical ways of winning the war. The men of the Six Companies who are no longer here were the same kind of men, and, were they alive, would have had the same burning patriotism and the same singleness of purpose.

There probably will always be a difference of opinion as to how the Six Companies started and how the members should be ranked. It is of relatively little importance, but I think it will be generally conceded that the Six Companies was originally conceived around the financial strength of the Utah Construction Company. This was followed very closely by MacDonald & Kahn, whose readily available assets were a tremendous contribution. Morrison-Knudsen had been discussing Boulder Dam with the Utah Construction Company for months, without thought of anyone else being necessary, and it was Harry Morrison who really brought MacDonald & Kahn into the picture. When it was realized that a combination would have to be made, everyone seemed to want J. F. Shea Company of Portland. Charlie Shea wanted C. F. Swigert, president of the Pacific Bridge Company. Felix Kahn had had some dealings with Henry Kaiser and suggested him as a good possibility. On further discussion with Kaiser, it developed that Kaiser and the Bechtels had been working independently on the same idea for several months.

The successful completion of this great project was in a great measure due to Frank Crowe, its manager of construction. His great slogan, which was placarded all over the job, was, "The hell with excuses—move the muck!" When Stevick asked Crowe how he could help most, Crowe replied, "By having all of your directors' meetings in San Francisco and not on the job"—but he laughed when he said it.

Crowe was also manager of construction for the great Shasta Dam, which came later, and, while looking over another large project in which he might be interested, he died of a heart attack. His funeral was one of the largest ever attended in Redding. I have before me the book on the Shasta Dam, which he inscribed to me in these words: "Greetings to you, Leland—the man who has always been helpful and kind to us old construction stiffs."

The details and the problems which had to be mastered by Crowe and the members of Six Companies are almost unbelievable. I never fly over Hoover Dam and Lake Mead without thinking of former President Hoover's smiling words when the name was changed: "What difference does it make—there it is."

For more than fifty years the possibility of a bridge across San Francisco Bay from San Francisco to Oakland had been discussed in one form or another. "Emperor" Norton, in his fantastic uniform and child-like vagaries, preached it on street corners with no idea at all as to how it could be done except by a wave of the hand. As I said earlier, my Grandfather Cutler prophesied in the California Legislature in 1858 the building of a bridge across the Bay, and he was called "Cutler, the Dreamer."

In later years various promotional schemes were launched and franchises sought from the San Francisco Board of Supervisors. All of these were haphazard, without sound planning and doomed to failure. The Army and Navy both opposed any bridge. While a director of the Chamber of Commerce in 1927, I was chosen to present the bridge case to Secretary of Navy Curtis D. Wilbur on one of his visits to San Francisco. Secretary Wilbur was a brother of Dr. Ray Lyman Wilbur, Stanford's President, and had been appointed Navy Secretary by President Coolidge. Legend had it that he was appointed by Coolidge on Mr. Hoover's recommendation and that Dr. Wilbur was the one intended for the appointment but that Coolidge got the names mixed. I always doubted that story, for Curtis Wilbur was an Annapolis graduate and quite a man in his own right; he later became a federal judge. I knew Curtis Wilbur well but made no headway on the bridge presentation. The Navy just wouldn't have it. The Army, whose permission had to be obtained for anything affecting navigable waters, was adamant and it looked as though there would be no bridge.

Shortly after Herbert Hoover became President, in 1929 to be exact, he appointed what was known as the Hoover-Young Commission to go into all matters affecting a bridge across the Bay and to settle the question once and for all. The Hoover-Young Commission reported to Governor Young of California and the President of the United States on August 6, 1930, and recommended the site of the present bridge. I became president of the San Francisco Chamber of Commerce at the beginning of 1930 and served for three terms. Bert B. Meek was a member of the Hoover-Young Commission and Director of Public Works under Governor Young. Charles H. Purcell was State Highway Engineer and had all along been in charge of bridge planning for California. The state Legislature had appropriated $650,000 for the preparation of plans, Mr. Purcell's engineers had worked diligently, and California would be ready whenever Washington was. We all looked forward to the passage of the Reconstruction Finance Corporation Act, which President Hoover had conceived and was pressing for passage. Mr. Purcell and I were in Washington when this Act was before Congress and helped to bring about an amendment to fit the case of the San Francisco–Oakland Bay Bridge. Senator Hiram Johnson, despite his antagonism toward President Hoover, used all of his great strategy to help us. Later Governor Rolph, who had followed Governor Young, made me a member of the Financial Advisory Committee of the Bay Bridge and I was vice-president of its Executive Committee, the other members being Harrison Robinson of Oakland, now deceased; Joseph R. Knowland, publisher of the *Oakland Tribune*; and George Cameron, publisher of the *San Francisco Chronicle*. Governor Rolph said he would put me on the state payroll at a dollar a year so that I could be reimbursed for the expense of the many trips I would have to make to Washington. He failed to do it and probably could not, under the law; but all in all I made about fifteen trips, a few of which were paid for by the Chamber of Commerce, but most of them I paid for myself.

Long after Mr. Hoover retired from the Presidency, in fact just a week before Mrs. Hoover died suddenly in New York, they were dining with us at our apartment at the Fairmont in San Francisco. We had a beautiful view of the Bay and the bridge. Mr. Hoover remarked, "That is a fine view of Le's bridge." I said, "No, that is Mr. Hoover's bridge." My son-in-law, Dick Ellis, who was present, said, "Jesse Jones says it's

159

his bridge." Mr. Hoover looked a bit quizzical and said: "When the RFC Act was before Congress, I needed Jack Garner's help to get it through and made a deal with him that if it did go through I would appoint Jesse Jones to the RFC. I did appoint Jones and I have never regretted it." I remarked, "Mr. Hoover, the only indictment I have ever heard of you is that you were not a good politician. If you made that deal I think you were a mighty good one."

Mr. Hoover went on to say that as soon as the RFC Act was signed and became law, people flocked to Washington, asking how much they could get and for what kind of projects. California, he said, knew what it wanted and was ready with detailed plans and specifications for the bridge, prepared at a cost of $650,000, which stood up under all the scrutiny the RFC could give them.

One day in the fall of 1932 Mr. Purcell telephoned me from Washington while I was still president of the Chamber of Commerce and asked me if I could come to Washington and help him. He said that he and his engineering staff had been there for several weeks and had not been able to get a hearing before the RFC directors. In my office at the Chamber I called a meeting of the Executive Committee of the Financial Advisory Committee of the San Francisco–Oakland Bay Bridge, and also asked Paul Shoup, president of the Southern Pacific, to attend. There had been persistent rumors that the Southern Pacific would oppose the bridge and, knowing Shoup intimately, I thought it wise to have an understanding before we started. In response to my rather blunt question, Shoup stated definitely that the railroad would not oppose the bridge directly or indirectly; that it was essential to the progress of California, and he added, "Le and I understand each other and he will take my word for it." Cameron asked Shoup to go further and "give us a leg up." I knew that was asking too much. President Hoover and Shoup were great friends but I would not ask him to do more than not oppose us, because he had his own problems. Shoup merely smiled and shook his head at Cameron, and that ended any plea for the Southern Pacific's help. Shoup and all the railroad officials kept their word to the letter, even when it later developed they had to give up their automobile ferries as one of the RFC conditions. Robinson and Knowland agreed to go to Washington with me, and Robinson undertook to secure from Governor Rolph credentials for our committee, which would give us official standing with the RFC. This he did by telephone, and he dictated for the Governor's signature what amounted to a power of attorney, which set forth unmistakably that California would ratify any engagement we might make with the RFC. We filed this document with the RFC and were accepted without question by that body as representing the State of California—an unusual procedure certainly, but effective and typical of the way Governor Rolph did things. Robinson also wanted to find a hardheaded business attorney who would be a good trader and whom we would certainly need later in working out matters with the RFC. He asked me to recommend one. That was a difficult decision for me because I had many friends among attorneys and of course intimate ones among Stanford men. It was like being on a jury where you do the thing you must do regardless of your personal feelings. I knew we had a gigantic task ahead, and without hesitation I recommended F. M. McAuliffe of the firm of Heller, Ehrman, White and McAuliffe. Neither Robinson nor Knowland knew him but we went immediately from our meeting to McAuliffe's office and I explained our situation. I knew McAuliffe very well and had for many years, but he was not a Stanford man and I knew many feelings would be hurt by his selection. Robinson and Knowland were both impressed and wanted to engage him on the spot, but McAuliffe would have to be an employee of the California Toll Bridge Authority, have the approval of the Governor and Attorney General Webb, and could not possibly expect compensation commensurate to the work that would be involved. McAuliffe called in his senior partner, Sidney Ehrman, and properly explained it as a public service that the firm was being called upon to perform. Lloyd Dinkelspiel, also a member of the firm, was sent for. Dinkelspiel was a young man, a fine, sound lawyer, with a knowledge of public affairs and a great knack of getting along with people. Ehrman made it clear that the firm could not spare McAuliffe for long stretches of time and that Dinkelspiel might very well "bat" for him at times and take up the burden later on. This was agreed to and was to take effect as soon as it could be worked out. The contract finally was in McAuliffe's name but Dinkelspiel had a great part in the negotiations. In my opinion, we might not have made the deal with its countless negotiations without these two men. This was nearly twenty years ago, but the men who worked with them in Washington still remember them with respect, and both continue to serve in every way for the good of California. McAuliffe is past president of the San Francisco Bar Association and the California Bar and a regent of the University of San Francisco. Dinkelspiel has had a great part in Jewish relief work locally, nationally, and internationally, and is now President of the Board of Trustees of Stanford University. I know I do not have to say that they are my close friends and that I have a great respect and affection for them.

Robinson and Knowland agreed to go to Washington with me the following day. I went to my bank to arrange some personal financing, for none of us knew how long we would be gone. The banker was and is one of the finest citizens of San Francisco, but even then he was getting pretty tired of taxes and didn't have much idea of how the bridge would be financed. After our small business was concluded I remarked casually, "I'm going back to Washington and get $75,000,000 to build a bridge across San Francisco Bay." The banker bellowed in a voice that could be heard a block away, "I hope you fail. There's too much progress in this town." I left the bank slightly puzzled and confused because that was not a very encouraging start for a young fellow on such a mission.

When we arrived in Washington, I found a message from Lawrence Richey, President Hoover's secretary, that the President wanted to see me right away. I went to the White House and had a long conference with him. He was of course fully informed, because it was he who initiated the Hoover-Young Commission and saw it through when all efforts toward a bridge in San Francisco were stymied. Those who know Mr. Hoover know that he is not the most patient man in the world and that he has a very expressive vocabulary. He knew that Purcell and his engineers had been in Washington for some time and he wanted action right away and told me how to get it in no uncertain terms. President Hoover explained that Harvey Couch, Democrat from Arkansas, whom he had appointed, was in charge of self-liquidating projects, and that was where I was to start. He also added that if I couldn't get at Couch that day, I didn't belong on the California Board and wasn't the Le Cutler he knew. He made it clear that he would help us in every way but that the President of the United States had quite a few things to do and wasn't an errand boy and that we would have to do our own work. He finished up by smiling and asking me to dinner that night, when I could give him a report—but that too is another story.

I left the White House and went directly to my old Stanford friend, Merle Thorpe, who was then editor and publisher of *Nation's Business*. I told him what I wanted, and while Thorpe said he made it a rule not to take advantage of his friendships and get into such things, he would go with me to Couch and I could tell my story in my own way. Thorpe and Couch were close friends. *Nation's Business* was the official publication of the United States Chamber of Commerce and Couch was a director of the Chamber. Both Thorpe and Couch belonged to the Burning Tree Country Club, played golf together, and, as I later learned to my sorrow, also played a little poker. Thorpe phoned that we were on our way and we were promptly ushered in. Thorpe said: "Harvey, I've known Le Cutler intimately for thirty years. He will tell you his story. Don't waste any time trying to outguess him or think he is trying to outguess you. I vouch for him and I want you two fellows to start from scratch." I've never had a finer introduction in my life. Couch was a big man, well over six feet, with a soft, Arkansas drawl, and all he said was, "What do you want, Sir?" I told him about the plight of our California engineers on the San Francisco Bay Bridge and that all we wanted was a chance to tell our story to the directors of the RFC, because Harrington, the RFC engineer, had not been too co-operative. I added, however, that I thought it was because he was overworked and everyone was crowding him. Couch simply said, "How about tomorrow morning at eleven o'clock?" Such is the magic power of friendship.

President Hoover had explained to me that Charles D. (Daddy) Marx was Chief Consulting Engineer for the RFC. Marx was dean of the School of Engineering at Stanford, where President Hoover as a young student had taken his engineering courses. He was on leave from Stanford. I knew him very well and had liked him greatly over the years. After leaving Couch I went to him and told him what I had accomplished, and he agreed with me that Harrington was being pressured from every source but fundamentally was all right, and that he would straighten him out and work with me for "old times' sake." I explained everything to Purcell, who was greatly relieved. The next morning at eleven o'clock we went to the Directors' Room of the RFC, a very large and imposing room. I felt that I was in the Court of the Chief Justice of the United States. The directors were all assembled. One of our engineers, a good one, had arrived first, however, and was leaning back in his chair with his feet on the magnificent directors' desk smoking a pipe! I corrected that rather angrily, but it did not help our situation. Jesse Jones was not then chairman. He was a new member and had been appointed by President Hoover about the same time Couch was appointed. Altee Pomerene of Ohio was the chairman. I remember he wore a stiff-bosomed shirt with a diamond stud in the center of it.

The first question asked us was by Judge McCarthy of Utah, one of the members. It was one none of us wanted to answer and couldn't answer because it was fatal to our bridge. The question was, "What was the total revenue from all the ferryboats last year?" The answer, of course, would have to be, "Not enough to amortize the amount we are asking for." We could see from the look in their eyes that they would get rid of the small-town Western boys in just a minute and go on about their business. The answer was, of course, that construction of a bridge accelerates traffic, which is strictly an engineering matter. While Purcell was trying to explain it, Harvey Couch gave me the quiet finger and I went over and sat beside him. He whispered, "Cutler, did you ever play football in college?" I whispered back, "Yes, Sir." "What did you play?" asked Couch. I said, "I played quarterback." He whispered, "Did you ever take time out when you got into trouble?" When I said yes, he returned, "You're in trouble now, Son; take time out!" I started to rise, but he patted me on the knee and said, "Take your time, Son." Just then Jones said: "They will do to San Francisco what was done to the bridge in Detroit. Somebody will build a tunnel under the Bay parallel to the bridge and get all the business." I was president of the San Francisco Chamber of Commerce at the time and told them so, and I said, "Please don't ever tell on me, but we can't have a tunnel under the Bay because we have earthquakes out there." When the laughter subsided, I referred to the first question they asked and said we should not waste their time on engineering matters, as they were problems for the engineers to decide.

164

Harvey Couch said, "I think that is very wise. I move it be set down for special hearing Thursday (two weeks later) at eleven o'clock." The directors were so glad to get rid of us that they all voted in favor of Couch's suggestion, and as I went out, Couch covertly winked at me. Two days later we came back and received conditionally $75,000,000. In those two weeks I did the most effective work of my life. Florence McAuliffe had arrived and he wanted action too. I saw President Hoover several times, and when I couldn't see him I saw Dr. Wilbur, Secretary of the Interior. He was President Hoover's closest friend and could talk to him when no one else could. I saw Arthur Ballantine, Under Secretary of the Treasury, who held the balance of power on the board, because Odgen Mills, the Secretary, was in San Francisco, where George Cameron, who had stayed behind, entertained him lavishly. Arthur Ballantine is a man I will never forget, and he was most helpful on every occasion while President Hoover was in control.

Harrison Robinson made a speech before the directors of the RFC, saying that we did not want the bridge particularly—all we wanted was to put men to work, and then he lectured the directors on their duty to do something about it. Cowles, a director from Iowa and a fine man, stood up and said the directors did not need anyone from California to tell them their duties, and he moved, as a matter of personal privilege, that the California delegation be asked to leave and not come back. He also asked that the sergeant at arms escort us out. The sergeant performed his duties promptly and we were escorted not only to the elevator but to the street. We sat on a bench, a dejected lot, and Robinson said we would have to get our reservations home, because clearly we were through. I told everybody to sit there and wait until I came back from the White House, because "when it was all over and done the bridge would be built" and we might as well finish our job. I went by Secretary Wilbur's office and asked him to go with me to President Hoover, because he could get in quickly and I couldn't. We had quite a talk, and on behalf of my colleagues I took a characteristic scolding from the President. When he was through with me he said he would talk with Cowles that night. Later he told me he had quite a bad time with him until midnight, because Cowles was greatly offended, and Mr. Hoover said he didn't blame him. The next morning, however, I had a call from Larry Richey. All was cleared and we were to go back to the RFC at eleven o'clock, but we must be very discreet and quiet, and—I say it modestly—I was to do whatever talking was necessary. As luck would have it, Cowles rode up in the elevator with us and did not even nod. Daddy Marx was there, as was Harrington, the chief engineer, with big circles under his eyes and looking very tired. He told me aside that he had been up all night under Marx's orders, checking and approving Purcell's plans, and he thought everything was all right. Still Cowles wouldn't speak to us but he voted "Aye" with the other directors and we were conditionally granted $75,000,000. I have a picture of Charley Purcell, now dead, then Director of Public Works of California, on my walls, and it is inscribed to me, "When all is over and done, the bridge will be built."

I did not know the RFC men then as I know them now, and of course did not dare to call them by their first names. Over the years I came to have a great respect and affection for them. Harvey Couch, who is dead now, Jesse Jones, Judge McCarthy, Sam Husbands, Carroll Merriman, Morton Macartney (chief loan agent), Senator Henderson, and many others connected with the agency. Always now, when I have nothing at stake, I visit them when I can because I like them.

Harvey Couch and Jesse Jones I had as my guests one year at the Bohemian Grove after the bridge bonds were purchased and the job finished. Harvey and Jesse were unobtrusive except that Harvey, being from Arkansas, quietly challenged everybody in our camp to a hog-calling contest and Jesse suggested poker instead. Mr. Hoover was at the Grove too and I took them to his camp and left them together. I would like to have listened to that one.

As soon as the RFC agreed to buy the bridge bonds conditionally, which was in September 1932, Jones called me into his office and asked me to put off the announcement until after the elections in November, on the ground that it might help President Hoover. I explained that we could not possibly postpone the announcement, that all California was waiting for it, and besides, I said, "Most respectfully, Mr. Hoover appointed you." "Yes," said Mr. Jones, "and I respect him, but I am a Democrat!"

The nearest I came to a bribe was from Harvey Couch after Jones

166

was through with me. He called Robinson, Knowland, and me into his private office. "Cutler," he said, "I have given up everything, presidency of the Arkansas Light and Power Company and a railroad, director of the Chase National Bank, and all I get is $10,000 a year. You have just gotten $75,000,000; don't you think I ought to get mine?" I was self-conscious and embarrassed and stammered something about "Yes, Sir, I do." He turned to Knowland and said, "You're an older man than Mr. Cutler and publish the *Oakland Tribune*; you think I ought to get mine, don't you?" Knowland stammered too and didn't know what more to say than I. Couch twinkled his eyes and said, "I have an old aunt in Sausalito who is seventy-three and never has had her picture in the paper. If you will send your society reporter over there and put her picture in your paper, Mr. Knowland, I'll figure I've got mine." Knowland could hardly wait to telephone instructions to his office, and Couch framed and had on his walls the article and picture in the *Tribune*.

The human side of Couch and Jones and the main directors was a source of great comfort and understanding to me. They were poker-faced and the only time I got into trouble was when I tried to play the game with them. They had a great sense of understanding and of humor, but saved it for those they trusted and respected. One summer morning at the Mayflower Hotel in Washington I was taking a shower and Mrs. Cutler answered the telephone. It was for me. Harvey Couch had come in on an early sleeper from Arkansas and asked me to have breakfast with him, and he said, "If that lady who answered the telephone so early is your wife, have her come too." When we went to his apartment I said, "This is my wife," and always after we jested about whether she was or was not the lady who answered the telephone.

Mrs. Cutler and I happened to be stranded at the Mayflower Hotel one Sunday. Harvey Couch and Mrs. Couch had all their family, and Mr. Justice Stanley Reed and Mrs. Reed, at a big table in the center of the Mayflower dining room. Harvey said grace very simply and carved a big turkey as he would at home. I wish there were more men like that. I wish there were more men like Jesse Jones. He knows me inside out, and I think I know him too. He is right in almost everything he does, and although I am a Republican, I would feel pretty comfortable having Jesse Jones as President of the United States. I hear from him at frequent intervals and wish that he and Herbert Hoover and other great men like them could live forever!

Jesse Jones in his book, *Fifty Billion Dollars*, the story of the RFC, relates the quarterback dialogue with Harvey Couch and says in part:

The San Francisco to Oakland Bay Bridge had been advocated by *Herbert Hoover* long before he became President. It had been recommended by a commission of which he and C. C. Young, who was Governor of California from 1927 to 1930, were the joint heads. It was, of course, enthusiastically supported as a project by the forward-looking businessmen of the San Francisco Bay Area. Three of these gentlemen, Leland W. Cutler, an insurance executive and civic leader, Charles Purcell, an engineer, and Joseph Knowland, publisher of the Oakland Tribune and father of United States Senator William Fife Knowland, brought the bridge dream to Washington and presented it to our board only a few weeks after we had begun making loans on self-liquidating projects.

Mr. Jones is right in saying that the San Francisco–Oakland Bay Bridge had been advocated by Mr. Hoover long before he became President. As a matter of fact, in 1922 he arranged that President Harding appoint a committee of Army and Navy officers to study it. On military grounds they reported against any site unless it be from Hunter's Point. In 1928 Mr. Hoover made a speech in San Francisco in which he promised to secure a solution of the problem. He followed this up by appointing in 1929 the Hoover-Young Commission, which I mentioned previously. This commission was made up of Army and Navy officers of a wider point of view. The commission was under the chairmanship of Mark Requa, with Admirals Standley and Gregory, Army Engineers Pillsbury and Daley, the civil members being George Cameron, State Senator Breed of California, who died this year at a very advanced age but always a great citizen, Daddy Marx, and Charles Purcell. On August 12, 1930, they reported favorably for a bridge via Yerba Buena Island. Mr. Hoover, I am sure, was behind the suggestion of Mr. Purcell that the Financial Advisory Committee appointed by Governor Rolph in 1932 go to Washington and negotiate with the RFC.

All in all, as I mentioned previously, I made about fifteen trips to

Washington in the interests of the bridge, and it was not until June 1933 that the RFC made a definite bid for the bonds—half an hour before the bids for the tremendous contract would open. I was in Washington at the time, working against the deadline, with Harrison Robinson and Attorney McAuliffe in Sacramento. It must be remembered that the banks had closed in the meantime, and there is no telling how much of an advance in price the contractors would have put in for a second bidding if such had been necessary.

I have often remarked to Jesse Jones in jest that the reason the Reconstruction Finance Corporation granted us $75,000,000 conditionally was because the directors required more than fifty amendments to the laws of California and they thought we couldn't accomplish it. The money was conditionally granted in September 1932, and all of California seemed to think the pile drivers would be in the Bay the day after we had the brass band and the parade. As to the brass band and the parade, I had to stay in Washington to gather up odds and ends. I received a telegram dated October 10, 1932, from Mayor Rossi, reading as follows:

OF COURSE WE ARE ALL DELIGHTED OVER THE ACHIEVEMENT AFFECTING OUR TRANS-BAY BRIDGE AND WHEN I CONGRATULATE YOU ON THE GREAT PART YOU PLAYED WITH OUR HONORED PRESIDENT AND THE RFC I FEEL I AM ONLY REECHOING THE FEELINGS OF GRATITUDE WHICH ARE IN THE HEARTS OF ALL SAN FRANCISCANS. WE SHALL GIVE YOU A GRAND RALLY ON YOUR RETURN, WHICH WE UNDERSTAND WILL BE SATURDAY. KEEP WELL.

ANGELO J ROSSI

I did not want a brass band and a parade or any ado, because I knew that we had a great deal to accomplish in the Legislature and that it would take many months and possibly a year. It was not until the following June that the Federal Reserve would respond to checks. In the meantime we had the state Legislature, bank-closing over the nation, many trips to Washington, and a change in administration. Also, I was walking down the back alleys at night to avoid the countless people who remarked, "I thought you were going to build a bridge?" I can never think of the bridge without thinking of Senator Thomas A. Maloney, then Speaker pro tem. of the Assembly, who authored and fought the legislation to successful culmination at Sacramento. Money for the approaches had to come from the state gas tax, and for road tax purposes the state was divided into District 1 of the north and 2 of the south. Los Angeles did not care about San Francisco or Oakland at all, as long as no money came out of its gas tax, but the rural communities, the so-called "cow counties," were hurt because their secondary roads would have to wait, as their funds came from District 1. Again do I think of the men in the Legislature who helped me: Senator George Hatfield of the San Joaquin Valley in California, one time United States District Attorney and later Lieutenant Governor—always a power in the Senate; Senator Tom McCormick of Rio Vista, Senator Rich of Marysville, and Jerry Seawell, whose mother and mine were little girls together. Many of the older Senators used to meet with me at a "Directors' Meeting" in my room at the close of day, for it was during prohibition and there were many things to be discussed. Senator Herbert Slater was really the dean of the Senate, and I had known and loved him from his early days. He was blind but had many compensating gifts and never asked odds from anyone. He always scolded me a little bit privately, but when the going was tough before committees or on the floor, he was always on my side. Senator Slater and his colleagues were of immeasurable help in getting the bridge bills through. In 1947, because of his age and blindness, Senator Slater was faltering a bit, and I wrote and Senator Hatfield read, under special privilege, a tribute that was printed in the *Journal* of both houses, and later embossed.

A TRIBUTE TO HERBERT W. SLATER

For a score and a half of years I have counted Herbert Slater as one of my close, true friends. He has been the friend of countless men and all of us like to think that we are within the inner circle of his heart. I know I am because I love him as a boy would love his father and as a man loves his comrade.

Close to Herbert's memory and mine are the members of the Board of Directors of the Slater School of Friendship—Tom Ingram, Fred Handy, Skip Nelson, Joe Nolan, Tom McCormick, Irwin Quinn, Dick Barrett, Dan Burbank, and in humble pride, myself.

Although God took from Herbert one of His greatest gifts, he gave him back a compensating one. Herbert cannot see the color and the form of life, nor with his eyes watch men come and go, but compassed clear within his mind is the understanding of it all. As men take pictures home to contemplate when the day is done, so Herbert in his blindness muses clearly all the things he loves.

God made him sensitive to fairness and to chivalry and to the quiet exchange of banter which only friends can give and only friends can take.

We want Herbert Slater to live beyond life's day but never reach the dusk, and as he travels toward the shadow of the night may the clear bright light of friendship's star twinkle fair above the tranquil dawning of an Everlasting Day.

Looking back over the whole history of the bridge, I realize that it could not have been built without friends who believed in it and saw it through. I give Mr. Hoover the greatest credit, for he cut all red tape and formed the Hoover-Young Commission to find a way of doing it. Mr. Hoover conceived the Reconstruction Finance Corporation, agreed to an amendment to fit the case of the San Francisco–Oakland Bay Bridge, and during our first onslaught on Washington, used his power with the RFC to help us at every turn. President Hoover also stayed up late at night and received me when I needed help and at any hour telephoned friends who might be needed. I think he knew he would not be re-elected and he wanted the bridge on its way before he was out, because he believed in it and in its part in the progress of the nation.

President Hoover wasn't popular in the country, and in fact nobody from California was. The RFC was an unheard-of thing and a new instrument of progress. I have before me two editorials from the *Chicago Tribune*. Shortly after the RFC had agreed to buy the bonds, I combined the editorials in one because the theme is the same: "The James Boys from California," and the date is October 3, 1932. The editorial said in part:

It would be instructive to know on what kind of a financial set-up this loan was authorized. The interest charges alone on such a project would be $3,000,000 a year. Another million or two ought to be added for amortization and at least a half-million for maintenance and operation, not to mention the sums required for interest during construction. It is significant that no banking syndicate in boom times when any kind of security was salable had the nerve to finance San Francisco's bridge with its staggering overhead. Uncle Sam, for motives which are purely political corruption, has now undertaken to sink 62 millions of the taxpayers' money in this scheme, which would probably land a professional promoter in the penitentiary if he tried to sell it to the public. . . . If there are any honest men in the region of the Bay, they have not been heard from at this distance.

The bridge was built by revenue bonds purchased en bloc by the Reconstruction Finance Corporation. The initial fare was set at sixty-five cents. It is now twenty-five cents, and the remaining bonds would have been retired but for very recent legislation to keep a bridge toll so that the other bridges can be built. Once the present bridge is free, no other bridge could be financed. It may be that the "James Boys of California" will ride again!

The actual consummation of the agreement with the Reconstruction Finance Corporation took many months and a tremendous amount of work. Florence M. McAuliffe and Lloyd Dinkelspiel worked on the project as though it were their own, both in Washington and in Sacramento. President Hoover was defeated for re-election and Mr. Roosevelt became President of the United States. Dire prophecies were made by Republicans that Mr. Roosevelt would throw out all negotiations and that the bridge would not be built. I was with Mr. Hoover in Washington for a few minutes on March 3, 1933, while he was packing up, and I mentioned that I had to catch the Liberty for Chicago right away. Mr. Hoover asked, "Aren't you going to stay over for the Democratic festivities tomorrow?" I remarked, "A Democratic inauguration is not my idea of a festivity." "Nor mine," said Mr. Hoover, and a little later he added something to the effect that the San Francisco–Oakland Bay Bridge, as conceived and negotiated, was certainly safe.

I caught the Liberty Limited. Banks were closed and confusion was in the air. In Chicago McAuliffe and I stood in front of a closed bank and watched a parade of schoolteachers demanding their pay, with banners and shouts from the marchers that were indescribable. In Washington a few months earlier, while Mr. Hoover was still President, an attorney for the RFC had said at a directors' meeting, when the money was granted conditionally: "This money, Mr. Florence McAuliffe and Mr. Leland Cutler, will not be put in California banks; it will be put in New York banks where it will be safe." "Mr. X," said Mr. McAuliffe, "my name may be Florence but I wear a 17½ collar. Out in California, we are not Liberia or France, we are a part of this great commonwealth. The money will be put in California banks!" It was.

Of course the bridge project, as Mr. Hoover said, was so sound that nothing should disturb it, but no one knew what President Roosevelt might do, because we still had several months to go with our negotia-

172

tions. Early in the spring of 1933 President Roosevelt sent for me and told me that he had heard we were worrying but that the bridge was the greatest achievement of the RFC, that he wanted it to be built, and if I got into trouble to let him know. I had not particularly told anyone that I knew Mr. Roosevelt before he had infantile paralysis and that from the time he left the Assistant Secretaryship of the Navy until he became Governor of New York, he was vice-president and director of our Fidelity and Deposit Company of Maryland, in New York—the same position I held in the West.

When Mr. Roosevelt was defeated for the Vice-Presidency on the Cox ticket, Van Lear Black, owner of the *Baltimore Sun* and chairman of the board of our company, made Mr. Roosevelt a proposition to join forces with the Fidelity and Deposit Company of Maryland and the American Bonding Company of Baltimore, our subsidiary. He, Black, had formed a friendship with Mr. Roosevelt which lasted throughout his lifetime. Mr. Roosevelt became a director and vice-president in the New York area and was in charge of our New York office. The job of course was a new one for him, and he very wisely kept away from the handling of technical matters because his familiarity with the surety business was so slight. The following summer he was stricken with infantile paralysis. He had been on Black's yacht, which took him to Campobello, the Roosevelt summer home.

Practically all of our officials, with the exception of Black and George L. Radcliffe, first vice-president, and later United States Senator from Maryland, were very skeptical of the services which Mr. Roosevelt could render after his illness. Black, however, told Mr. Roosevelt that the company would continue to pay him his salary of $25,000 a year. This was done for a period of eight years, although Mr. Roosevelt for a while was a complete invalid and not in a position to render any real service. I never saw a man more cheerful or one who made a more determined and tireless effort to recover his health and physical activity. He swam constantly and worked on parallel bars. He resorted to every expedient he could think of to help his recovery and was very jubilant over every bit of progress made. He did not know whether he was building new nerves or reinvigorating the old, but he was constantly getting more use of himself. One time at 120 Broadway, our New York office, when he was on crutches and could barely touch his toes to the floor, he said, "Le, if I get the partial use of one leg before I die, I'll be satisfied—and," sticking out his jaw, he added determinedly, "I'm going to get it!" He used the parallel bars not only to strengthen his chest muscles but to train his legs to support his weight.

I went to a dinner with him one night where he was to speak. He arrived early before the crowd assembled and the speakers' table was banked with flowers. Mr. Roosevelt took his weight off his feet by lifting himself with his fists on the table, which no one could see, and talked for ten or fifteen minutes with a smile on his face. No one who knew him in those days could help but have a great personal admiration for the fight he made against such overwhelming odds. He had a devastating personality and charm and in the White House loved to reminisce with me about his days with the Fidelity and Deposit Company. His photographic memory would come to the fore and at the sight of me would give him an inexhaustible list of personnel and of a hundred incidents of the old days, as though he were a vital part of the company.

We paid Mr. Roosevelt his salary of $25,000 per year from December 1920 until he became Governor of New York at the end of 1928. We then gave him an additional bonus or severance pay of $50,000. This was a quarter of a million dollars with no taxes, such as there are now.

What gave the old-timers in our company apoplexy at mention of his name as President of the United States was that in *Who's Who*, where the subject furnishes his own biographical data, there was no reference whatever to his connection with the Fidelity and Deposit Company of Maryland. Probably this had something to do with the Free State of Maryland going for Mr. Hoover in 1928, and Senator Radcliffe successfully managing Senator Tydings' campaign, when Mr. Roosevelt went into Maryland personally to purge him.

Naturally I felt better after President Roosevelt's talk with me about the bridge project, and instead of penalizing he helped in every way he could. The banks, however, were closed and it was not easy for contractors to arrange their financing. It was in June 1933 that bids for the purchase of the revenue bond issue were opened in Sacramento.

174

Harrison Robinson was there and I was in Washington urging the RFC against the deadline. Of course my surety company was interested in the bonds on the contractors, but again it was not a question of how much we could get but how many surety companies would come in. The Six Companies group of contractors split up and bid against each other. The Columbia Steel Company wanted to bid on the superstructure, a contract of about $15,000,000. Ordinarily, that might have been all right, but with the banks closed I had, in addition to work with the RFC, to secure the indemnity of the United States Steel Company. This I obtained with the help of my great friend, William A. Ross, president of Columbia, and its attorney, Walter Shelton. My company, however, had to take 17½ percent of all the bids when we only wanted 10 percent. This was to make possible a legal opening on the day advertised and avoid a readvertising. Later, after the bids were awarded and the banks reopened, we cut our company down to the 10 percent we considered sufficient.

I have many files before me attesting to the human side of the bridge negotiations and countless humorous notations and memories. I still carry as a means of identification, or evidence of egotism, Pass No. 1 signed by Charles H. Purcell, and dated "until revoked." On the reverse side is written: "Permanent pass. Kindly permit the bearer and party to drive private car on the east and west crossways of the San Francisco–Oakland Bay Bridge." Apparently this is still good, but I have never used it. I merely keep it for sentimental purposes. Charley Purcell was, however, always No. 1 in my book!

The important thing is that the bridge was dedicated and opened on Thursday, November 12, 1936. This brought all of the temperaments of the United States and the Bay Area into action. Mr. Hoover was to be there, and though by this time I had resigned with my fellow members from the Financial Advisory Board and had no official standing, I thought that Mr. Hoover should be invited to ride in the parade, as should Charles D. (Daddy) Marx of Stanford, Consulting Engineer of the RFC. I think I went so far as to invite them both without consulting Governor Frank F. Merriam, who didn't get along too well with Mr. Hoover. Governor Merriam said he had been advised that President Roosevelt would be in San Francisco for the occasion, or his personal representative, Senator McAdoo. I happened to know that President Roosevelt would not be West at all, and some of the bitterness of the occasion was expressed in a letter from Mark Requa, Mr. Hoover's life-long friend. "I note that on November the twelfth at 10:00 A.M. the bridge opening ceremonies take place and that Governor Merriam cuts the chain. Merriam had as much to do with this as a resident of China. The man that ought to cut that chain is Herbert Hoover."

Senator McAdoo arrived, but he was no problem at all, although Governor Merriam insisted that he ride in the parade instead of Mr. Hoover. Both Senator McAdoo and George Creel, his friend, took a hand in dissuading the Governor, and although he called me at my Woodside home at midnight, both former President Hoover and "Daddy" Marx rode in state in the parade across to the Oakland side and back. Daddy Marx wore his high silk hat and after a wonderful reception and lunch in Oakland, at which Mr. Hoover spoke, all sat with me on the San Francisco side at the ceremony, where I presided. All had a chance to speak, even Senator Charles B. Henderson, chairman of the RFC, who had succeeded Jesse Jones, and who was destined to be quite a factor in the further negotiations we would have to have with the RFC in putting interurban facilities on the bridge.

Senator Henderson had been United States Senator from Nevada in the 'nineties, and the Henderson home was always well known in Elko, Nevada. When Harvey Couch resigned as a director of the RFC and Senators Johnson and McAdoo were trying to make up their minds whom to recommend for appointment, Senator Key Pittman of Nevada moved in on President Roosevelt and asked for the appointment of Henderson. Assistant Secretary of the Navy Roosevelt and Senator Henderson of Nevada had been old friends—and so are such things accomplished.

It so happened that Mrs. Cutler and I went back on the train that picked up Senator Henderson at Elko, Nevada. Of course it was by appointment all around. We had a delightful trip across the continent, and when we came into the Mayflower Hotel at Washington, Senator Henderson registered from Hillsborough, California. I said, "Don't forget, Senator, you were appointed from Elko, Nevada," so he scratched it out and registered from Elko.

176

The next night I wangled an extra invitation to the Gridiron Dinner, then held on the top floor of the Willard Hotel. Senator Henderson and I were a little late in getting there and came through the service quarters where a ramp had been laid down for President Roosevelt. The secret service men held us back until the President, who had not seen Charley Henderson for twenty years, stopped everything by grasping his hand and greeting him as "Charley" and asking him to be sure and see him the next day.

Much has been said about the interurban railway on the bridge, particularly now about its obsolescence. This was an extra matter with which the Financial Advisory Committee had to deal, over and above the $61,400,000 for the bridge proper, involving $15,000,000 and extending through 1934. I set down the recommendations that Harrison Robinson, Joseph R. Knowland, and I made to the Governor of the state of California and the Toll Bridge Authority, along with Exhibit A of the Reconstruction Finance Corporation, Exhibit B of the Railroad Commission of the state of California, and Exhibit C representing our summary (see Appendix). All of these meant a great deal more work with the RFC and the California Legislature, and cost the three of us money; but there the bridge is and—whether rightfully or wrongfully—there is mass transportation across it, and a terminal has been provided.

On the walls of my office I have a pen-and-ink sketch of the bridge. It is about six feet long and was made before the bridge was built, but it looks like a photograph of the bridge today. I took it to Washington in a roll under my arm to show the RFC what the bridge would look like. It is now covered with signatures of those who had a part in it, including President Hoover and President Roosevelt on the one document. At the outset, I asked Mr. Hoover to sign, which he did, on the lower left-hand corner. All the rest of the space was vacant when I took the roll to Senator Hiram Johnson's office for his signature. The Senator's secretary, Miss Connor, called me later that it was ready and not to tell the Senator she told me, but for me to notice where he had signed. She said he had remarked he wanted to get as far away from President Hoover as he could, and so with all that space available the Senator signed on the lower right-hand corner. I am sure it was all right with President Hoover for Johnson's signature to be six feet away!

Despite the work and maneuvering involved, over a period of years I formed friendships that nothing can take away from me. Robert J. Cummins, of Houston, Texas, was a consulting engineer, suggested by Jesse Jones to look us over. He is one of the finest men I know and our friendship has continued throughout the years. The RFC always relied on him because he is a sterling citizen and an outstanding engineer. Morton Macartney in 1935 was chief engineer of the RFC, and until very recently chief loan agent. No better man could have been in charge of things in Washington. Macartney and Cummins were like brothers and there were no tricks or guile in their make-up. Incidentally, Macartney is an excellent baritone singer and Mrs. Macartney a wonderful accompanist; Mrs. Cutler and I can never forget an evening we had in their home.

Countless letters and telegrams in my files attest to the friendships and humor that went hand in hand with the work, and that continue now that the work is done. Resolutions and testimonials by the score from state and government and civic bodies more than compensate for the fact that we paid our own expenses, and any time my grandchildren get ambitious I will provide plenty of dividends by way of material for their scrapbooks.

While I was in Washington on bridge matters I was steadily working for the Fidelity and Deposit Company, of which I was vice-president. Through our Washington office several years before we had written the blanket bond for the RFC, covering its employees all over the United States. The premium was about $50,000, and President Miller of our company told me one day that this was overdue and if the occasion arose to see what I could do about it. Shortly thereafter I was in Jesse Jones's office and asked him about the surety bond which we had written. He of course knew nothing of it but asked Costello, his right-hand man, to get him the file. Jones read the file without changing expression and said, "I'll tell you one reason we haven't paid the premium. We asked for a list of your reinsuring companies and you named ten; nine of them we are loaning money to to keep them alive. If that is the best protection you can give us, we will probably never pay you." As a matter of fact, we got our check a week later. Also I learned a lot about our competitors whom Jones discussed naïvely and whose confidence I never abused. Most all insurance companies were in trouble and the fear was that if one failed all might fail. Jones told me that he was under instructions from President Roosevelt to do anything that Senator George Radcliffe of Maryland, and our first vice-president, might ask. Jones further said, "And George follows me around like a snake." (This was the first time I ever knew a snake followed anybody.)

The next day I was in New York for reinsurance on a large risk we had in California. I was talking to the president of a surety company and he was lecturing me and finding fault with the underwriting of our company generally. I said casually, "Anyhow, Mr. X, the Fidelity and Deposit Company did not have to borrow $10,000,000 from the RFC." He exploded and wanted to know how I knew, and many other things, but I just shook my head. When the sputtering was over he shook his finger at me and said, "It takes a good company to borrow $10,000,000 from the RFC. The Fidelity and Deposit couldn't do it." We did not have to borrow, even ten cents, but the failure and reorganization of the other company added to the troubles of necessary suretyship for the bridge contractors, for Mr. X's company was one that had accepted reinsurance and failed just before the bids were to be opened.

One night in Washington I was called on the telephone from San Francisco by Mayor Rossi, with Alfred Cleary, of the Chief Administrative Office of the City and County of San Francisco, and Bert B. Meek, formerly State Director of Public Works. These men, all good friends of mine, wanted me to be president of an exposition to celebrate the building of the two bridges.

Early in 1933 talk about such a project had started. I believe Joseph Dixon, in a letter to the *San Francisco News*, was the first to propose it. I paid practically no attention to it because I was busy trying to get the bridges built. The Chamber of Commerce became actively interested, as did the San Francisco Convention and Tourist Bureau. I have always given the San Francisco Junior Chamber of Commerce credit for starting the whole thing, and principally among them Henry Eickhoff, Jr. (whose father was one of the stalwart citizens of San Francisco and my good friend).

The Shoals, just off Yerba Buena (Goat Island), had for years been accepted as belonging to the Navy or the Army. When I was president of the Senior Chamber, the Junior Chamber boys investigated and found the Shoals belonged to the State of California. The Airport Committee of the Junior Chamber had a "wild" idea of reclaiming the Shoals and using a man-made island for an airport. I had gone to the Legislature with the young men and presented the matter to the appropriate committee. I will never forget the incredulous look on the faces of the members. "You mean," one legislator asked, "this is in the middle of San Francisco Bay under water and you want us to give it to San Francisco for an airport?" The answer was a quiet "Yes"; and the answer of the legislators was, "It's all under the Bay; give it to them," with the clearly unexpressed thought, "—if they're that crazy." And so the Shoals was deeded by the State of California to the City and County of San Francisco for airport purposes. There could not have been, in my judgment, an exposition except via the airport route, and there would have been an airport via the exposition route, as was intended, but for causes which got out of hand. Later when I was working almost daily with President Roosevelt, he would smile and remind me, "Le, I know you're thinking Exposition, but I'm thinking airport."

In the middle of 1933 Mayor Rossi, at the instigation of the Board of Supervisors, appointed a "Bridge Celebration Founding Committee," and of course the first thing to be determined was the site. Ward Mailliard was the head of this committee and its driving force. I have in my files a telegram he sent me from Washington urging me to fill in the Shoals as the site of the Exposition, and this was before the committee had filed its report as to the site or I had been formally chosen as president of the Exposition. There isn't any question, as a matter of fact and of my knowledge, but that Ward was first to think of it and propose it. Of course he did it as Ward Mailliard to Le Cutler and off the record and before I was in it at all, but many things are accomplished that way. Ward knew me so well that he knew sooner or later I would be in the thick of it, and there wasn't any question in his mind from the start that if we were to have an exposition the Shoals was the place for it. I certainly consider him the father of the idea. Every citizen in San Francisco had his own pet choice. Improvement clubs, neighborhood associations, real estate men, landowners, even some of the supervisors waged active campaigns for their favorite spots, ranging all the way from Golden Gate Park and Lake Merced, to North Beach, China Basin, the stockyards, and Candlestick Point. The committee selected George W. Kelham, who had been intimately connected as an architect with the 1915 Exposition, and W. P. Day, a sound architect as well as an engineer, to report specifically on the matter of the site. They came up with Yerba Buena Shoals, which wasn't even in sight at low tide—and the war was on!

A year and a half elapsed while the study was going on and before the committee gave its approval. In the summer of 1934 the San Francisco Bay Exposition began its real work with a Board of Directors consisting of the outstanding businessmen of the city. I had been formally elected president, although already working for some time. Atholl McBean was made chairman of the board and John F. Forbes treasurer and comptroller, with an Executive Committee composed of Atholl McBean, Alfred J. Cleary, R. B. Hale, R. F. Allen, Colbert Coldwell, J. W. Mailliard, Jr., Allen L. Chickering, John F. Forbes, B. B. Meek, and Leland W. Cutler, ex officio. Subsequently, when in full planning and operation, we had a Board of Management which met daily at lunch. This was composed of James B. Black, Colbert Coldwell, K. R. Kingsbury, J. W. Mailliard, Jr., and myself. Upon Mr. Kingsbury's death in 1937, while I was in the Orient, Philip Patchin, also of the Standard Oil Company, was selected to take Mr. Kingsbury's place. Patchin was an unusually good public-relations man and helpful at every turn. In fact, if I had another exposition to build and operate—which heaven forbid—I would ask nothing better than that these same men without exception be with me. That particularly goes for John Forbes, who as treasurer and comptroller had a colossal task, because an exposition is a spending institution and we were always short of money. Naturally we had many differences of opinion every day, but the men on the Management Board and Forbes and Milton Esberg, who was head of our Exhibits and Concessions Committee and in fact a tower of strength to me on everything, allowed no rancor to enter into our deliberations but kept their minds on the accomplishment we were after.

Financing was our number one problem, and although I was a Republican and a friend of Mr. Hoover's, my thoughts turned to Washington and the federal government, having in mind an ultimate airport for San Francisco. I have touched on my long acquaintanceship with Mr. Roosevelt and that we had been together in the Fidelity and Deposit Company. In May 1935 W. P. Day was selected as director of works of the Exposition, Kenneth Kingsbury, president of the Standard Oil Company of California, as chairman of the Finance Committee, and George W. Kelham, as chairman of an architectural commission consisting of Arthur Brown, Jr., Lewis P. Hobart, Timothy Pflueger, Ernest Weihe, and William G. Merchant, who had been raised by Bernard Maybeck in the 1915 Exposition. While working on the financing of the bridge, I learned the value and necessity of having working plans ready for Washington consideration.

I want to say at the outset that I could not have accomplished anything without George Creel. He had been chairman of the Committee on Public Information under Woodrow Wilson in the first war. Creel has been frequently labeled as being in charge of propaganda at that time, and probably was, but he was more than any of that—he was a confidant of President Wilson, a powerful figure in politics, a great American, and my good friend of many years' standing. I say in affectionate jest that I doubt that Creel ever spoke a kindly word to me or I to him. We did not have to because we understood each other. During the Exposition, a friend remarked to me aghast: "Did you hear what George Creel said about you yesterday?" I remarked that if George could say anything behind my back that he hadn't said at one time or another to my face, I would love to hear it.

Creel had been a candidate for Governor of California, was a staunch Democrat, and was probably in the beginning closer to Mr. Roosevelt than anyone. I turned to Creel immediately, and, although the motto of the Bohemian Club is "Weaving spiders come not here," we had our first discussion of our problems of financing an exposition while at the Bohemian Grove. Creel was a true San Franciscan and he agreed to help in every way possible. He then represented *Collier's* in Washington and had been one of its chief editorial writers for many years, in addition to authoring many books. While Creel wasn't too sanguine, I had an idea I could get building money for the Exposition from the Public Works Administration (PWA), of which Harold Ickes was the head. Both Creel and I knew that a sponsor's fund would have to be put up by someone. With the PWA it would amount to 55 percent, and with the Works Progress Administration (WPA) only 20 percent. Harry Hopkins was head of the WPA, and I did not know him. Creel, of course, did, and at that time they were close friends. I had known Senator Hiram Johnson since I was a boy, and although he didn't like my friend Mr. Hoover, I once remarked that I was one of the few men left who could see good in both of them. Again every man to his own experience. Johnson had always been very friendly with me and, although a prosecutor at heart, had a great and kindly sense of humor, which always appealed to me and helped to balance his vindictiveness. I decided to go to Johnson and ask for his help. He said an astonishing thing which later I understood. He told me that he was probably closer to Ickes than anyone else; that he had recommended him to the President for his place, and was responsible for his getting it. Ickes had been manager of the Bull Moose Campaign in Illinois, when Theodore Roosevelt and Johnson ran for President and Vice-President of the United States. "But," said Johnson, "the closer you are to Ickes, the more he suspects you, and if I took you to him you wouldn't have a chance." Johnson, I soon learned, wasn't ducking it; he was telling me the truth, and he suggested my best chance was to go to Harry Hopkins of the WPA, whom he said he didn't know. Robert H. Hinckley was then regional head of the WPA for the Western states. He was a native of Utah, a resident of Ogden, and among other things a regent of the University of Utah. He was and is a sound Democrat and he and Creel agreed on many things and worked together. Hinckley is a Mormon and as a youth had gone on a mission to Germany for the Church. Marriner Eccles had gone at the same time to Italy, and from the telling I am not so sure a few of the minor rules of the Church were not broken when these two boys joined up in Rome for Christmas and so far from home. Hinckley is now a director of Eccles' Utah banks; and although he tried at various times to leave government service, he was, after leaving the WPA, a member of the Civil Aeronautics Commission, then its chairman, and the Assistant Secretary of Commerce. He resigned and became vice-president of the Sperry Gyroscope Company. Mr. Roosevelt recalled him and made him director of War Contract Termination, probably the toughest civil job then in America. He finally got loose from government and is now vice-president and director of American Broadcasting Company, with his old friend, Ed Noble, whom he succeeded as chairman of Civil Aeronautics. I mention all of this to indicate the two powerful men I had on my side, Creel and Hinckley, and to emphasize that while I did countless things to bring about the Exposition, I could not have accomplished anything unless these two had made it their business, with their friendships and connections, to see me through. Hinckley and Hopkins were close friends and during Hopkins' frequent illnesses Hinckley spent much time with him at Mayo's playing gin rummy and keeping him cheered up.

Creel and Hinckley paved the way for me to Hopkins on our first project, the reclamation of the Shoals and building Treasure Island. As I recall, they did this by letter, or verbally perhaps when I was not present. I was to tell my own story and make my own way. I went to Washington and directly to Jesse Jones and Harvey Couch of the RFC. Of course they knew Hopkins well and took me to him. They gave me practically the same introduction that Merle Thorpe had given me to Couch several years before. "Harry," they said, "we have dealt with Le Cutler for several years on the San Francisco–Oakland Bay Bridge, involving $75,000,000. He lived up to every engagement he made with us, and the State of California backed up every representation he made. He has something on his mind and will tell his own story, but take our word for it, you can believe him." "And Le," turning to me, "you can believe Harry. Now you two fellows go to it." A wonderful introduction truly. Hopkins said simply, "What do you want?" I told him. He said it was not a WPA project but he would see what he could do, and turned me over to Jay Cooke, one of his assistants, as I remember. I told Cooke my story in detail. I had maps and estimates and sketches, and in a month or so saw Hopkins again. I argued that, regardless of WPA or PWA, union or nonunion, if he would start us off with reclamation of the Shoals we would spend $50,000,000 and put men to work. Hopkins was an idealist, almost a fanatic; I think his philosophy of government was all wrong. He never hired a man in his life or had to meet a payroll, and he was poor as a church mouse. Hopkins was a

184

very sincere man in his own thinking, but he didn't work for the United States of America, although he believed in it in his own way passionately. He worked for Franklin D. Roosevelt. Later, when I got to know him better he said to me one day, "Le, you wouldn't have any man working for you who didn't believe in you or what you were trying to do, and you wouldn't work for any man whom you didn't believe in and the things he is doing. I believe in Franklin D. Roosevelt and everything on his program, and I won't have anyone in my employ who doesn't believe the same way." Despite his philosophy of government, terrible and dangerous as in my opinion it was, I came to have a genuine affection for him personally.

Negotiations with the WPA took about six months, with many trips back and forth between Washington and California. One night when I was in a room at the Mayflower Hotel with Hinckley and one of his assistants, they called Hopkins at frequent intervals while both figured with big sheets of paper, blueprints, and a great many pencils. Along about three o'clock in the morning I asked, "What is the best thing I can do?" Hinckley replied: "I think the best thing you can do is to go home. Don't forget, you are a Republican." I left that same day and when I reached San Francisco, Creel showed me a telegram from Hopkins declaring the building of the island a WPA project. The telegram specified that $3,800,000 would be granted to the City and County of San Francisco for the building of an airport and that Cutler, representing the Exposition group, would put up the sponsor's fund of 20 percent or $760,000.

As far as the Exposition group was concerned, it was a gentleman's agreement and I had nothing whatever in writing. I had told Roosevelt and Hopkins, however, that if they would grant the money to the City and County of San Francisco, I would see that $760,000 would be paid by the Exposition group in thirty days, which we all know is the shortest time known to man. I telephoned Kenneth Kingsbury, chairman of our Finance Committee and president of the Standard Oil Company, and without telling him what I had in mind asked for a meeting. He called it for the same afternoon, and present in addition to him, as I remember, were Atholl McBean, Milton Esberg, and John Forbes. I explained that I had obtained a grant to San Francisco of $3,800,000 for building the island, that the Exposition's share was $760,000, and I had promised the money within thirty days. Kingsbury was an imposing man; he sat behind an imposing desk and had a superlatively imposing office. The ceiling of his office was a normal one, but he hit it. "What right did you have to promise $760,000 in behalf of the Exposition—who gave you the right? You were not authorized to do it," and so on ad infinitum. I was angry too, but I kept my temper, as I found later I had to do every day throughout the Exposition. I said as calmly as I could: "Ken, I'm president of the Exposition. Maybe I'm not the man to be president, but I am. You keep asking me every day, 'Why don't you do something?' All right, I've done it; I've got $3,800,000 to build an island that you can see out of that beautiful window of yours. All you have to do is to raise $760,000, and if you are going to turn me down I'll get a megaphone and go on top of your roof and yell 'Fannie!' at everybody in San Francisco and I'll get the money! What do you say?" All of the men present chimed in and congratulated me and said of course they would find some way of getting the money; that I had done a good job, etc. Then Kingsbury said: "Le, what have you got to show for it—let's see the agreement." I said: "I have the word of Harry Hopkins and President Roosevelt—nothing else." All present hit the ceiling again, and being Republicans said they wouldn't believe either one of them under oath. When all was quiet, Kingsbury said he would call a meeting of prospective donors for two days later in the Standard Oil directors' room. If the president's room was impressive, the directors' room was much more so. Kingsbury, on two days' notice, assembled sixty people and I presented the case. Kingsbury was impressively nonchalant and asked each one for $15,000. A. P. Giannini, now dead, stood up and said if the sixty present didn't give $900,000, he would give it all. Of course in such a setting and with such a background, the sixty leading citizens pledged $15,000 for themselves or their corporations, to be repaid out of the first moneys raised under the leadership of Kingsbury, who announced that he was going to start a campaign for $7,500,000.

I returned to Washington with convincing assurance of $760,000 for Hopkins' grant, but I wanted the government's money turned over to the United States Army Engineers, where it would be safe and where

186

the work could be done by contract. I reminded Hopkins that he himself had said at the beginning that it was not a real WPA project, to be built with buckets and brooms and shovels. He agreed but said that only one man in America could have the money transferred the way we wanted it, and that would be the President of the United States by executive order. I thought about going myself immediately to the President because I was always welcome but generally for reminiscing purposes. I located George Creel in Kansas City and told him my story. He flew to Washington and we immediately went to see the President. I was somewhat afraid and argued with Creel to wait until we had an appointment and could rehearse our case. All Creel wanted to know was whether I knew my facts, and when I assured him I did he called a cab and we went.

Creel did not need an appointment even in those days. Marvin McIntyre, Steve Early, and Pa Watson, the President's secretaries, could have paved the way for him, but they didn't have to. All of the secretaries waved him in, and with Cordell Hull and J. F. T. O'Connor, Comptroller of the Currency, waiting, Creel walked right into the President's office with me trailing behind. After greetings were over, Creel very seriously said, "Mr. President, Le wants to ask something of you." I told him of Hopkins' grant of $3,800,000 and my request that the money be transferred to the United States Army Engineers and the work done by contract. I recited the reasons for it and the necessity for an executive order. Creel pounded the table in his own convincing fashion and together we made a very logical presentation. The President sat back smoking a cigarette in his long holder and told us a funny story, very much to the point, about a Negro in Georgia. He asked me for the project number, etc., and wrote, "Project X43 WPA—grant to the City and County of San Francisco for construction of Island $3,800,000 to be constructed by Army Engineers O.K.," signed FDR. This he tossed over to me and the whole transaction had not taken over ten minutes. I was elated and walking on air. As we started for the door, President Roosevelt said, "Le, there's just one catch to that; you have to get by Controller General McCarl and General Markham, Chief of Army Engineers." What took ten minutes with the President took several months with those two gentlemen. Both were fine men for the

United States and, in addition, General Markham was an excellent piano player! The transfer was eventually accomplished. Creel in his excellent autobiography, *A Rebel at Large*, says: "Leland Cutler descended on Washington with a bland request for millions," and "The President was not any too enthusiastic at the outset for New York was also begging funds for an Exposition in 1939 but he softened considerably when we pointed out the benefits that would accrue. Aside from providing employment for five thousand men and pouring large sums into the Federal treasury by a tax on admissions, there was the added inducement that the island would be turned over to the Navy at the Exposition's end." We offered it to the Navy for $1.00 per year as long as they might want it, pending its ultimate use as an airport, which Roosevelt never lost sight of and all of the money granted was for airport purposes. "A wonderful and necessary base . . ." wrote Creel. "Under the spell of Le Cutler's oratory, the President approved allocations of $8,545,000 and along with the grants came the suggestion that I take the post of United States Commissioner."

I quote this to indicate how closely Creel and I worked together—I could not have accomplished the Exposition without him. Previously I had urged him to come to California and take the federal commissionership. He stated flatly that he could not do it because of his connection with *Collier's* and his deep sense of obligation to them. One night at dinner in the Mayflower, he succumbed and told me he had figured out that he could continue his writings and be Commissioner too—that he had a "loose foot" and of course a great love for San Francisco. I immediately started to work on the President to include Creel in our program and to appoint him, and also urged Secretary Roper to use his influence. Creel had a hard time getting his release from *Collier's* because he was *Collier's* springboard to the administration and his lifelong friend, Editor William L. Chenery, relied on him greatly. Creel and I felt certain that we could work out the financing with the federal government but we could not tell San Francisco so. No one likes to be told ahead of time that he is going to give money before definite arrangements have been made. We avoided any statements to San Francisco and in response to direct questions from civic bodies replied that we had no commitments from the federal government whatever. The

188

Exposition group had no official position; as far as we were concerned, we merely had a gentleman's agreement without anything in writing, and it is a fine commentary and a refreshing one to look back and realize that everyone lived up to his agreements.

There were six parties involved: the WPA, the War Department, the PWA, the City and County of San Francisco, represented by the Public Utilities Commission, the Exposition, and the Navy. The varying interests of these different factors obviously presented quite a problem in the administration of the project. The War Department through the Corps of Engineers was responsible for the actual construction work, including control of expenditures, engineering, and supervision of personnel. The Exposition company had to produce the finished appealing picture and yet the only authority it had was derived from a resolution of the Board of Supervisors of the City and County of San Francisco on November 5, 1935, and signed by Mayor Rossi, appointing the San Francisco Bay Exposition as its agent to "plan, arrange for and conduct said Exposition on said site, but without authority to incur any obligation on the part of said City and County of San Francisco."

Concerning the $760,000 raised by the Exposition for the sponsor's fund, I went to Washington and pointed out to General Markham that the War Department would use that money without any of their own and keep the work going for six or seven months. I proposed that our contribution be 20 percent of work done each month, the Exposition to make the money available ten days after the day bids on any contract were opened, and that if any time the Exposition failed to put up the necessary sum on time, the entire amount of the $760,000 still unpaid would become due and payable. After considerable negotiation, this was agreed to and our first month's contribution was $13,373.79 and we had the balance in reserve. Payment of the sponsor's contribution was spread over the life of the project and our agreement was lived up to in the most minute detail.

The whole approach of Creel and myself to the federal government was that the reclamation of the Yerba Buena Shoals was entirely justified in the airport which would result and in creation of facilities for national defense, and that thereby the project should be supported by the Navy, by the Army, and by President Roosevelt, who was intensely interested in both airport and a national defense site on San Francisco Bay. Later developments showed that he was farsighted in helping us, because no one knows what the Navy would have done without the island as a receiving station during the war.

Creel and I enlisted the support of such powerful figures as Brigadier General W. E. Gillmore, U.S.A. (Ret.), Assistant Chief of the Air Force, Maurice Harrison, Colonel Harry Roosevelt, Secretary of Commerce Daniel C. Roper, Admiral William H. Standley, Senator William G. McAdoo, Senator Hiram Johnson, Representative Florence P. Kahn, Congressman Richard J. Welch, and Robert H. Hinckley, regional director of the WPA and later chairman of Civil Aeronautics. The emphasis which was to be placed upon the desirability of the reclamation of the Shoals from a naval standpoint is indicated by the presence of Colonel Roosevelt, Assistant Secretary of the Navy, and Admiral Standley in this group. We also stressed the desirability of the project because of the number of men who would be put to work. The high degree of mechanization of doing the work by dredges caused the proportion of expenditures for labor to be too low, compared to those for machinery and equipment, for the job to be classed as a relief project. However, Major General Lytle Brown, then Chief of Engineers, United States Army, did state that 51 percent of the money spent in dredging operations went to direct labor. He also estimated that 25.8 percent of the money went to indirect labor. While this total of 76.8 percent did not place this type of work in the relief category, it did indicate that such an expenditure resulted in desirable employment of labor, which Harry Hopkins with his sincerity and idealism believed in.

It was intended to award the contract for the island by call for bids. The Navy asked for a turning basin, a change in the construction of the sea wall to permit dredging of the basin to a depth sufficient for the maneuvering of naval vessels (sixty feet in depth for submarines). The development of the airport could be an integral part of the grounds of the Exposition but a rock wall was necessary for the sand fill to be dredged from the Bay. Trees, plants, and shrubs had to be provided, as well as the construction of a roadway and trestle from Yerba Buena Island—architectural and engineering work and water supply and drainage.

Private dredging interests who were solicited for submission of bids refused to do so, with the result that the Army Engineers handled the work themselves. Work was started in March 1936 and the fill required approximately eighteen months to complete. The fill was made by suction dredges operating on a twenty-four-hour schedule. Sand for the fill was pumped from adjacent areas four to twenty-five feet below sea level and sluiced to the Shoals until the fill rose approximately thirteen feet above the average low-water level. Approximately 25,000,000 cubic yards of sand were required for this purpose, comprising over 400 acres of ground. The required area was surrounded by a rock retaining wall of almost three miles and consisting of 287,000 tons. The total cost was $3,809,200, of which the Exposition contributed $760,000. The Army Engineers were the contractor and, like all contractors, divided the appropriation by the yardage.

The local dredging concerns issued a joint letter indicating that their refusal to bid was based on their inability to reach satisfactory terms with rock contractors and their doubt that the money available was sufficient to do the work. Being in the surety business I knew all of the contractors intimately. They knew where all the dredges were, and I am sure they believed that by holding out they would be in a position to obtain higher prices on a rebiding, or in any event they would be able to lease their dredges to the government at a satisfactory price and make up for the long idleness. The latter proved to be the case. Every available dredge was used by the Army Engineers and I think there was general satisfaction all around. Even the rock men got together in their bid and four of the biggest operators entered a single bid. Five hopper dredges and three pipeline dredges of the government were used during the life of the reclamation project, and in addition the dredges and equipment of the American Dredging Corporation, the San Francisco Bridge Company, and the Hydraulic Dredging Company were rented to supplement the government equipment. Bonus arrangements above certain guaranties were entered into and this assured a reasonable expectancy of income to the dredging owners and protected the interests of the United States.

There was a WPA requirement that at least 90 percent of the labor employed on any project of that federal agency be taken from the public relief rolls. Because of the scarcity of laboring men on relief rolls with the training and experience necessary to man a dredging operation, an obvious difficulty was encountered by the Army Engineers. As in countless other matters which had to be straightened out, Creel and I attacked the problem and in April 1936 obtained from Thad Holt, assistant administrator of the WPA, a letter to Major General Markham, Chief of Army Engineers, "For the purpose of continuing the employment of regular crews of government dredges and attendant plant, except that additions and replacements as may be needed will be taken from public relief rolls if qualified relief persons are available, I hereby exempt this project from the requirement of paragraph C, Part III of Executive Order 7046, that at least ninety percent of the persons employed on a project shall be taken from the public relief rolls."

It can be imagined that a project of this magnitude and character took a great deal of work and much maneuvering behind the scenes, both in Washington and at home. Both Creel and I believed in working quietly. I took all of the work possible off Creel's shoulders and left him to his work with *Collier's*, because I knew his deep sense of obligation to its editors, Chenery and Colebaugh, and their great dependence on him. Also, nothing as yet was settled about his federal commissionership. In the pinches, however, Creel helped me as though it were his own personal project and I will always be grateful to him. Ascertaining that I might wangle an expense account for the purposes, we gave a big luncheon in the private banquet room of the Carlton, giving the chef carte blanche, and all of the power of Washington was there. George was in his element and took charge but called on me to explain what we were after. While my speech was apparently extemporaneous, I had worked on it carefully, and all in all the occasion was a great success and lasted until late in the evening.

One of our troubles was that New York was holding an exposition the same year. I had attended a dinner given by Grover Whalen, New York's president, to the ambassadors and bigwigs at the Mayflower Hotel, which was quite elaborate and must have cost New York at least $35 a plate. So quietly did we work that we had a resolution through Congress declaring us an International Exposition, a proclamation from President Roosevelt calling on all the nations of the world to participate, and a gross total of $6,456,631.18 from the WPA and $7,376,-875.26 from the PWA six months before New York found out about it. The WPA was very sympathetic and did everything to help us. Ickes and the PWA were different and difficult. Ickes seemed to have a grudge against anything having to do with California. He had a big map in his office with red thumbtacks marking all of the California spots where government money had gone, and he had charged up to the Bay Area as a loan or grant the $75,000,000 of bridge money—which was no concern of his at all. I tried to tell him that it was a purchase by the RFC of revenue bonds. I knew, because I was head of the Financial Advisory Board which had assisted the state officials in negotiating the transaction. I made no headway whatever and he was always belligerent at every meeting I had with him. I could not afford to fight with him because we needed PWA money for our buildings after the island was built, but the PWA grant carried a 55 percent sponsorship and was costly to the Exposition. Again the PWA grant was to the City and County of San Francisco, the work was handled on a contract basis, and all contracts were let by the Public Utilities Commission of the City and County of San Francisco. As in the case of the WPA grants, with a 20 percent sponsorship the city did not put up a cent of money. It all came from the Exposition group. Colonel Allen G. Wright was attorney for the Exposition, as he was for the Chamber of Commerce, and did yeoman service for us in all our dealings with the city. E. G. Cahill was manager of public utilities and constantly grumbled at being a "rubber stamp" in certifying our estimates. His grumbling was of the kind, however, that didn't hurt, for he was a sterling public official, loyal to his city, the Exposition, and to me, and one of my firm friends of today.

The original PWA grant referred to buildings to be built "on reclaimed land belonging to the City and County of San Francisco for construction of airport and recreational facilities" and required that contracts be let and work begun by January 15, 1936. I went to Washington to gain an extension of time from Ickes, for we hadn't even started work on the Shoals. Ickes refused me in no uncertain language and I was desperate. Ed Foley, whom I had known as an attorney for the RFC, and a good friend, was attorney for the WPA and is now

Under Secretary of the Treasury. Ed followed me down the hall from the meeting and suggested that we amend the grant to read "on re-claimed land or other land belonging to the City and County of San Francisco," and that if this were done, starting any part of the work before expiration of our time would be construed as substantial compli-ance and would hold the original grant until we could build the island. I hurried back to San Francisco, and with Mayor Rossi and Cleary, of the Chief Administrative Office, and Joe Philips, in charge of city real estate, made a tour of the city and looked over every possible site. We chose a site at the corner of Bush and Stockton which was owned by the Board of Education, and though we had no money because our finance campaign was just being organized, we decided hurriedly to build an administration building to house the workers during the con-struction of the Exposition. On January 14, one day before our grant from the PWA was to expire, I took a cab to the office of Lindgren and Swinerton, low bidders at $174,000, and asked Al Swinerton to sign a contract with us and get steam shovels on the job, have pictures taken and the date certified to. I had gone to Stanford with Swinerton and knew him very well. "Have you the money?" he asked. I said, "We haven't a cent but please sign the contract; do as I ask and I'll find the money." Swinerton did just that, and then I asked him to loan me $5 so I could pay for the taxicab which I had waiting outside. Although Ickes did not like it, the deal went off on schedule. Lindgren and Swinerton were paid and Al got his $5 back from me personally.

About this time Grover Whalen came to life and apparently real-ized that we meant business. One day my telephone rang, and without any salutation an angry voice said, "What does San Francisco mean by having a world's fair the same year as New York?" I said, "The only answer I can think of, Mr. Whalen, is, what does New York mean by having an exposition the same year as San Francisco?" Rather pom-pously came the reply: "Ours was ordained by George Washington 150 years before," and without even a comma or pausing for breath he added, "and we postponed ours a year on account of San Diego's fair." I said, "What did Washington think about that 151 years ago? Let us co-operate and work things out together." Whalen replied that "The world is our field and we will knock on every door." I said, "When you

194

do, you will find that the Fuller Brush salesman from San Francisco has been there just ahead of you—let's go to it." It was of course childish talk on both sides, but we did not work well together at all. The day of world's fairs was over with before we started and neither one of us knew it. Whalen did not come out to see us although Mrs. Whalen, who was a lovely, gracious lady, did, and she had with her some of the New York officials and quite a delegation of New York newspapermen. I remember one of the dinners we gave her party at which Charley Driscoll, the New York columnist, was toastmaster. He paid our Exposition the greatest compliment it ever had when he said amidst laughter, "Leland Cutler is not as beautiful as Grover Whalen, but his Exposition is!" Mrs. Cutler and I visited the New York Fair twice, once incognito when we could see it as we wished, and the next day when Whalen received us formally with an honor guard of Indians on cow ponies, as befitting a country boy and girl from the West. Immaculate in his frock coat and striped trousers, he surprised me with a newsreel in which he lauded the greatness of the New York Fair and said in effect: "Of course if you want to see a nice little country fair, visit San Francisco—if you have the chance." I was taken off my guard but replied as best I could that "Our Exposition was not the biggest, it was only the most beautiful. The reel was shown in many theaters, and San Francisco did not fare too badly. The *New York Tribune*, in commenting on our visit, said in part:

With a tact that should qualify him for the diplomatic service after his own fair closes next December, Leland W. Cutler, president of the San Francisco Exposition, visited the New York World's Fair yesterday and even dared to give his impressions of the rival extravaganza.

"You have me, gentlemen," Mr. Cutler said with a mock rueful smile as he was introduced to reporters on the balcony of Perylon Hall, where he was awaiting Grover A. Whalen, the Fair's president. Then he proceeded to compare, contrast and praise both Fairs with a suavity that would have offended neither a rabid Californian nor a partisan of New York's three-ring circus.

Although his first visit, officially, was yesterday he said he had done a "sneak preview" the night before, paying his own way through the gate—he had a ticket stub to prove it—and touring the grounds incognito with Mrs. Cutler.

"It is a marvelous show," he said, "especially at night with the colored lights on your Perisphere, the fountains and the vast stretches of buildings and walks.

"Our exposition is considerably smaller in area, you know, 400 acres compared to your 1600 (he was 400 over the actual acreage—a good diplomatic stroke, even if accidental), and where you have had to spread your effects we have been able to mass them.

"But there should be no necessity to either compare or contrast the two. This country is big enough to support two World's Fairs the same year and the American people will be falling down on the job if they do not.

"They should be proud of the fact that they have two such wonderful expositions to visit. We've done a good job on one coast and you've done a grand job on the other."

The *New York Times* in an editorial said:

It was not Diplomats' Day at the World's Fair when it was visited by Mr. Leland W. Cutler, President of the San Francisco Exposition. But it should have been. When Mr. Cutler interviewed our newsmen the word tact gained fresh nuances. In the first place, he had qualified himself to express free and untrammeled opinions by becoming a paying guest the day before. His impression was one of vastness. "Our exposition," he admitted, "is considerably smaller, you know—400 acres compared to your 1600 acres." Masterstroke or mistake, this added 33-1/3 percent to the New York acreage right off the bat. But he was quick to add that "where you have been compelled to spread your effects we were able to mass them." Other than that he refused to compare or contrast. But was there something significant in mentioning, just at the beginning of our hot season, San Francisco's "cool nights"? If so, he politely refrained from observing that at this season by the Golden Gate every day is a fair day.

I wrote previously that the day of world expositions was over before either one of us ever started and we didn't know it. I used to see people drive around our grounds early in the morning so that they could be in Los Angeles by night and then when they would get back home in the Middle West say, "Sure, we saw the Frisco Fair!" I was in the lobby of the Biltmore one day in New York and I heard a group of fine-looking men and women discussing how to spend the afternoon. One man remarked, "Let's go out and see the Fair," and the rest of the group demurred—"No, we saw the Fair yesterday." It used to be that people would travel long distances and take a month or two to see a world's fair going every day. My mother went to our Exposition every day. She would welcome anyone going with her to the entrance gates and then she insisted on being on her own, for she planned just what she wanted to see. When I was a boy, if I had a rope and a piece of stick, I could play with it for a month. Now we give our children all the modern and fantastic toys in the world and in an hour or so their cry is, "What can I do now, Daddy?" Children now can see artificially done in the movies things more wonderful than can ever be assembled in a world's fair. I would not prophesy that there would never be another world's fair, for we all know that "never" is a long time, but to be successful it would have to be planned along lines entirely different from any that have gone before. When I was chosen president of the Golden Gate International Exposition, I went to Rufus Dawes, president of the Chicago Exposition, whom I had known for many years, and asked to go over his plans and to get all the help he could give me. He gave me many of his men and everything I asked for, but said, "Le, it will not do you a bit of good. Times change rapidly and you will have to plan yours entirely different from what Chicago did." He added that when he was chosen president of the Chicago Fair he came out to San Francisco to learn from C. C. Moore, president of the 1915 Panama Pacific Exposition. Moore helped him in every way but gave him the same information—that he, Dawes, would discard everything he would learn from San Francisco. I think now that I would know how to put on an exposition—which again heaven forbid—but I did have to discard everything that Dawes showed me.

· The time came when New York and San Francisco felt that one or the other should postpone. Of course, in New York's mind, that should be San Francisco. Certainly two world fairs in the same year was not a sound program. President Roosevelt very wisely advised us both to continue. He pointed out that the country had been surfeited with world's fairs—San Diego, Chicago twice, Cleveland, Fort Worth, and Dallas. Roosevelt said, "If you wait another year neither one of you will get a cent from Congress or any federal agency. You two men get together and make of 1939 an exposition year. Get a round-trip fare to both expositions; Grover, you convince America that New York has the best, and Le, you do the same. I know you both and you both can do it. Now go to it." Of course the President was right and any postponement would have meant the end of the one who yielded or lost the throw of the dice.

While New York had an issue of $22,000,000 or thereabouts in debentures bearing 2 percent—most of which had to be repudiated, I believe—San Francisco's campaign was for $7,500,000 with no guaranties whatever. We thought we would gain an airport. We knew our Exposition would help the state generally and our only engagement with the subscribers was to repay in proportion to the profits which we might make. We raised $6,500,000 by popular subscription instead of $7,500,000, and the $6,500,000 was lost, but in the main everyone was satisfied.

Our Finance Committee was headed by Kenneth Kingsbury, president of the Standard Oil Company of California, with Henry Q. Hawes as vice-chairman, and Ray W. Smith, who had been with me most effectively in two Community Chest campaigns as executive secretary. The other members of the Finance Committee were:

Wallace M. Alexander	John E. French
R. F. Allen	A. P. Giannini
James B. Black	Samuel Kahn
A. B. C. Dohrmann	J. R. Knowland
Milton H. Esberg	Roger Lapham
Herbert Fleishhacker	A. D. McDonald

George D. Smith

Ex officio:

Atholl McBean, chairman of the board
Leland W. Cutler, president
John F. Forbes, treasurer

Later Colbert Coldwell and Allen L. Chickering resigned as members of the Board of Directors and Executive Committee, and Kenneth R. Kingsbury and George D. Smith were elected to fill the vacancies created by their resignations. Still later, Mr. Coldwell was re-elected as a member of the Board of Directors and the Executive Committee, at which time Mr. Kingsbury and George D. Smith and Milton H. Esberg were elected to the board and Executive Committee. Mayor Angelo Rossi was elected an honorary member of the committee. The untimely deaths of B. B. Meek and Kenneth R. Kingsbury created vacancies in the membership of the committee and James B. Black, president of the PG & E, and Philip Patchin of the Standard Oil Company were elected to fill the vacancies. The sudden death of Milton H. Esberg left still another vacancy, which was filled by George Creel; Major Charles Kendrick was elected a vice-president of the corporation, filling the vacancy caused by Mr. Kingsbury's death.

With the unanimous approval of the members of the board, George W. Kelham was appointed chairman of the Architectural Commission, with the following members: Arthur Brown, Sr., Lewis P. Hobart, Timothy Pflueger, Ernest Weihe, William G. Merchant. After the passing of Mr. Kelham, Arthur Brown, Jr., was appointed chairman of the Commission. At approximately the same time that the Architectural Commission was appointed, W. P. Day was appointed director of works and was subsequently also elected a vice-president.

In order to alleviate some of the burden of the Executive Committee and officers, the members thereof by resolution created an administrative committee of five members as follows: John F. Forbes, K. R. Kingsbury, Atholl McBean, J. W. Mailliard, Jr., B. B. Meek, Leland W. Cutler (ex officio). Later, a Board of Management was elected consisting of James B. Black, Colbert Coldwell, K. R. Kingsbury, J. W. Mailliard, Jr., Leland W. Cutler (ex officio), and, upon the death of Mr. Kingsbury, Philip Patchin was elected to succeed him.

H. C. Bottorff was, from the inception of the Exposition, assistant treasurer and controller and bore the brunt of all complaints—lack of money and complaints of concessionaires and exhibitors—and did a remarkable job. Colonel Allen G. Wright was general counsel for the Exposition from the beginning and steered us through many a difficulty. Bottorff and Wright and I met daily and ironed out many things which might not have been according to Hoyle but which kept the show moving. The Finance Committee in its subscription campaign, while not reaching the goal of $7,500,000, did produce $6,500,000, and this could not have been accomplished without very systematic planning. The prospects were for subscriptions of $25,000 and over and were set up by classifications, as follows:

Foods and beverages	Gas and electricity
Hotels, apartments, restaurants	Real estate
Oils	Construction
Retail	Communication

Wholesale and manufacturing	Insurance
Automotive	Investments
Amusements	Business and professional service
Import and export	Newspapers and printing
Transportation	Advertising
Banks and loan companies	Mining

Naturally a great deal of personal work was done by the members of the committee. Each man was assigned an industry and held responsible for quota being maintained. The Exposition was looked upon as a civic project and thus received the support of the community. Once the campaign was under way, the solicitors could point to those concerns who had already subscribed, as an inducement for the prospective subscribers. Also, the subscribers expected some real return on their investment and believed that the Exposition would act as a sufficient stimulus to business in California and the Bay Area through an influx of tourist travel, and that the money expended on the construction of the Exposition would ultimately bring a return to the individual businesses of the subscribers. That belief can in part be attributed to the reputations of many of the men active in promoting the Exposition, to the promotional and publicity program which was carried on in conjunction with the subscription campaign, and to actual estimates made by civic organizations, such as Californians, Incorporated. Also, those who put up the $6,500,000 had in mind an airport, and the Finance Committee did a remarkable and almost unbelievable job.

I was a constant commuter to Washington, D.C., because of the multitudinous things that needed attention there; also matters were not going too well at home. Although we were asking the City and County of San Francisco for no money, the permission of the Board of Supervisors had to be obtained before we could have state legislation to use the Shoals for Exposition purposes. Temperaments, selfish interests, and politics developed rapidly and undoubtedly delayed the construction of the Exposition for a year. There was quite a bit of opposition to the Shoals, and in June 1934 Adolph Uhl of the Board of Supervisors of the City and County of San Francisco introduced a resolution before the board protesting the Yerba Buena site, although at that time the Kelham-Day report had not been released, and the Exposition authorities had made no official decision as to the site. Since the Shoals had been deeded to the City and County by the state in 1933, the approval of the board seemed essential to the use of this site; hence there was considerable apprehension toward this countermovement. In spite of this protest, or possibly because of it, the directors of the Exposition did not make their official decision until February 28, 1935, when, as president of the San Francisco Bay Exposition, I wrote a letter to the Honorable James B. McSheehy, president of the Board of Supervisors. This letter followed two meetings of the directors of the Exposition Corporation in which the site problem was discussed, with the proponents of all sites being heard and a mail ballot being taken. The ballot was unanimously in favor of the Shoals, the majority of those voting expressing the opinion that if the Shoals could not be had there should be no exposition because of the likelihood of financial failure. My letter stated:

The officers and directors of the San Francisco Bay Exposition, a non-profit corporation, have reached the conclusion, after careful study of all available sites and consideration of the factors involved in bringing about a successful exposition in 1938, that the Yerba Buena Shoals is the best possible location.

As the result of our studies, which have covered engineering, construction, transportation, and financial problems, we believe that the Yerba Buena Shoals is the only site which can be successfully financed without recourse to a bond issue.

This decision favoring Yerba Buena Shoals is based entirely upon the conviction that the site offers the best location from the standpoint of setting, surroundings, and accessibility, and is the only possible location providing that guaranty of financial success which would justify the assumption of leadership and responsibility of the citizens of our community who make up the directorate of our corporation and would have to bear the burden of private financing.

The title to the Yerba Buena Shoals site is held by the City and County of San Francisco and so we respectfully ask that the City and County of San Francisco call upon the Legislature of the State of California to pass whatever permissive legislation may be necessary to make the use of the Shoals possible for exposition purposes and to aid actively in bringing this legislation about. We also respectfully ask the City and County of San Francisco to indicate its willingness, as owner of this property, when called upon, to further the negotiations of the Exposition officers and directors for Federal funds for the reclamation of the Shoals, bearing in mind that the reclamation of the Shoals will, at the conclusion of the Exposition, give to the City and County of San Francisco an airport with an estimated salvage value of at least $3,500,000.

With this cooperation from the City and County of San Francisco it is the opinion of our directors, that an exposition of unusual attractiveness can be financially successful and that transportation costs to and from the site can be held at a minimum and within reach of all . . .

These men feel that San Francisco should not be burdened with a bond issue and that her taxes should not be increased for exposition purposes. It is the judgment of these men that an exposition on Yerba Buena Shoals site only would be financially successful, and accordingly they would be willing to arrange for a certain amount of private financing there but would not feel justified in doing so on the other locations suggested. It is a matter of judgment as to whether these conclusions are correct, but they are so arrived at as a result of careful and thorough study and in all sincerity. This group feels that such private financing as is necessary could better be pro-rated voluntarily than assessed in the form of taxes over all of our citizens. Also as a result of their investigation, these men have reason to believe that the Shoals are more susceptible to Federal financing than any other location.

I wrote a succeeding letter to McSheehy on March 1, summarizing the factors upon which they based their selection of the Yerba Buena Shoals. The letter was unsuccessful, and on March 4 the Board of Supervisors adopted the following: "The Board of Supervisors of the City and County of San Francisco respectfully endeavors to induce the Directors of the San Francisco Bay Exposition, Inc., to reconsider its action adopting the shoals to the north of Yerba Buena Island as a site for its proposed exposition in 1938, in favor of a more suitable and accessible site on the San Francisco peninsula within range of a five cent street car fare."

On March 7, 1935, Adolph Uhl, chairman of the Public Welfare Committee of the Board of Supervisors, wrote the directors of the Exposition Corporation asking, "Do you feel that if the Board of Supervisors should fail to grant the Exposition Company the right to use the Shoals in San Francisco Bay for the site of said Exposition as requested, that you would not favor any other location on the main land within the boundaries of the City and County of San Francisco?"

All directors were again canvassed, but no change in opinion was expressed. I responded to Uhl that "Every Director would, as good citizens of San Francisco, assist any responsible group who might undertake a worth-while Exposition on any site. The responsibility for the undertaking elsewhere, however, would have to rest upon other shoulders than the Directors of our Corporation. I know that no one of the Directors would decline to help. Their declination is only one of assumption of responsibility for any other site."

After considerable bickering back and forth, in which the supervisors continually asked for reconsideration of other sites and the directors declined to accept responsibility for the Exposition on any site but the Shoals, I went out to the Board of Supervisors one afternoon at two o'clock accompanied by Florence McAuliffe and made a personal plea. The supervisors met as a committee of the whole and the chambers were packed. We left at quarter of three in the morning. In the meantime I was subjected to quite a bit of abuse and my motives questioned. Chairman McSheehy, well known for the quirks in his language, left the chair and came down on the floor. He said, "Everybody knows Le Cutler and we all love him but he don't know the rump of the common people like I do." I readily agreed to that. One man shook his fist at me and said that I had gone East and got $75,000,000 for the Key Route and the Southern Pacific (referring to the $75,000,000 that I had helped to get for the bridge), and that now I wanted to build an island in the middle of the Bay so that the Southern Pacific could have it for a terminal! The entire audience was hostile, and McAuliffe and I could see that we were making no headway at all, although I think we could have had a majority vote if we had not declared a recess about quarter of two in the morning. Supervisor Warren Shannon I think really meant to vote for us, but the relaxation of the recess thickened his tongue and on reconvening he said, "I change my vote from "No" to "Aye" and vote "No"!

Even in the face of the decision on the part of the Exposition group, the supervisors decided to have a vote of the people. A special city-wide election was held and the following questions placed on the ballot:

1. Shall an exposition to celebrate the completion of the bay bridges in 1938 be held on the mainland of the City and County of San Francisco within the range of a 5¢ car fare?

2. Shall an exposition to celebrate the completion of the bay bridges be held on Yerba Buena Shoals?

3. Will you favor a bond issue, if needed, to finance an exposition on the mainland?

George D. Smith accepted the chairmanship of a committee known as "Save the Exposition League," and with Howard Freeman of the Exposition staff set up headquarters, and conducted an aggressive and intelligent campaign, although a fast and bitter one. The results of the vote demonstrated the confidence of the people in the Exposition authorities as to site, and the financing was blithely left to them:

		Yes	No
1.	Mainland	54,450	69,133
2.	Shoals	79,197	47,719
3.	Bonds	36,800	87,753

A bill was introduced in the state Legislature granting the use of the Shoals for Exposition purposes pending its ultimate use as an airport, and this was passed and signed by Governor Merriam. Following this, the Board of Supervisors adopted an ordinance authorizing the lease agreement between the City and County of San Francisco and the Exposition company for the Shoals site, and the way was cleared for more hard work on the part of the Exposition management.

I returned to Washington and, always with the help of George Creel, obtained approximately $2,000,000 from the Public Works Administration administered by Harold Ickes. This was for the Administration Building, two hangars (one of which we used for the Art Palace), ferry slips, paving, and various buildings we used for the exhibit.

Our whole approach was on the basis of securing federal funds for an airport. We seldom discussed Exposition in Washington and when we did it was as the means of eventually securing an airport; at all times we were sincere in that ambition and had no other thought. President Roosevelt kept saying to me: "Le, I know you are thinking Exposition but I am thinking airport." From the standpoint of an airport it was a little incongruous that we would have to have trees, plants, and shrubs—the very things that would be in the way of an airport. Hopkins told me that if I would write him a treatise on the subject justifying the planting of trees, he might be able to give us some more money. I put my soul into the presentation to Hopkins, and the WPA granted us $1,874,988 for planting. The technical description finally arrived at was, "Trees, plants, and shrubs for airport and recreational area for the City and County of San Francisco involving the early growth and care, boxing, etc. preparatory to placing on reclaimed areas selected for the airport." Hopkins granted this most willingly, because it was his one chance in the whole Exposition setup to put WPA laborers to work. All of the beautiful, seasonal flowers and shrubs were started in special areas in our parks, which of course required constant care and much labor, unskilled as well as skilled. This was an excellent arrangement for the Exposition and provided one of the most beautiful and outstanding features. We started a quiet campaign for donations of trees and secured a whole olive orchard, the trees of which lined the principal thoroughfare. Countless other donations of rare trees came in, and the WPA appraised them and accepted them as our sponsors' contribution. In this way the whole planting cost us practically nothing in money, gave continued employment to many, and will always remain one of the most beautiful memories of the Exposition.

President Roosevelt had agreed that in addition to the money we received from the WPA and PWA for "airport purposes" we should have $3,000,000 for federal participation in the Exposition and that George Creel would be the federal commissioner. New York was to have $5,000,000 because, as the President explained, they had had no other money from the government and of course New York was the larger city.

After making the arrangement, the President asked me to stay in Washington for a week or so while he went to Warm Springs for treatment and rest. When he returned he sent for me, and with him was Acting Director of the Budget Daniel W. Bell. Pointing his long cigarette holder at Bell, the President said, "Le, my boss says $3,000,000 is too much for you; we will have to cut you down to $1,500,000!" I cried and pulled out all the organ stops I could find, but to no avail. Roosevelt kept referring to what his "boss" said and added that tax receipts had not come up to anticipation but if they did later Bell might restore us to the original amount, etc. I was clearly beaten, and the President did it most adroitly and blamed it all on the Acting Director of the Budget. I could do nothing but accept the cut, but I had to get in a fling at New York. I said, "It is an unworthy thought, Mr. President, but what about New York?" "Oh," replied Roosevelt, "we are going to cut New York to $3,000,000. Somehow I felt better but said, "It is still an unworthy thought but does Grover Whalen know it?" The President called in Marvin McIntyre and told him to telephone Whalen and tell him about it. I immediately amended the bill which we had before Congress, changing it from $3,000,000 to $1,500,000, and went to New York. I saw Whalen and asked him if he had heard from the White House. He said he had but that he was not going to change his bill. I said it was none of my affair but I was sure the President would veto his $5,000,000. Whalen said, "He wouldn't dare veto a bill for New York. Of course he would for San Francisco." However, I returned to Washington and the next morning Senator Johnson telephoned me that our bill for $1,000,000 would shortly be on the floor, but he added, "You told me it was to be for $1,500,000." I asked him to hold it and went immediately to the Senate. Johnson and Senator Joe Robinson of Arkansas, the floor leader, came out, and Senator Robinson showed me in Roosevelt's handwriting a brief memo reading, "$1,000,000 for San Francisco Exposition OK," signed FDR. I asked them to hold it up while I located George Creel, which I did in Kansas City. Creel flew to Washington and we went to see the President without an appointment, but Creel in those days had no trouble getting in. George pounded the table and minced no words. I talked as best I could, and in between the President told us stories. In about an hour we had our bill back to $1,500,000—which is what we got, with Creel as federal commissioner. Whalen forced his bill for $5,000,000 along and had it passed, but in the end had to start all over again and be content with $3,000,000. I never thought of accusing Roosevelt of double-crossing me, because I and what I represented were the beneficiaries of all he was doing. I have not been able to satisfactorily explain to myself, however, why he should forget a half-million dollars in such a few hours.

With federal financing for the Exposition assured, I turned my attention to our own state Legislature. I gave a dinner to the San Francisco delegation at the Family Club and had with me the veteran campaigner and legislative representative of the Chamber of Commerce,

Richard W. Barrett, who had been my close friend for many years. Dick was a most effective man in the Legislature and had the confidence of everyone, and we had worked together for many years. Our San Francisco delegation promised its support, and as several of the legislators were from the University of San Francisco, there was much bantering about my arranging a football game between Stanford and U.S.F. in return for the support. The next day I went to Sacramento and discussed our needs with Governor Merriam. He was cautiously noncommittal but asked for a memorandum of what we wanted and promised to consider it. That was where I made my mistake and it taught me a lesson. The Legislature convened in a few days, and I returned to Sacramento with a memorandum which I gave to the Governor and leaders in both houses, setting forth that we would need $1,200,000 and showing specifically what the money would be used for. As the session progressed it became apparent that with proper maneuvering we might possibly get an appropriation of $5,000,000 if it were not for my memorandum asking for $1,200,000 which had been so hastily and prematurely drawn. The money of course was for state participation and not a grant to the Exposition, but it was of tremendous value to the whole show. Harry Chandler, publisher of the *Los Angeles Times*, and a fellow Stanford Trustee, was in San Francisco, and at breakfast one morning in my suite at the Fairmont Hotel I asked his support of a $5,000,000 program. He readily promised it and said, "You go ahead, Le, and have the Exposition in San Francisco; Los Angeles doesn't want it. You will have all the grief and headaches and every visitor who comes to your Exposition will go on down to Los Angeles and spend his money there and stay longer with us than he will at your show." Chandler was right and that is what happened. With the support of the Los Angeles papers and legislators and much work on the part of my friends in the Legislature and George Creel's Democratic friends, we were able to wangle a $5,000,000 bill onto the Senate floor. I appeared before all committees of both houses and had to stand up under a lot of questioning—not all of it good-natured—over my written request for $1,200,000. We passed the Assembly and eventually were set for special order in the Senate. I was tipped off at the last minute that Senator Culbert Olson of Los Angeles, later Governor of

California, would offer an amendment to cut the appropriation in two and give $2,500,000 to Los Angeles for a year-round mart, which had been under discussion for some time. As Senator Olson was going into the Senate I cornered him and asked him bluntly if he was going to introduce the amendment. He denied it vehemently. I told him I would be sitting right behind him and on the lookout. Within five minutes the Senate convened and our bill was called up, and Olson was on his feet offering his amendment. He was shouted down by an avalanche of protests and our $5,000,000 appropriation went through overwhelmingly. Such is the way of politics.

I have never felt right about the way our legislators were treated. The Board of Management of the Exposition had decreed that there should be no passes for anyone. Rufus Dawes, president of the Chicago Fair, and Frank Belcher, president of the San Diego Fair, both warned me that we would have to come to passes sooner or later and that we had better profit by their mistakes and grant a limited number at the beginning. To wait would merely cause irritation and dissatisfaction which a delayed granting could not overcome. Our board was adamant, and this went beyond the Legislature to the Army and Navy, the federal government, and our own Governor. I bought my own pass, and many others which I could ill afford, just to keep the peace. I paid $20 for a season pass, I remember, for Governor Merriam, who couldn't understand why he shouldn't be granted one. Later on, when the damage was done, we capitulated and supplied a properly chosen list with season passes, but many of the legislators were so disgusted they mailed them back with sarcastic letters. That episode is not a pleasant memory. Also probably every legislator had in the back of his mind that we would be able to employ some of his friends. We had in all over 380,000 applications for jobs. I was too crowded to look into them personally, and I will always feel that we did not do enough for the men who made the $5,000,000 state participation possible, or for the government officials, or for the fine Army and Navy men who made our Exposition so colorful. Governor Merriam appointed me a member of the state commission that was to administer the $5,000,000, and when Governor Olson came into office he promptly removed me. This made no difference, of course, because I was the president and had a hand in everything. Olson in fact removed all of Governor Merriam's appointees with the exception of George Creel.

It should be remembered that New York and San Francisco were putting on their expositions the same year. For many years a "League of Nations" in Europe has had the power to endorse or not endorse world fairs. It really is a protection to the various countries of the world, which would much prefer to be let alone and spared the great expense of participation. We sent George Creel to Europe to represent us, but New York had the inside track and received the endorsement.

209

X

THE ORIENT

COLBERT COLDWELL of our Board of Management, a former president of the Chamber of Commerce and always a farsighted citizen, insisted that we turn our eyes toward the Pacific and make that our theme. Up to now we had just been working for an Exposition really without any theme. Coldwell urged that we build a Pacific House, which should be the center of the cultural side of the Exposition and in effect a justification for it all. After much discussion we agreed on that and had a public contest for a name. This resulted in "The Golden Gate International Exposition" with the subtitle of "A Pageant of the Pacific." Our corporate prosaic name was "San Francisco Bay Exposition."

Mrs. Leslie Van Ness Denman, wife of Judge William Denman, Presiding Justice of the United States Court of Appeals in San Francisco, was the moving spirit in Pacific House. Both Judge and Mrs. Denman had been most helpful to me in Washington in the groping stages of the Exposition, and Mrs. Denman's interest in the Exposition as a Pageant of the Pacific never flagged, and she was at all times a most gracious hostess for outstanding occasions at Pacific House.

It was vital to our success that we secure the participation of the countries bordering the Pacific, and the board decided hurriedly that I should immediately go to the Orient. I went home on a Wednesday, as I remember it, and told Mrs. Cutler that we would leave for Japan on the *President Hoover* on Saturday. The Chinese Incident was on, which Mrs. Cutler could not distinguish from war; our children were small, and, after talking far into the night, she decided that she could not go and leave them. She agreed with me, however, that I could not very well tell my board that I could not go just because my wife would not go with me. This was one case where, like all salesmen, I figured that if I went myself I could get the countries in. Paul Sexson, who had been Mr. Hoover's secretary, was now mine, and he was to go with me.

On Friday I came home and explained to Mrs. Cutler that there was a jurisdictional strike on the water front, that the sailing of the *President Hoover* would be delayed until it was settled, and that I had been chosen to arbitrate it. Mrs. Cutler thought for a minute and said, "I think we will be safer in Japan, war or no war; I don't want you to arbitrate any strikes—I am going with you." A few days later we got away, and Mrs. Sexson went along with Paul. They were delightful companions, and although there was a great deal of intense, hard work involved, we had a trip that will always remain in our memory. I was fully accredited by the State Department and the President and had known Ambassador Grew for some time. I gave Sexson the title of "Commissioner," and he wore the striped trousers and high hat whenever I did and went everywhere with me. At night when festivities were over, he would get out his trusty typewriter, and with our coats off we would many times work far into the morning.

Although I know the Japanese as well as, if not better than, most Occidentals, I found I did not know just how the Oriental mind works. I thought I could state my case as we would do in this country and get an answer in a day or so. Because we had originally planned to visit Japan only, I had reservations back on the same ship. I soon found that I had to drink saki or, as I later discovered to my betterment, tea in the offices, and be polite and patient for weeks before they would talk business at all. I once remarked to Mrs. Cutler that I was so tired of being polite that I was certain to beat her up once we were again on shipboard!

Ginjiro Fujihara, later Minister of Munitions under Tojo, was the leading industrialist of Japan and president of the Ojai Paper Company, which had a monopoly throughout the Empire. He was a superior man in every way, although almost cruel in his belief in the self-sufficiency of Japan to stand alone against the world industrially, if necessary, and he had written several books on the subject. He was president of the Exposition which Japan was planning and also president of the Olympic Games slated for Japan four years later. I had met Fujihara in this country when he was the guest of Albert Schwabacher on his yacht at a party given him by the Zellerbachs. Fujihara took immediate charge of me and assigned his right-hand man, Yasumosuke Fukukita, to go with me everywhere and plan my stay in Japan. This was a particularly happy arrangement for me because I had gone to Stanford with Fukukita, where he had majored in English, and I had known him well. I later realized that we saw the silk mills and potteries and paper mills, and the like, but inquiries about steel mills and airplane factories were cleverly brushed off by vague rejoinders that they were "down Osaka way." Tokyo, and the various cities of Japan, were beautiful places, and we were royally entertained and met everyone of consequence except the Emperor. We were all being so polite that I was not making much progress officially in getting Japan signed up for our Exposition. I appealed to Ambassador Grew and asked him for a suggestion as to whom I should concentrate on to bring our matters to a conclusion. Grew said the one man who would have the most to say and who was probably the most nearly pro-American in Japan was Minister of Commerce and Industry Yoshino, now a life member of the House of Peers. Paul Sexson and I donned our striped trousers and went forth to meet him. His office was large and imposing, and many military caps, capes, and swords were hanging in the anteroom, indicating that an important conference was under way. We were ushered into a drawing room, which is always a part of the principal Japanese offices, and the inevitable saki was brought in. By now we had learned that if we did not touch it for a certain length of time the saki would be removed and tea brought in. With the tea came Minister Yoshino and an interpreter. We had not talked very long before I realized that Yoshino was understanding every word I said and did not need an interpreter. I asked him if that were not so and he replied in English that it was. He went on to relate that when he was a boy in his teens he was attached as a clerk to the Japanese Commission to the 1915 San Francisco Exposition with instructions from his government to forget the Exposition once he reached San Francisco and to study English and political economy at the University of California. He then talked very freely to me in English about C. C. Moore, president of that Exposition, W. H. Crocker, Reuben Hale, and many others. Yoshino and I got along excellently. He sent to one of his homes in Osaka for some choice beef and personally cooked a real sukiyaki dinner for Mrs. Cutler and the Sexsons and me. Mrs. Yoshino was president of the Japanese YWCA and was touring America. I cabled my sister,

212

who was president of the San Francisco YWCA, and she met Madame Yoshino there and entertained her during her stay. Unfortunately the Japanese papers played up her arrival in San Francisco as being greeted by tomatoes and egg-throwing on the part of our longshoremen, but my sister said that there was no truth to it, and on my return I could find no one who knew anything about it. Yoshino was perturbed for several days but later told me he had heard from his wife that the story was sheer fabrication on the part of the Japanese press.

From then on we made good progress, and Yoshino agreed to come into our Exposition for a total investment of $1,400,000—dollars, not yen—and that is a lot of yen in any man's country. We had to agree that the Japanese building would be constructed in Japan to give Japanese employment and shipped to San Francisco in a knocked-down condition, with fifty Japanese workmen to assemble it. That meant of course negotiations with our labor unions, but with the help of Jack Shelley, then head of the Building Trades Council and now congressman, we were able to work it out readily. Later the building, all of the art objects to go in it, the workmen, dancers, and entertainers all came over in one big shipload, and quite a ceremony was had, and an international radio hookup with Japan was arranged with many speeches. The last I heard the FBI was still looking for some of the passengers!

After our success in Japan, my Board of Management cabled me to keep going. Albert Lasker and his daughter and Gene Sarazen and Mrs. Sarazen were with us in Tokyo and went on to Manila with us. We boarded the ship at Kobe, and Lasker and I solemnly agreed that no major power ever need fear Japan. Sarazen, being a hardheaded, practical fellow as well as a good golfer, said we were crazy; that Japan someday soon would threaten the whole world. Incidentally, while in Japan I asked Fujihara if he thought they would really have their exposition and the Olympic Games. He hesitated a moment and then replied, "Frankly, no; we talk about them but I am certain they will never be held because the militarists do not want the minds of our youth distracted and taken off our main objective, the Chinese Incident."

The night before we left Tokyo I gave a formal and well-arranged dinner in the Imperial Hotel for seventy-five high-ranking Japanese with whom I had dealt. Ambassador Grew, Paul Sexson, and I were

213

the only Americans. Everyone was in dinner jackets, the table had been beautifully decorated by the maître d' and it was an outstanding occasion. There was one Japanese whom I had decided not to invite. He was Mr. Kasai, a member of the Diet of the Lower House. He was a graduate of Harvard and had gotten his Master's degree at Columbia. He more or less forced himself on me, and in a memorandum which I prepared during the war for a governmental agency, I facetiously and, as it turned out, mistakenly referred to Kasai as the "Huey Long of Japan." At the government's request, I prepared about thirty memoranda of top Japanese whom I had encountered, because our government thought it might have to deal with some of these men after the war. Later a government official told me I had missed it on Kasai in saying I did not trust him, as he had been imprisoned by the Japanese for being too pro-American! Anyhow I did not invite him to the farewell dinner, but while I was dressing for the occasion Kasai telephoned and asked me if he should wear a black tie or a white tie. That was too much, and of course I capitulated and told him to wear a black one. In the course of the dinner he suddenly had a violent nosebleed, and it happened right in the midst of my speech when I was waxing poetical and speaking of the beautiful relationship between Japan and the United States. Holding a napkin to his nose, Kasai advanced to the head of the table, apologized, and asked permission to leave. Of course the thread of my peroration was broken and I was flat. Kasai was not too popular and everyone was smiling. Fujihara arose and said something in Japanese which caused a hysterical outburst of laughter and destroyed any chance of continuing my speech. I asked Fujihara for a translation and he said brokenly, "Many a time have I heard Mr. Cutler speak and bring tears to the eyes, but this is first time I ever see him bring blood to the nose." The dinner ended on that note and not even Ambassador Grew could restore any semblance of solemnity.

In Manila, President Quezon, whom I had met previously in New York when he was on his way to the coronation in England, and a number of times in San Francisco, reiterated his promise of a million pesos. This he had solemnly assured Herbert Fleishhacker and me would be forthcoming. In Manila he said he would make it an administrative measure, which he did, and later cabled me in San Fran-

214

cisco that the bill had passed. He then vetoed the bill. Quezon used to work for Fleishhacker and Alfred Sutro, so every afternoon we would telephone him. Fleishhacker, calling him Manuel, talked very straight and practically accused him of double-crossing us. I was more polite, and finally Quezon said the State Department would not permit him to use the money. I found out the State Department had nothing to do with it but that it was under the Bureau of Insular Affairs. With the help of my old friend Joaquin (Mike) Elizaldi, High Commissioner to the United States, we straightened Quezon out and got the participation.

While at the Palace in Manila with President Quezon one day, I slipped on the highly polished floors and dislocated my shoulder, with the result that my arm was strapped to my side all the time I was in the Orient. I was most uncomfortable because, linen suits or no, it was very hot and humid.

From Manila we went on a Dutch boat to Saigon, Indochina. There in my halting, academic French I negotiated a contract for participation, because the officials with whom I dealt could not speak a word of English. The contract held up and we had an excellent exhibit.

We then went overland to Siam and, because of a festival in Pnompenh, Cambodia, with hotels crowded, stayed with the only white missionaries in all the province. They had a beautiful home with a Frigidaire as proud as a baby grand piano in the living room. It was a revelation to come out of the jungle after crossing muddy rivers and rice paddies and see the beautiful paved streets of a modern city. All food and green vegetables have to be boiled in that country, and the missionaries had a native convert whose invariable prayer of grace before every meal was, "God bless this food and protect us from it, Amen"!

The next day we set out by motor for Siam, with a two-night stay at the fine hotel near the famous ruins of Angkor Wat. It is almost unbelievable that these massive stone buildings in a rectangular enclosure nearly two miles in each direction could have remained in the jungle undiscovered for so many centuries. No cement was used, which makes the construction all the more remarkable. What civilization they harbored is unknown, as is the source of the stone, for Indochina has none of consequence. Monkeys swing from the trees and the only sound is their chatter. Elephants prodded by elephant boys roam in the moats surrounding the great buildings, and I have never seen anything more mysteriously impressive. The only distraction to me was the countless bats winging their way through the long corridors. Historians say they were built about A.D. 860 and were discovered only about sixty years ago.

Early in the morning, again by automobile, we drove to the border of Siam and, after a good breakfast of American ham and eggs, took the train for a daylong ride to Bangkok, arriving in the evening. We were met by the number one Americans and American Minister Neville and Mrs. Neville. Bangkok is a most fascinating city but like all places in the Orient not too clean. Open canals through the streets used jointly for bathing and washing clothes make cleanliness impossible. Because of the countless rice paddies close to town the water in these canals and streams is always muddy. The hotel facing the river was spacious and most comfortable, but we slept beneath netting to ward off the bugs and lizards, and whenever or wherever we sat down a boy would appear with a covering for our legs to afford the same protection.

After cocktails at the Polo Club, which was most fashionable, with smartly dressed women and well-mannered men, we were taken to dinner at an American home. During the evening I opened a wrong door and saw a basement flooded with muddy water almost to the top step. It was explained that this was an overflow from the rice paddies. Lizards were on the wall, and a gibbon, which is very much like a monkey although of the ape family, perched on my shoulder at dinner and then decided he liked Mrs. Cutler better. She was quite vocal in expressing her terror of the family pet.

Minister Neville told me confidentially that a revolution was in the making and that he doubted the officials to whom I would talk would be in power at the time of our Exposition. This proved to be the case, although we were able to get a few works of art and examples of Siamese culture, which were dressed up to appear as the Exhibit of Siam. The Nevilles had two sons in school in Connecticut. They told me there was so much looting and graft in the various governmental departments that they did not dare risk sending gifts to their boys, even under the protection of the United States, and asked me to mail several for them when I could return to our own country.

We had expected to rejoin at Bangkok the Dutch ship which had carried us to Saigon. It was too heavily loaded, however, to make the river and had anchored in the Gulf of Siam. A good-sized tug took us down the river, a ride of four or five hours, and we boarded our ship in the late afternoon.

A swarm of Indians, turbaned, white-toothed, and ingratiating, were waiting for us in small boats surrounding the ship. They clambered aboard and began crying their wares of precious jewels. They spread them on the deck in gleaming white handkerchiefs and the jewels were dazzling and sparkling and of all colors. I think I have never seen such an array. Under my urging, Mrs. Cutler bought quite an assortment, as did Mrs. Sexson, because they were quite reasonably priced, considering their brilliance and attractiveness, and the Indians were also open to a little bargaining as the time for sailing drew near. Later in Hong Kong the ladies went to a jewelry store of repute to have their collection set and found that every piece was pure and unadulterated glass. I still get the credit for this.

The next day we were in Singapore, which will always be to me a fascinating city. The American Consul General and his wife met us and took us to their home, a lovely, rambling place equipped with large and lazy ceiling fans in every room. We were asked to sign their guest book. Just above our name and the last entry of a day or two previously was the signature of Amelia Earhart, who had just flown off over the Pacific, never to be seen or heard of again.

I called on the Sultan of Johore, whose principality is connected with Singapore by a causeway. I had met the Sultan and the Sultana when they were in San Francisco under the guidance of Renee May, the San Francisco partner of Getz Brothers, importers and exporters, and a big factor in the Far East. I had taken the Sultan and his party down to Palo Alto to visit former President Hoover, who had been in Malaya many times as a mining engineer, and felt free to ask Johore to participate in our Exposition. L. L. Goodman was a partner of Renee May and made his home in Singapore. His influence was far-reaching and he was held in the highest repute. He invited me to a Chamber of Commerce lunch and afterward set about persuading the Sultan to join us. Johore did come in, with a specially constructed building and exhibits from Johore, and the Sultan sent his nephew and his nephew's wife to the Exposition to represent him. This could not have been accomplished without Goodman and May, and I will always be grateful to them. Goodman was a lieutenant commander with the United States forces during the war, stationed in San Francisco, and for a time gave some special courses at Stanford University.

Also at Singapore I met representatives of Australia and New Zealand who later also joined our Exposition. The only disappointment to me in all Singapore was a Singapore Sling, of which I had heard most of my life but which I hope I will never have to taste again!

From Singapore we went to Batavia in the then Dutch East Indies. I considered our chances of getting them to participate rather desperate because New York was their natural trade port and they had already signed with the New York Fair. The New York Commissioner had been months ahead of me in every country I visited, which did not make my work any easier.

I called on our American Consul General, Dr. Foote, very early in the morning. Because of the heat, his office hours were from 5:30 A.M. to 10:00 A.M. I presented myself on the dot of 5:30. Dr. Foote told me it would probably take me a week to gain an audience with Dr. Von Mook, the Lieutenant Governor and also Minister of Commerce and Industry. I had other ideas because our schedule was so tight it called for only two days in Batavia. I went back to the Hotel Des Indes, where we were staying, and telephoned Henry Van C. Torchiana, the Consul of the Netherlands in San Francisco and my close friend for thirty years. Torchiana had been born in the Dutch East Indies and was a boyhood friend of Von Mook's. He told me to give him an hour and then make my call with every assurance that I would be well received.

The Hotel Des Indes was a beautiful hotel with an extra-large bedroom, sitting room, and screened porch to each suite. Our only criticism, and that applied to most hotels in the Orient and the Far East, was that the bathroom either did not exist at all or was across an alley. Mrs. Cutler threatened to write a book on "Bathrooms I have known or could not find."

218

Sexson and I dressed formally for the visit and, debating between a cab or a limousine, decided on the latter. We gave instructions to the driver to take us to Von Mook's office, which was right around the corner, not over a hundred feet from the back of our suite.

We were received most cordially by Von Mook and his chief deputy. I recognized Von Mook, a man I had met a number of years before at Stanford where he was the guest of Alonzo Taylor, head of our Food Research Institute, as one of the great economists of the world. We naturally talked Stanford for a while and then got down to Exposition business. Von Mook pointed out the many advantages of trading with New York and that Batavia was already committed there. Looking back, I think I made my best selling talk of the entire trip. Von Mook said he would give us his answer the next day and invited us to the Dutch Club for luncheon. After luncheon he said that he would have to be going to the ship that was taking hundreds of Hollanders back to Holland for Christmas, and that it was always an outstanding gala occasion. For the first time I confessed that we were going on that ship also as far as Singapore, where we would change to another one for Manila. I had not wanted Von Mook to know that we were spending so little time in Batavia and in effect were just taking a flyer there. His promise to give his answer the following day changed all that.

The answer the next day at lunch was "yes," and in fact we got two buildings and had a very satisfactory relationship. I will always remember Batavia and the surrounding country as rich, beautiful, and clean. This is with the exception of the canal of muddy water down the middle of the main, paved street, where children bathed and washed their teeth, while their mothers did the family washing beside them, using the stone steps, which were at every block leading into the canal, as a washboard. I suppose it is the same now that this vast country of 70,000,000 souls is Indonesia.

Returning to Manila, Mrs. Cutler and I were with High Commissioner Paul McNutt and Mrs. McNutt at Baguio one week end. Mrs. Cutler and Mrs. McNutt at breakfast were joking with me half seriously about the Japanese spy who had attached himself to me in Tokyo. I was defending him and explaining that he was an old college mate. McNutt's aide interrupted and handed Paul a sheaf of cablegrams. McNutt looked very grave and announced to us the bombing of the American gunboat, the *Panay*, in Chinese waters. As I recall, he added that we should face whatever was ahead and get it over with.

We all felt that it meant war. We drove to Manila, about 150 miles away, and there found screaming headlines all pointing toward war. We had planned on going home by way of Japan, where our contract with the Japanese government was to be signed. As though the bombing of the *Panay* was not enough, the *President Hoover*, on which we had passage home, had gone on the rocks off Formosa. The *President McKinley*, a freighter, was the only American ship in the vicinity. It was standing by the *Hoover* and was not due in Victoria or Vancouver, B.C., until February, while we had counted on being home for Christmas. I put in a telephone call to Tokyo for Minister Yoshino, and when he came on the line, blurted out most unwisely, "In view of what has happened, do you think it safe for me to return to Tokyo?" Yoshino asked, "What happening?" I said, "The bombing by Japanese planes of an American gunboat in Chinese waters." Yoshino replied that he had heard of no such happening. There was then a click on the line. The chief operator later told me we were not cut off but that someone from Tokyo came in on the line. In the five minutes or so before Yoshino was back on I had a chance to gather my wits and explained that I knew nothing about "the happening." I had just seen some headlines and had not even read a paper. Yoshino kept insisting that I give him details, but I knew nothing and stalled as best I could. I told him that Exposition matters called me home immediately and I wanted to know if Mr. Sexson, as my commissioner and representative, would be acceptable to the Japanese government in concluding our arrangements. Yoshino said that he would cable me as soon as possible. Fourteen hours later I received a cable from him that the news of the unfortunate accident had just been released coincident with the profuse apologies of his government, that Sexson would be entirely acceptable, and that he felt the best interests of his country could be served by my returning and properly presenting the cause of his people to my people. I think this last thought came as the result of many speeches I had made in Japan. I was asked at an official banquet what I thought of the many missions which Japan was sending to Europe and elsewhere. I replied that I thought they would accomplish nothing at all; that if Japan treated me right—and I believed in Japan—I could do more good than all the missions they might send. I believe that was the right approach, for time and time again I was asked to repeat this statement, and here it was coming to light in Yoshino's cable.

Sexson got passage for himself and Mrs. Sexson on the *Chichibu Maru* to Tokyo. Possibly the fact that by now we had accumulated some twenty pieces of baggage which Paul would have to wrestle with influenced me to hurry him on his way. Neither Mrs. Cutler nor I had ever been up in a plane, but without telling her I bought passage on the Philippine Clipper, which later was riddled and escaped from the Japanese at Wake Island. When I told her I had tickets home on the Pan American Clipper, her eyes filled with tears for a moment until I said, "Honey, I'm just as scared as you are but let's get out of here!" In those times the Clippers flew only in the daytime and stopped overnight at the comfortable Pan American hotels at Guam, Wake, Midway, then Honolulu, and the long hop to San Francisco was practically a day and a night.

We were to leave the next morning shortly after midnight and reach Guam at 4:00 P.M. A big party was given for us by the T. J. Wolffs (whom we had known for many years) at the Manila Hotel, with everybody in evening dress. Although we stayed at the Manila Hotel, Tommy and Caroline Wolff practically made us their house guests during our stay in Manila. They had a beautiful home—probably the most outstanding in Manila. Tommy was, and is, number one American, and their hospitality is fabulous and their friendship precious. Wolff had stayed on in the Philippines after the Spanish-American War, was chief of the constabulary at one time, and in later years was head of the American Red Cross for a long time. He and Caroline knew everybody and were known by everyone. Wolff particularly knew the Oriental mind, which I didn't, and shook his head at my procedure many times, but was most patient with me and helped me greatly to accomplish what I was after. Both Tommy and Caroline, who is a gentle, lovely lady, were interned in Santo Tomas during the war, and the ordeal they were forced to undergo was almost unspeakable and certainly unprintable. Wolff has long been a member of the Family Club in San Francisco. They visit America frequently, and Ethel Jane and I cherish their friendship greatly.

I guess we took it for granted that there would be berths aboard the Clipper and that we could change and go to bed. We went directly from the party to the plane, and Mrs. Cutler sat up in her long evening dress until we reached Guam. I still had my arm strapped to my side and my evening clothes did not feel too comfortable either. I had tried to cheer Mrs. Cutler up by reminding her that we did not know anybody in Guam and that we could bathe and change and rest and be on our own until morning.

As we taxied to the dock we saw a lot of gold braid, and as we went ashore the braid saluted and said, "The Governor's compliments, Mr. Cutler, and you and Mrs. Cutler are expected at the Governor's mansion immediately and for dinner." I will not repeat what I muttered under my breath. We pleaded for an hour's rest and change, but time limitations were such that we could only take half an hour—and we had really nothing to change to anyhow. Visitors to the island were few and the officers' wives undoubtedly made the most of every occasion. It turned out that I knew the Governor who was an old friend, and I was at ease; but Mrs. Cutler has insisted that she couldn't reconcile herself to the light, airy dresses of the ladies invited to meet us while she felt so crumpled. Of course she didn't look that way to me, but I doubt I could persuade her ever to visit Guam again.

Shortly after we left Midway, Captain La Porte, in command of the Clipper, told me that if head winds were against us from Honolulu to San Francisco, he would have to take on more gasoline and leave us behind. We would be the ones put off because we had been last to book passage from Manila. The *Lurline* was sailing from Honolulu the afternoon of the day we were to arrive and there would be no other ship for two weeks, which meant we would not get home for Christmas. I did everything I could to draw out the captain on his guesses about the head winds, but of course he had no means of knowing, and it could not be known until we reached Honolulu. I asked permission to wireless the president of Pan American, whom I knew. Captain La Porte readily granted this but expressed the opinion that the matter would be left entirely to him and that he did not want to leave us behind if it were at all possible for us to continue. The captain and I had become very friendly and I believed this, but I wirelessed Juan Trippe, telling of my troubles and of my anxiety to be home for Christmas. The reply came promptly and very properly left the decision entirely in the hands of the captain. The *Lurline* was to sail at four o'clock, which was the time we were due to come down at Pearl Harbor. I had to make the decision, and no one knew how the winds would be. I wirelessed William Roth, president of the Matson Steamship Company and an old friend, asking him to please hold the *Lurline* for us. His reply was that the ship would be held in port for one hour, which would give us time to get from Pearl Harbor to the Honolulu docks.

Shortly before we reached Honolulu, Captain La Porte told me that someone had stolen some official papers from him and that he would not let anyone off the Clipper until he found them. He said the document was most important and had been entrusted to him for delivery, that he was a commander in the Naval Reserve and would be court-martialed if he lost them.

We offered our baggage for inspection, but he waved it aside and said he did not suspect us but would have to keep all aboard until the papers were found, and he expressed his deep regret over interference with our Christmas plans. He then announced to all the passengers what the situation was, and the crew and captain began the search for the missing document. We landed in Pearl Harbor and floated around for an hour biting our nails while the search continued. Finally one of the crew found the papers in the bilge. It was a big official-looking document covered with seals and of course oily and soaked in bilge water. Captain La Porte was one of Pan American's best captains and was transferred shortly thereafter to the Atlantic side, so I never heard the story behind the stolen papers. The Clipper carried only twelve passengers, but some of them were a bit mysterious to us. Parades, Philippine Commissioner to the United States at one time, and later in trouble with the Philippine Commonwealth after the Japanese invasion, was aboard, as was the grandson of Sun Yat-sen and his bodyguard. We were in a big hurry to get off, and now there seemed to be little chance of getting aboard the *Lurline*. We were rushed through customs and into a waiting car, which our old friend, Ed Harrison, had ready for us with the motor running. We also had a Kanaka traffic officer go ahead with his siren open and another officer at the wheel. I have always considered that ride from Pearl Harbor to the Honolulu docks the most thrilling part of our trip. When we reached the docks the *Lurline* was in the stream and off Diamond Head. We threw our baggage into a motor cruiser which Harrison had waiting for us and caught up with the *Lurline* after another fast ride. A Jacob's-ladder was lowered over the side. It should not be forgotten that looking up at the side of a ship from the water is a terrifying thing. It is worse than the wall of a tall building. Mrs. Cutler and I climbed up that swaying rope ladder, were dragged through a porthole by deck hands, greeted courteously by Captain Berendson—although he probably didn't like us at all for delaying him—and we reached San Francisco in time for Chirstmas. Mrs. Cutler has always regretted that our children could not have seen her climbing the Jacob's-ladder, for they express doubts about it to this day.

All of this was in 1937, fourteen months before the Exposition was to open. I had secured participation of all the Oriental countries I visited, which enabled us to provide a proper background for our theme of a Pageant of the Pacific, and other countries were coming in under the impetus of the start we had. Construction of Treasure Island had started in March 1936 and was certain to be ready in time for buildings and planting.

Although we had a department of exhibits and another handling concessions, with Emory Wishon supervising one and Milton Esberg the other—both outstanding citizens and loyal friends of long standing—I was constantly traveling East and to Washington, to interest corporation executives whom I knew. Also, there were countless details at home which had to be handled. Colonel Dorst of the United States Army Engineers, although very friendly with me, early refused to deal with our director of works and insisted on clearing everything through me. That was absurd because I was not a construction man and it added greatly to my burdens. If it had not been for Major, now General, Fred Butler (Ret.), who was in actual charge of the work and most co-operative and efficient, we would have had a really serious condition as a result of the impasse.

George Creel and I had persuaded President Roosevelt to visit the Exposition when he could. He demurred for a while because he wanted to get away for a rest and board the cruiser *Houston* at Galveston and not come to San Francisco at all. We stayed with him until he accepted, but it was for a date before the Exposition would open. The Administration Building, one of the permanent buildings on the island, and a magnificent structure, was finished and we decided to have a big luncheon for Roosevelt there. Governor Merriam and Mayor Rossi, although agreeing to share in the expense, shied away from having their names used in the invitations because of the pressure they knew would come from thousands who could not be accommodated but who would insist on being included. George Creel and I, quite reckless by this time, issued the invitations in our names and soon found out what Merriam and Rossi had in mind. It was a gala affair, with George Smith of the Mark Hopkins Hotel doing the catering from San Francisco, and it was of course expensive.

We met the President and his party at Crockett at six o'clock in the morning, because a long tour through Mare Island and neighboring towns was laid out for him. The President looked very tired and drawn as he came down the ramp from his private car with the vast crowd staring at him. I have always regretted that Creel and I did not leave him alone for a chance to get his well-deserved rest aboard his beloved *Houston*.

He did go aboard the cruiser after the lunch, and I secured permission to borrow his secretaries Marvin McIntyre, Pa Watson, and Steve Early, and the newspapermen for a round of entertainment. We repaired to the Bohemian Club and later to the Bal Tabarin where we had an excellent floor show and practically all of the occupancy. It can be surmised that the President's train was quite late in getting away for Yosemite that night, but I was assured by the President that all was forgiven.

During this pre-Exposition period the Hearst papers were not warming up to our efforts, and I asked my staunch friend, Herbert Fleishhacker, to intercede with Mr. Hearst personally. In short order Hearst asked Fleishhacker, James B. Black, chairman of our Board of Management, and myself to San Simeon for a week end on condition that we would bring our wives. We had a fabulous week end and won Mr. Hearst to our side. I want to say in passing that from the time the Exposition was conceived until it closed and the lights were out, Herbert Fleishhacker guided, cajoled, and helped me constructively into progress. The gem of the Exposition, the Italian Art Exhibit of the old masters, was due to him. In my book Fleishhacker will always be one of the most constructive citizens the West has ever had, and he has always been my true friend.

The Exposition opened its gates on the day we had planned long in advance, February 18, 1939. We had chosen that date out of sentiment, because it was on February 18 that the very successful 1915 Panama Pacific International Exposition opened in San Francisco.

The day before the opening I was so certain of an overwhelming crowd that after conferring with my board I went on the radio and made an appeal for people to bring their lunches. We had many fine restaurants on the grounds but I did not see how they could handle the crowds, and I feared that inadequate eating facilities on the opening day would adversely affect future attendance.

I had a beautiful office in the Administration Building with well-arranged sleeping quarters, for many nights I stayed on the grounds.

We had a big force which worked all night of the seventeenth, and I worked with them, my janitor experience of early days standing me in good stead.

The Administration Building had a balcony which ran the entire length of the building and overlooked the grounds and the approaches from both San Francisco and Oakland. Opening day was a beautiful one and I paced up and down on the balcony and waited for the over-flowing crowds. Even now I have a sinking feeling as my disappointment comes back to me with the memory of the realization that the public was indifferent and was not going to respond to our years of effort and planning. New York discovered that too. The day of world's fairs was truly over. We had an attendance of 130,000 on that opening day. This is a lot of people but it didn't make much of a showing on our four hundred acres of grounds.

There were colorful opening ceremonies, at which Governor Olson and I cut yards of ribbon, and many speeches by dignitaries of our own country and from abroad.

I am not going to attempt to cover the many crowded days and months of the Exposition. I had looked forward to it after all the years of effort as something which would be a lot of fun. I told Mrs. Cutler later that I was like a kid who looked forward to the picnic and the day of the picnic it rained and he didn't have any fun at all.

If we could have had Tom Watson and his IBM Days with Grace Moore and Lawrence Tibbett, and the Japanese Days with their great crowds, George Creel and I often agreed the attendance would have topped all records.

No world's fair has ever had money enough, and we had less than most. Two years before the Exposition opened, we made a deal with the San Francisco Labor Council and the San Francisco Building Trades Council that there would be no strikes by any of the crafts doing work at Treasure Island. Jack Shelley and the other labor leaders saw to it that the agreement was lived up to, and our building program was probably the largest union-made job on record in the western United States. However, we did have many union troubles behind the scenes, most of them in my office. Also, I was slugged twice. A police inspector who had been a friend of mine for many years put one of my assailants in the hospital for a couple of weeks. We had temperaments at every turn. Once the Exposition was under way, it belonged to the public. I was the only one who could not afford to lose his temper. Every time I went out on the grounds to look things over or get a little relaxation, I would be besieged by well-meaning people who wanted to tell me how to run the show, and I would have to take refuge in my office again. With all of the detail I had to handle, I was having to appear at two and sometimes three lunches and dinners a day, greet innumerable dignitaries, dedicate buildings and exhibits, attend cocktail parties and two or three radio hookups daily, and listen to complaints of concessionaires and exhibitors. Looking back, that part of it is a cross between a nightmare and a kaleidoscope. I did not keep a diary because I did not have time, nor did I have a register book for our countless guests. It seemed as though I met most of the people of the world, and I enjoyed them, and many of their personalities are still strong upon me. In any number of cases the chance meetings of those days have developed into fine friendships which grow with the years.

As time goes on, all the grief seems to have faded away and only the beauty of the Exposition remains—the beauty of flowers and trees and sky and the magnificent lighting at night, which I doubt can ever be equaled.

The humor of little incidents stays with me too. My daily standing at attention in frock coat, striped trousers, and high hat, with General Bowley in full regalia; and our carrying on a running commentary out of the corners of our mouths while we waited to greet visiting potentates and high officials. The magnificent drill team of the Thirtieth Infantry would fire the proper salute, and after greetings we would ride slowly to the Federal Building where Commissioner Creel would go through his honors and, often with a sly flutter of his eyelids, take over for a round of formal entertaining.

Once early in the Exposition when General Bowley and I were at attention for a Maharaja entitled to eleven guns, the Infantry fired twelve. General Bowley did not change expression and barely moved his lips but said distinctly to me, "Damn it—there goes another four dollars." The next second we were shaking hands smilingly with the Maharaja as though the Army had not wasted a shot.

And there was the time when Senator and Mrs. Taft visited us, and I yielded to Republican pressure and proclaimed it Ohio Day. Mrs. Cutler and I gave them a luncheon in the beautiful Yerba Buena Club, and I learned that Senator Taft wanted to make a speech on the grounds. Exposition crowds don't go to hear political speeches. However, Edgar Bergen and Charlie McCarthy were giving a free show in the Temple Compound and generally had an audience of about fifteen thousand. Bergen used my sleeping quarters and kept Charlie there between shows. It was easy to arrange for Bergen to leave the outdoor stage by an unknown exit and not return for an encore. I did not tell Taft anything about it and ushered him in by another entrance just as Bergen went out. Fifteen thousand people were applauding for Bergen's encore, and Taft thought the applause was for him. I held aloft the gold spade with which the Senator's father, President William Howard Taft, had turned the first shovelful of earth at the 1915 Exposition and very quickly introduced him. If he had made a short speech all would have been well. Puzzled looks began to appear on the faces of the crowd and there were not fifteen thousand in the audience when Taft finished.

Later that afternoon, George Creel had the Indian Chief, his squaw and papoose, and other Indians of the Federal show at his fine quarters in the Federal Building with Edgar Bergen to entertain them. Bergen had the papoose on one knee and McCarthy on the other. I have never listened to such dialogue or seen such wonder as was in the Indians' eyes. Such was Bergen's sense of the proprieties that Charlie said nothing fresh or out of the way, and the little papoose had all the best of it, greatly to the Indians' delight.

With a flow of pleasure I remember the many times Creel would have unexpected guests of distinction and invite me over and stress that I was to bring a few chickens with me so that lunch could be served. Creel was particularly good at starting the conversation on a high, serious note and keeping it there. Such was the day when Mrs. Roosevelt and Miss Thompson appeared at Creel's unexpectedly and I was invited with four chickens. I saw Mrs. Roosevelt in a new light that day which lasted, with just the four of us, until late in the afternoon. A large range of subjects was covered entirely different from "My Day," as I read it, and I can understand some of the reasons now why Mrs. Roosevelt has such a place in the world.

One big disappointment to me was Hoover Day, for which I had made the most careful preparation. I was called to Washington unexpectedly but boarded a plane the night before and expected to be back to preside. We were grounded en route and I wired George Creel, a thoroughgoing Democrat, to take over. George handled it so well that everyone was delighted and did not miss me at all! Mr. Hoover told me afterward with something of a twinkle that Providence had helped ground me.

Again there was the inspiration of Ambassador Grew, who was with me at a stirring performance of the "Calvalcade of the Golden West." At the end when the Star Spangled Banner was played and we were all standing, Grew, who had endured so much in Japan, said to me with a choke in his voice and tears in his eyes that it was worth the long trip just to be there that one time.

These are trivial things, but they indicate how pleasant memories alone have survived the stress and strain and grief of an Exposition which a little group of us seemed to be carrying on our shoulders.

The Exposition closed October 29, 1939, with the closing ceremonies in the Federal Plaza and every foot of the area filled. Those who could not find standing room heard the ceremonies over the public address system throughout the grounds. At the close of the final ceremonies and just before the lights were extinguished for the last time in 1939, I said in part:

The Golden Gate International Exposition was the dream of many—states and cities and counties, and boys and girls and men and women. Lights are made by men in beauty and last for just a little while. Memories come from God and live forever. So will our memories of this beauty live until Time's End!

The question frequently arises as to whether the Exposition was worth while and the effort and expense justified. Thousands of letters in the files from people all over the world who had the good fortune to visit the Golden Gate International Exposition attest to these from both an educational and business standpoint. One distinguished visitor said, "We who have had the privilege of visiting the Golden Gate International Exposition realize that in no other way could we have seen the latest achievements of science, such wonderful collections of art, such horticulture, and such lighting effects." Based upon interviews since then, the general consensus of opinion is that the Golden Gate International Exposition was an educator from the beginning of its organization to the closing of its gates. It has left a picture of beauty in structure, arrangement, and illumination. Its conduct has added a new chapter of progress in art, science, education, and business. The report on the Exposition by Californians, Inc., a separate and reputable organization of long standing, said: "Today, with Treasure Island deserted and the crowds gone, we miss the tourists. They helped us to a feeling of living more broadly. They made our cosmopolitan city feel still more cosmopolitan, entertaining, and important, and their expenditures of almost $65,000,000 in the Bay Area were a tonic to local business."

It was thought for a time that there would be no second year. With

230

the island built and all the buildings there, an enterprising group, spear-headed by George D. Smith, decided that nothing could stop them. John Forbes agreed to continue as treasurer and controller, with H. C. Bottorff as assistant treasurer and controller and Colonel Allen G. Wright as counsel. The Executive Committee did me the honor of asking me to continue as president and tried to prevail upon me to accept it. I had been with the Exposition from the creation of the corporation, was tired physically and mentally, and knew that my company had been very lenient and patient with me in allowing me to serve the Exposition for so long. I therefore declined with a big feeling of relief and submitted my resignation. The Executive Committee thereupon created the office of honorary president and unanimously elected me to that office. A resolution was adopted, which read in part as follows:

Leland W. Cutler, as President of this corporation, steered its course through many stormy seas with rare skill and he was from the inception of this corporation down to the closing of the Exposition in 1939, ever attentive to the many problems of the Exposition's building and operation. It is in grateful appreciation of his many and varied services that he is at this meeting elected Honorary President of this corporation.

A new Executive Committee was created consisting of G. W. Brainard, Clarence B. Eaton, Harry H. Hilp, D. M. Messer, John R. Cahill, Alfred J. Cleary, George Creel, Leland W. Cutler, John F. Forbes, Edward H. Heller, Dan London, George D. Smith, Russell G. Smith.

George Creel and I were asked to see if we could prevail upon Marshall Dill, then president of the Chamber of Commerce, to accept the Exposition presidency and bring William W. Monahan, general manager of the Chamber, with him to be manager of the Exposition. Creel and I called on Dill and, wearing our selling clothes, arranged it. J. W. Mailliard, Jr., although having no part in 1940 management, helped out in new bank and corporation financing, and the 1940 Exposition was on its way.

As this goes to press I have just come from laying George Creel to rest. Without his help it is my firm belief that there would have been no Golden Gate International Exposition. George belonged to America and to the world. His countless friends will not know a man who did as much for his beloved San Francisco. His City's generation will smile and reminisce about the many unbelievable things he accomplished. As Larry Harris, who had known him for fifty years, once said to me, "Don't ever ask George to do anything you don't really want or if you're not in earnest, because if he believes in it, he'll embarrass you by doing it."

Creel was sturdily honest and a man of high ideals. He was an out-and-out Democrat but did not ever hesitate to espouse the Republican cause if he thought the Democrats were wrong. He was sincere in everything he did. My copy of his *Rebel at Large* is inscribed, "To Le Cutler, with the love of his friend, George Creel." I will always miss him.

XI

AT LARGE

ALTHOUGH Mrs. Cutler importuned me not to take on any more public jobs and I had more or less promised to ease up, I did agree to help out in the movement for a World Trade Center in San Francisco. Captain Robert Dollar and Wallace Alexander had talked to me about such a venture some thirty years before. Pacific House at the Golden Gate International Exposition was an idealistic expression of the project, and after the Exposition closed we kept the idea alive for a while (through the enthusiasm of Mrs. Denman), with quarters in the Palace Hotel and a small subsidy from the State Department.

In 1945 O. C. Hansen of Frazar and Hansen, importers and exporters, and chairman of the Foreign Trade Association of the Chamber of Commerce, had organized the San Francisco World Trade Center, Inc., a nonprofit corporation, with Ira Lillick, Ernest Ingold, Leland Kaiser, and M. A. Cremer of the Marine Exchange, as officers. He and Mr. Lillick, a fellow Stanford Trustee and outstanding admiralty attorney, had called at my office to ask me to help them set up a World Trade Center. I explained my promise to Mrs. Cutler that any more public work was out for me but that I would give them the benefit of such experience as I had accumulated. I steered the World Trade Center plan into the Chamber of Commerce, and the first Board of Directors of the nonprofit group was named by that body. They were (in addition to Messrs. Hansen, Lillick, Ingold, Kaiser, and Cremer) A. H. Jacobs, Edward H. Tickle, Ray B. Wiser, Harry S. Scott, Frank K. Runyan, William G. Merchant, B. F. Modglin, Harvey Hancock, M. J. McCarthy, A. McKie Donnan, and Leland W. Cutler.

Shortly after this I left for the East, and while I was away I was elected president of World Trade Center, Inc. I did not take this seriously at first, but I don't like to be beaten at anything—no one of us does—and in 1946 I had formulated an idea of how to proceed. I talked to J. W. Mailliard, Jr., an old friend and president of the Board of State Harbor Commissioners, which controls the water front (because San Francisco is a State of California harbor and not operated by the City). Mailliard was a former president of the Chamber of Commerce and we had worked together on many things. With his blessing I gave a resolution to the ever-faithful assemblyman, Thomas A. Maloney, to introduce in the 1946 budget session of the Legislature. This was passed by both houses and it called upon the Harbor Board to "investigate the desirability and feasibility of a World Trade Center for San Francisco and report to the 1947 Legislature prior to January 15th of that year." A report of two hundred pages was prepared by an economist then in state employ, Dr. T. B. Spitzer, and edited for practical consumption by several of us who were interested. The report was most comprehensive, so much so that the Legislature hardly knew what to do with it. I then had Speaker pro tem. Maloney introduce a bill creating a World Trade Center Authority for San Francisco. Los Angeles fought us bitterly, and, as that city had the balance of power in the Legislature, we amended the bill so that Los Angeles could have a Center too, and after a hard fight led brilliantly by Maloney, the bill was passed and signed by Governor Warren. Los Angeles hasn't known what to do with it, and the Governor has not appointed for that city the members of the Authority as set up in the statutes. For San Francisco Governor Warren appointed the following: Leland W. Cutler, chairman; Floyd M. Billingsley; Paul L. Davies; James S. Dean, State Director of Finance; Thomas J. Coakley, president, Board of State Harbor Commissioners (Mailliard having by that time resigned); James A. Folger; Ewald T. Grether; Charles Howard; L. K. Marshall; Charles H. Purcell, Director of Public Works; and George Pollock.

The following year, by arrangement with the Harbor Board, legislation was enacted transferring funds from the Harbor Board to the San Francisco World Trade Center Authority for architectural, engineering, and promotion expense, and the Harbor Board in addition agreed to provide a site adjacent to the Ferry Building. Preliminary architectural plans were drawn by William G. Merchant, a magnificent architect, who had been on my architectural commission at the Exposition. Once we were committed to a World Trade Center, Merchant and I agreed that we would see it through and also modestly agreed that it couldn't be built unless we stayed with it. It was contemplated that the first unit would cost approximately 6,000,000, with an over-all ultimate structure of approximately $75,000,000. This has been changed somewhat, but we are very close at this writing in 1954 to the financing and erection of a structure where the nations of the world, especially those bordering on the Pacific, can display their wares and in one place view the products of our own country. Also quarters will be provided for cultural organizations to meet in an atmosphere of trade and discuss the peace of the world, for it is almost trite to say that peace and trade go hand in hand.

This is fascinating work, but it has been a hard, grueling task, where an immense amount of pioneer work has had to be done. We now see light ahead and are confident of success.

Our official brochure, published in 1951, has the endorsement of Secretary of Commerce Sawyer; Nelson Rockefeller, chairman of President Truman's International Advisory Board; Mayor Robinson of the City and County of San Francisco, dean of the Consular Corps of San Francisco; and the president of the Latin-American Association. In the Preface Governor Warren wrote:

> On behalf of the people of California I take pleasure in extending an invitation to the nations of the world to become familiar with the World Trade Center program we are developing in the San Francisco Harbor.
>
> San Francisco is a major gateway to and from the countries of the great Pacific Basin—countries which have an aggregate population of more than a billion persons. I am confident that the development of the World Trade Center, with its convenient and economical means for the interchange of products, will contribute greatly to the encouragement of trade in this vast area.
>
> The San Francisco World Trade Center is an agency of the State of California, and the resources of the state government are pledged to make it a success. We offer our full cooperation to representatives of governments and of commercial firms who have need for facilities such as those to be offered by this important new trading center.

At the beginning of 1952 Mrs. Cutler and one of her sisters, Mrs. Blanche Sample, and I started on a trip around the world in behalf of ensuring participation in the Trade Center. I visited most of the countries of Asia and Europe. I saw wealth of raw material and poverty of people beyond description. I became firmly convinced that if trade did not cross borders armies would and that where trade flourished there would be no room for armies. I was brought up to believe in the protective tariff—and still do to a certain extent—but I became convinced that the peoples of the world cannot buy from us unless they can sell to us; that our economy can absorb their goods, and that it will be far better and cheaper to allow them to sell and get dollars than to keep pouring our millions into their countries as recklessly as we have been doing over the years. In other words, "Trade Instead of Aid" should be our slogan and should guide our conduct. Even the priming of a pump must produce water sometime or there will be a desert waste. I saw communism in all its ugliness—countries at the bow-and-arrow stage who want to fly airplanes; countries with recent "independence," which to them means license to do as they please and without strong men to guide them. The communistic countries are just waiting to see where the strength lies because they want to be on the winning side, and the strength of the world lies with Russia and the United States of America.

I was accredited by powerful governmental departments, as I was when I went to the Orient in behalf of the Exposition in 1937. I visited over thirty countries and personally had conferences with the leaders of all nations. No one over there likes America. They just want more. Many years ago Mr. Hoover told me that Europe was not ready for democracy and did not want it, and that we should not try to force democracy upon them or boast about the things we had or try to raise them to our standards. I was in Paris when General Eisenhower transferred his command to General Ridgway. We went to one of the homes of the American Embassy for dinner, and the home was behind locked gates. We started to leave our car outside, but the gatemen told us to bring it in. The day before, one car was outside for an hour, and it was painted red with the words in white scrawled on it, "Ridgway, Le Pest, go home." Children went together to school for protection under guard with crowds following them and taunting them with the cries of "Americans, go home."

Most of America doesn't know anything about Asia or Europe. I know that frequently in reading the newspapers in America when I

236

noted a foreign date line I would turn to the sports pages. I never heard of Kuala Lumpur, for instance, and yet it is the hotbed of communism. Norman Cleaveland, an old Stanford friend, read about us in the Singapore papers and wired us an invitation to fly to Kuala Lumpur and visit his tin mines. Singapore friends advised us not to attempt it because it was too dangerous; driving was out of the question and no one took the trains because they were attacked and derailed every day by the Communists. Unexpectedly we put in at Port Swettenham, which is only forty miles from Kuala Lumpur; we were to stay two days and load rubber. Cleaveland came aboard and invited us to stay all night with him at his home but said it would not be safe to be on the road after five o'clock. It was just that hour when we got ashore and Norman's driver started out, with Cleaveland holding a Tommy gun at his side and watching the jungle all the way. No untoward incident occurred and we arrived safely at Cleaveland's lovely home adjacent to the clubhouse and race course. He is a bachelor, and sitting at ease with his feet on an ottoman and a drink in his hand he remarked, "I lead the life of Riley." He showed me a manifest where for the protection of his seven tin mines and a rubber estate of his cousin he had imported from the United States 811 machine guns, any number of sawed-off shotguns and smaller weapons, and a quarter of a million rounds of ammunition. Not my idea of "the life of Riley." He told us we would have to pick up an armored car at his office only four miles away; that several times he had rescued the police with it when the constables were surrounded by Communists. He said if we heard shooting in the night not to worry, for the Commies never came to Kuala Lumpur proper. The ladies were nervous, but we started out the next morning, reached Cleaveland's office, where he strapped on a gun (as he said, for effect), then followed the armored car to one of the mines, which was surrounded by barbed wire. Ten constables and the chief were aboard, and they deployed to protect us while we went in a sampan to the artificial lake where the dredge was located. Between the mine and the jungle was a watchtower with armed men. The day before, five Commies were killed in a skirmish, and three of them had Cleaveland's work tags on them. It used to be that the Commies were afraid of an armored car and would not attack it, but London sent General Temple out to take charge, and he

237

tried some measures which didn't work. I read a few days ago that the Commies in retaliation attacked an armored car and killed forty-five. Later in London at a luncheon with the Lord Mayor, I sat next to the Prime Minister of Malaya, who knew Cleaveland well and had been in his home many times. He told me the Commies had put a price of $3,500 on his head—"the *life* of Riley."

Our ship called at Belawan, Sumatra, to load rubber. The Goodyear Rubber Company has a plantation there of 67,000 acres. I met the managing director, Mr. Titus, in Singapore, and became well acquainted with him. He carried a Tommy gun with him, too, in a small satchel which looks like a brief case. He has quite a bit to look out for, as his plantation has 40,000 employees and families to take care of. Quite a responsibility, and it is no small tribute to him and his company that, despite the grief he must have had, he steered his plantation through the uprising without being seized.

I was told that the longshoremen get the equivalent of $1.00 per day, twenty-five cents of which they are allowed to keep, and out of this they pay their union dues. The remaining seventy-five cents is managed by the unions, which feeds, houses, and clothes the stevedores. The clothes are about as big as a pocket handkerchief! A handful of rice feeds them and they sleep on the ground. This was the first time a passenger ship with white people had been in the harbor for twenty-five years, and only the unending vigilance of the ship's officers kept them from picking up everything in sight. Swarms of them—a sorry-looking lot—stood at the deck's gate and pressed their faces against the windows of the ship's lounge, staring at the passengers inside. Soldiers detailed to guard us stole cameras and desk clocks and vanished. One could hardly blame them, for the soldiers, except for a few at the top, we were told, hadn't been paid for a year. We got away with a sense of relief, because we all had felt uneasy and sensed the unstability of the country, and the soldiers all had itching trigger fingers. Without strong men I do not see how this vast country can emerge to independence. Certainly they are very close to the other side, if not already there.

Ceylon has an extremely busy port. I counted at least twenty-five large ocean-going vessels of all nations. It seemed to out-rival Singapore, certainly in appearance. There appeared to be enough trade in these faraway ports to fill several world trade centers. Of course many barriers and uneasy conditions will have to be overcome. So much of trade is traditional and much of it is artificial. It is more than a phrase that "peace and trade go hand in hand." It is not easy to make it work when the mind of the world is on armament.

Cochin, India, voted Communist overwhelmingly. It is the center of the cashew nut industry, and the nuts there are easiest to load because they are packed in uniform fifty-pound boxes. Immediately the result of the election was announced, however, orders went out from the loaders to use low gear on the winches, and this prolonged the loading. The ship was at the mercy of the loaders.

Bombay is most depressing since the British have withdrawn—a big, swollen city with great poverty and hunger. Everywhere countless people sleep on the streets or sidewalks and in window sills, because they have no homes and are weak from hunger and exhaustion. In the morning the dead wagon makes its rounds and carries them away. Any description of Bombay I might essay would be trite because the city has been described in books many, many times. Despite the great commerce undeniably there and the fine buildings which have been created over the years, I was depressed and glad to get away.

Karachi, Pakistan, was different despite the terrible slaughter when the partition came. The country, I think, is past the blueprint stage. Its docks and loading facilities are modern but its principal beast of burden is the ancient camel. These camels are everywhere and draw unbelievably heavy loads. I saw one hitched double with a cow, and in contrast little donkeys hardly bigger than rabbits drawing loads just as heavy. Pakistan, too, has its refugee and poverty problem with plenty of dirt and filth, and the country cannot possibly get along without America's help. We went to a trade fair at night dominated by the People's Republic of China Building and its exhibit. The impression was given that China was not only the founder of civilization but easily the leader today. Everything was manufactured and furnished by East Germany, and you and I know that until Russia stepped in China's boasted invention of gunpowder was used only for firecrackers. Down a little, narrow street earlier we saw within a block every possible form of transportation—camels, donkeys, bicycles, ponies, rickshas, man-pushed carts, streetcars, bullock carts, and we were riding in a brand-new automobile—a decidedly mixed metaphor, but the Tower of Babel on the ground. Food has to keep up with all this somehow if the country is to emerge from chaos, but I have a feeling it will. The "overflow" population is the problem, and that is a little outside my jurisdiction. Pakistan has a long way to go, but I think it will go steadily ahead. Famine is very close, it would seem, and refugees with nothing to do and precious little to eat and the flimsiest of thatched covering against the elements should be easy prey to the Communists, but somehow I feel the country will make it. There must be something in their religion that has held the people together over the years.

Europe was refreshing after my experiences in Asia, but to me even Europe was extremely tiresome. I could not have accomplished what I did if it had not been for the services of Colonel John D. Hartigan, whom I had known many years ago at the University of California. Colonel Hartigan was thoroughly experienced in trade relationships and protocol and spoke all of the languages that seemed to be used in Europe. He had gone over to Europe ahead of me and made my appointments for me. Because of delays on the part of our ship in reaching Europe, many of these had to be changed on short notice, and I must accord to him that he did a magnificent job. My schedule was very heavy, and I couldn't get away from the fact that despite America's great help to all the countries of Europe we were not liked and every obstacle seemed to have been placed in our way. I flew from West Germany to Amsterdam and some bombastic official held the plane for fifteen minutes and berated me because I couldn't account for three dollars of my own money. I had cashed one of my own ten-dollar traveler's checks and used the three dollars for tips and porters. I was forced to interview everybody at the airport and made to feel like a criminal. If it had not been for Colonel Hartigan's military air and a few ill-chosen words of my own to the effect that if it were not for America they "would be in the salt mines or in chains or at the bottom of the ocean and I am going to Amsterdam right now and work my way out of the three dollars," we would probably still be in West Germany. I had no trouble in Amsterdam.

Most of the grief has faded away, and as I write this in 1954 the

World Trade Center has been financed and the bonds certified by the Supreme Court. So the dream of Captain Robert Dollar and Wallace Alexander thirty-five years ago will be a reality and I am very happy about it although still a little tired. Also, with due credit, I am not so sure that we would be as far along as we are without John Hartigan.

While it had nothing to do with world trade, it was in Cairo that I had my greatest uplift which made the trip forever unforgettable. We had talked of visiting a church for Easter, but strangely as the day turned out we could not have had a more impressive Easter Sunday anywhere in the world: the great Egyptian museum filled with the golden tombs and beautiful things prepared for the afterlife of the occupants; King Tut's exhibit with its priceless accompaniment for his life forever. The things of antiquity have always interested me and here they all were before my eyes and they were created three thousand years before Christ! We went to the Pyramids, built 4,700 years before Christ. We went inside the one built by Cheops, and to the sepulcher where he was buried. We visited the Sphinx. We saw the site of Old Egypt which has been dead for a thousand years but which surely will someday be resurrected. We went through narrow streets with people living on one side and tombs on the other—the living and the dead. In many cases the families live above the tombs and know they will be with their families in a happy world later. We went to the oldest church in Egypt, a Coptic Orthodox Church where services were going on and little children were making palms to carry. This church is built above the cave where Mary hid Jesus, according to legend, on her flight from Palestine to Egypt, and we were taken down to the hiding place, now sacred, and shown the little niche where Jesus was hidden, and the hollow scooped out from solid rock where Mary bathed Him. It is now a baptismal font. Then a few steps away was the oldest synagogue in Egypt, built on the place where Moses prayed before he led the children of Israel out of Egypt and into the Promised Land. In the morning we had seen Moses Island, in the middle of the Nile, where Moses was found by Pharaoh's daughter. We went to the Citadel, which was armed at the time of the Crusades, and into a most magnificent mosque. It was one of the five worshipping hours, with Mohammedans prostrate and facing Mecca and praying. We could see the Pyramids and all of

Cairo from the Citadel, and the palace of the King within a stone's throw of where Napoleon lived for three years and where his troops were bivouacked and where he said, "Soldiers, from yon Pyramids forty centuries look down upon you." We visited the burial place of Egypt's kings, grand and beautiful beyond description. I thought of the rulers buried under the Pyramids, and of my Grandfather Durham, who visited there sixty years ago. I told the story of how, walking from the Pyramids, he plucked a black lily from the sand. An irate Arab shouted and shook his fist and started after him. My grandfather dropped the lily bulb and ran. The Arab threw the bulb, which hit Grandfather on the heel and broke in several pieces. On the run he picked up a small piece, carried it in his pocket when he returned on a slow boat all the way back to our home in Irvington, California, and planted it. The next year we had a full-grown lily, and on the old farm there is a whole bed of them. My mother had a garden of them in San Francisco, and over the years she gave many to friends. In our garden at Woodside was a cluster of beautiful black lilies from this shattered bulb grown in Egypt sixty years before. Using this for a text, my grandfather, who was a minister, preached a powerful and convincing sermon on immortality which I shall always remember. Blanche and Ethel Jane and I felt that we had an Easter Sunday which nothing can ever take away from us and which we will always remember.

XII

STANFORD AND THE
LOWER DIVISION

AS I review a busy and a happy life, I look upon my Stanford trusteeship as the greatest honor that has ever come to me. I was President of the Board for twelve terms, and the close association with Mr. Hoover and Dr. Wilbur, for both of whom I had a great admiration and affection, was an experience which nothing can ever take away from me. For thirty-four years I have tried to serve Stanford as Trustee, and I have been re-elected to my fourth ten-year term. Stanford has been the greatest part of my life. I entered as a student when I was seventeen, knew Mrs. Stanford, took courses under David Starr Jordan and Dr. Branner, and as a Trustee served with several of the Life Trustees whom the Stanfords appointed before the University began. In my own university days I had seen what outstanding teachers of maturity and understanding could do for youngsters in their teens, and I came to feel that the Lower Division had a definite place in Stanford's program. Dr. Jordan talked about a university of high degree, which we all believe in, but he made no real move to eliminate the first two years and make it a graduate school. President Wilbur did, and I opposed him and led the fight for the preservation of our Lower Division work. At an alumni meeting Dr. Wilbur announced that as of a named date there would be a reduction in the number of men students in the Lower Division and that eventually it would be abolished.

The Trustees, on October 13, 1927, under President Wilbur's dominance, resolved that there should be further reduction in the number of men students and that the number to be admitted in October 1928 should be reduced to 350. I did succeed in having the resolution state that "no determination be made at this time of the question of the elimination of the Lower Division," but every one who knew Dr. Wilbur well knew that he was merely biding his time. Alumni protests from all over the United States poured in. The Alumni Association requested that three chosen representatives be permitted to appear before the Board and present the case against elimination. This was unheard-of and was agreed to only after much debate, for the Trustees, as a body, did not relish having their sacred halls invaded by vociferous alumni. Timothy Hopkins, a Life Trustee, declined to be present when the alumni appeared. It was all to no avail, and the minutes of January 5, 1928, show the following:

Protests of various alumni relative to the elimination of the Lower Division were read and the Secretary of the Board of Trustees instructed to send them the following letter:

At a meeting of the Board of Trustees, held on the 13th day of October, 1927, the President of the University reported that the enrollment of students at the University for the academic year 1927–1928 had already reached such proportions that, in his judgment, it was advisable to reduce the number of new men students to be admitted to the Lower Division standing for October 1928 to 350, instead of 450, as theretofore.

For the reasons stated above, that recommendation of the President was adopted.

Your communication under date of November 14, 1927, was read and fully discussed at a meeting of the Board of Trustees held upon January 5, 1928. A reconsideration of its action in the matter was not deemed advisable.

In taking this step, the Board has acted upon the facts as they now appear. As has heretofore been pointed out, the Board has merely decided upon a reduction of admissions to the Lower Division for the academic year 1928–29, and has not reached or announced any decision upon the questions of further reductions or the ultimate elimination of the Lower Division. If hereafter conditions should indicate the wisdom of modification in any direction, the Board will, from time to time, take such action as may seem to it to be in the best interest of the University.

In the meantime Herbert Hoover had been elected President of the United States, and before he was inaugurated in March he asked Dr. Wilbur to be his Secretary of the Interior. Dr. Wilbur at first chose to stay with the University, but telephone calls from Mr. Hoover to several Trustees decided the matter, and the Board granted him a leave of absence for two years. Robert E. Swain, executive head of the Department of Chemistry and a Stanford graduate of the Class of 1898, was named by Dr. Wilbur to be Acting President. Dr. Wilbur had always opposed having a vice-president. It was soon clear that Dr. Swain would not take any stand of consequence without consulting Dr. Wilbur. This was undoubtedly natural on the supposition that Dr. Wilbur would return to the University in two years. When it became evident that the President was probably planning on keeping Dr. Wilbur in his cabinet for the full four-year term, the Board requested me to go to Washington and tell Dr. Wilbur of our conviction that he should return to Stanford.

I of course went to see Dr. Wilbur first. I was convinced that consulting his own personal feelings he wanted to return. Mrs. Wilbur was in wretched health. She and Mrs. Hoover had been girls together and classmates, but the Secretary of the Interior and his wife stood at the end of the receiving line and the President and his wife at the head. Dr. Wilbur was taking no salary from Stanford and allowing and encouraging his two fine sons to continue their long medical courses and be married and raise families while they were doing it. Despite his closeness to the President, it could not have been a happy situation for him. My simple argument was that we were then a fifty-million-dollar corporation and needed a President and the Trustees wanted him back. Also that six months in excess of our two-year leave had already gone by. I think Dr. Wilbur wanted to come back, but he told me I would have to talk it over with the President. This I did that same afternoon without making much headway. In fact President Hoover was pretty stern with me and with the Board for even thinking of such a thing. No one who knows Mr. Hoover ever has any doubts about his ability to express himself clearly and forcibly. After a distinctly unpleasant afternoon, he smiled and asked Mrs. Cutler and me to have dinner with them that night, adding that he and I would continue while the ladies did something else.

When dinner was over, the President took me up to the Lincoln study and said, "Le, people forget that Dr. Wilbur and I have been close friends for forty years. In this job I need a friend. Borah is unreliable, Hiram Johnson is vindictive. I can talk to Dr. Wilbur without fear of being misunderstood and he can talk to me. He never repeats anything I say. I need him."

I reminded the President as respectfully as I could that he and I were Trustees of a great University and that he proposed to keep our President away from us for four years. President Hoover replied with a wry smile that he had resigned as Trustee when he became President of the United States, and I countered with the fact that we had not accepted his resignation. In the end I told him that we could not deny him the one friend he wanted and asked for, but that, with great respect, he, as President of the United States, would have to write a letter to the Board requesting Dr. Wilbur's services. The President demurred at this and asked in effect, "Why should I?" He said he would think it over and let me know. I said as strongly as I could that with Dr. Wilbur in Washington, the Trustees were going to run the University, that I was going to continue to fight for the preservation of the Lower Division, and that I thought the Board would support me and adopt strengthening resolutions to that effect.

The next day I received a letter from the President, and it is to be noted that he stated our case entirely from his viewpoint and put in quotation marks the statement that he wanted us to make. It is a tribute to Mr. Hoover's will that we made practically the statement he outlined for us and granted leave to Dr. Wilbur for the remainder of the four years. The letter follows:

THE WHITE HOUSE
Washington
May 4, 1931

MY DEAR LE:

I have been giving thought overnight to our conversation of yesterday and it seems to me that the following is the best analysis of the matter as I see it.

The Board is practically unanimous that Dr. Wilbur is irreplaceable as President of the University and they desire that he should remain on as President for the balance of his serviceable life. I have requested that he be given a further eighteen months leave in order that as Secretary of the Interior, he may further develop the program of vast importance to the whole educational and public health interests of the American people and for the great service he can be to me in the responsibilities of this position.

The trustees agree that this is a service which the University should contribute to the nation and that they should facilitate such an arrangement. The only difficulty that arises is the arrangement to be made for conduct of the University over the 18 month period.

246

One of the suggestions is that Dr. Wilbur should resign and be reappointed at the end of the period, it being the idea that this would impose full responsibility upon Dr. Swain and make for better internal administration of the University. It seems to me there are many difficulties in the way of such a course. There would be no added potency to Dr. Swain's position if it were known that he was to be relieved. Unless it were made public it would place the trustees in the position of lack of frankness, and if it were kept secret there would immediately be the question as to whether Dr. Swain was the man to be permanent President of the University. All together, if such a course were followed it would be necessary in the interest of the University to announce that Dr. Wilbur was going to be reappointed. This would not seem to me to be any material change from the leave of absence as I think Dr. Swain could be induced to take entire responsibility for the institution in any event. I know perfectly well that Dr. Wilbur would like to be relieved of all consultative or other relationships in matters of administration.

There are also some objections to the idea of Chancellorship as it would likewise have to be announced that at the end of the stated period Dr. Wilbur would again take the position of President. Otherwise this also might be challenged as a lack of frankness. Furthermore both these methods would at the time of reappointment be a reflection on Dr. Swain unless it had been through advance understanding.

My conclusion is that if the Board of Trustees wish to be of service to the public and to myself, it would be much better for them to meet the cheap political attacks now in progress by a perfectly frank statement that "the trustees wish to retain the service of Dr. Wilbur as permanent President of the University; at the same time they wish to make an appropriate contribution to public service and they are confident they can be of no greater service than to grant to Dr. Wilbur a further leave of absence; that in the meantime Dr. Swain will take over the responsibility for the administration of the institution; that they are confident the University can make this sacrifice without harm to the institution whose program is well established and will go forward without any difficulty."

Yours faithfully,
HERBERT HOOVER

I replied to this on May 6, 1931, while still in the East:

MY DEAR MR. PRESIDENT:

Regardless of how I think the matter we discussed should be handled, please be assured that I will do all in my power to arrange it in accordance with the views expressed in your letter of May 4th. We are in entire accord in our purpose and the result to be obtained.

247

I am sorry that Mr. Shoup could not have been with me, but he telephoned today that he would be in Washington Saturday. I have told him of our conversation and your conclusion, and I know he will want to express his views as you have permitted me to express mine.

Mrs. Cutler and I are leaving New York Saturday on the *California* by way of the Canal and will be home the latter part of May. With the benefit of Mr. Shoup's discussion with you meanwhile, I am hopeful we can determine matters at our Board meeting early in June. There are many factors to be considered in the West and we want to do this in the best possible way. I will write you before our meeting if any difficulties develop.

Please know that whenever I can be of service you have but to command me.

Respectfully,
LELAND W. CUTLER

I of course reported the result of my interview to Dr. Wilbur and stressed as strongly as I could what I hoped to do about the Lower Division. When I returned Dr. Wilbur wrote me making in the main two points: (1) that most of the grants we had received from various foundations had been made upon his assurance that the Lower Division would be abolished, and (2) that many educational and other opportunities had been offered and declined by him because of his belief that the Lower Division would be done away with and he would have a graduate school to work with. I replied rather bluntly as follows:

October 21, 1931

DEAR DOCTOR WILBUR:

You are so well acquainted with my views on the matter of the Lower Division and of the question in the minds of the Trustees as to the wisdom of the policy of its elimination, that I am sure it is not necessary for me to attempt to comment in detail on yours of October 14th. We all recognize the difficulties of your position and we do not want to add to those difficulties. I was expressing the unanimous wish of the Board when, a few months ago, I urged you to come back to the University and plead with President Hoover to permit you to come back. As embarrassing as it may be to do so in your absence, the Trustees must continue to carry on as they think best.

I am sure you did not mean to imply that the Board is obligated to eliminate the Lower Division because of our knowledge of the many educational and other opportunities which you have had and which we have from time to time urged that you not accept.

I am certain that the Board has had no knowledge that pledges from the various foundations have been solicited upon the assurance that the Lower Division would not continue. I do not see how this could be because the Board decreed by Resolution in 1927 that "further reduction in the number of students to be admitted to the Lower Division be carried out by you at such rate and to such extent as might from time to time be authorized by the Board and that no determination be made of the question of the elimination of the Lower Division at any specific period."

The Board would not attempt to say that the Lower Division should never be eliminated. The necessity of it might come in a very few years or be delayed, but a considerable number of the Trustees firmly believe that the necessity is not now and that it is important to set at rest the doubts concerning the Lower Division. The mere statement that the Lower Division is to continue until some later date is not, in the minds of many of our Trustees, sufficient.

Upon receipt of your letter I discussed the matter fully with Doctor Swain and at his suggestion conferred with a number of our Trustees on the idea of postponing our special meeting until Doctor Swain could have a chance to discuss the whole matter with you in Washington next month. In their opinion it seemed best, however, that the meeting should be held and allow the Board in session to determine the matter of postponement. I will, of course, read your letter to the Board and have asked Doctor Swain to be present and fully present his views. It goes without saying that if a conclusion is reached to continue the Lower Division, no announcement will be made until you have been fully advised. The manner of the announcement would be very carefully studied and safeguarded in every possible way.

With kind personal regards, I am

Sincerely yours,

LELAND W. CUTLER

Subsequently the Board restored the number of incoming freshmen to 450 and adopted this resolution:

WHEREAS, it seems desirable, in connection with the presentation, from time to time, of the Leland Stanford Junior University's educational program and its present and future needs, more clearly to define the policy of the University respecting the continued maintenance of research work, graduate departments and undergraduate instruction, including the lower division, and the proportionate balance of these various phases of university activity; and

WHEREAS, it now appears that applications for admission to the upper division have not increased at the rate indicated by previous forecast studies, and that the total undergraduate enrollment for the current year, as compared with the previous year, has decreased;

Now, therefore, be it resolved:

(1) That the Leland Stanford Junior University continue its policy of developing and maintaining a university of high degree, with research projects and strong graduate departments.

(2) That the University also recognize the splendid opportunity which it has with its unique campus, ideal student living conditions, and relatively small classes, to maintain concurrently undergraduate instruction, including the lower division.

(3) That, in pursuance of this policy, the lower division be continued at the Leland Stanford Junior University with such increases as the administrative officers may determine can be accommodated, having in mind the total enrollment in all divisions, and the advisability of accommodating as many worthy students as the University's resources and facilities reasonably will permit.

(4) That all previous resolutions and actions in conflict herewith be, and they are hereby, rescinded.

There the matter stands at this writing at the beginning of 1954. None of these differences brought about any change in the friendship and affection which Dr. Wilbur and I had for each other until his death, nor in that relationship which I am proud to say I have with Mr. Hoover to this day. I did learn, however, in this and many other matters over a long period, that a trusteeship is everything the word implies.

When I retired as President of the Board of Trustees I received a longhand note from Dr. Wilbur, written May 22, 1942, as follows:

DEAR LELAND:

This is just a line to thank you for your years of unselfish service to Stanford as Chairman of the Board. Over many years you have always been ready and willing to do anything you could. I know of no one who has made such a fine record of voluntary contribution to us.

Am glad you are to continue to help us. Tresidder ought to be a good man to succeed you. Hope you will be back soon.

All good wishes and my keen personal appreciation of what you have done.

Yours,

RAY

One time the *Stanford Alumni Review* devoted its entire issue to Dr. Wilbur and asked me to write something in verse about him. I chose the form of a sonnet, which is a particularly hard medium and was especially hard with Dr. Wilbur as a subject. Here it is:

RAY LYMAN WILBUR

He is so lank in visage and so stern
Of stature, first meeting does forbid
A knowledge of the kindness which is hid
Within his heart and mind; of fires that burn
Restrained, impatient of control and yearn
To flame a pyre for ignorance, and rid
The world of dry and rotted growth, amid
The truths which he would have all youth to learn.
Yet thousands know he reaches to the skies
To gain Truth's raiment and its colors fair
Of lasting pigment woven pure and gay.
And this he gives to youth with twinkling eyes—
A close-spun garment as a shield to wear
Against all wrong forever and a day.

I also wrote the Trustees' memorial resolution at the time of Chancellor Wilbur's death. The resolution read in part:

Dr. Ray Lyman Wilbur was chosen in nineteen hundred and sixteen to be President of Stanford. With the Trustees' increasing confidence and respect, he served twenty-eight terms. During that time, in the years nineteen hundred and twenty-nine to nineteen hundred and thirty-three, the Board was proud to grant him leave to occupy the post of Secretary of the Interior of the United States in the cabinet of President Herbert Hoover. In nineteen hundred and forty-three, upon his retirement from the Presidency, he was named Chancellor of the University.

From the day he entered Stanford, Dr. Wilbur's life became closely linked with progress of the University. As an undergraduate he soon evinced those qualities of leadership and intellectual integrity that made him in later years a leader not only in the University but in his profession and the nation as well. Friendships he made upon the campus in his student days ripened into associations that ultimately changed the history of the world. His worth as a young alumnus quickly was recognized, first by appointment as teacher and University physician, and soon thereafter as Dean of the Medical School. Of his fifty-seven years at Stanford, far more than half were served as President and Chancellor. From the beginning to the end of his association with the University, Stanford held in his mind and heart a place of deepest devotion.

There was no phase of Stanford life or of the Founders' hopes that Dr. Wilbur did not understand and endeavor, with all his mental and moral resources, to formulate into a sane program of educational guidance for young men and women. In them he saw the future hope of America, and his unwavering purpose was to develop in their consciousness those integrities of principle and purpose that must prevail if our civilization is to endure. He was impatient of superficiality, yet he understood youthful exuberance so well that he could smile with young and old in common understanding of it all. His counsel was direct, explicit, and wise, and upon acquaintance illuminated by flashing wit and good humor. His many public addresses were examples of concise, clear thinking and farsighted vision.

The Trustees take deep satisfaction in the knowledge that during the years of his Chancellorship he maintained his office near that of his friend of undergraduate and later years, Herbert Hoover, in the tower of the Hoover Library. Dr. Wilbur said at its dedication, "This is a great shaft of light up into the blue for the long look of history," and he added, "We need that long look."

The Board of Trustees of Stanford University in grateful acknowledgment of the long look that Ray Lyman Wilbur gave in behalf of the youth under his guidance at Stanford and of the people of his country, and in respect and love of him, caused this Resolution to be adopted and recorded in the minutes of its meeting on this twenty-first day of July, nineteen hundred and forty-nine.

Dr. Donald B. Tresidder succeeded Dr. Wilbur as President of Stanford. Tresidder was a young man and a graduate of Stanford. He had great personal charm, knew his University thoroughly, and with the educational opportunity of a lifetime within his grasp was stricken by a heart attack in New York City.

I had something to do with the selection of Dr. J. E. Wallace Sterling to succeed him, and President Sterling is now at the helm. He is a great President and has the full confidence of the Trustees, faculty, students, and alumni. Everyone connected with Stanford feels that the University will go steadily forward under his leadership. The problems of a privately endowed university in these troublesome times are almost overwhelming, but President Sterling is equal to any challenge and is gaining new support in every move he makes. He and Mrs. Sterling are a great couple to lead the University. He was a graduate student at Stanford and with Mrs. Sterling is very close to the young men and women in the student body, and both have full knowledge of the progress that must be made from graduation on.

I do not feel that my life is finished or my work is done; with eight eager-eyed grandchildren, I am daily reminded that the world is ahead and that I can still have a part in it. I shudder once in a while when I think of the mistakes I have made and the opportunities I failed to grasp or handled passably when I might have carried them out to the full.

I spend very little time, however, in bemoaning anything, for with all the world's confusion and tragedy and heartaches, it is a good world and somehow I feel that we will muddle through. America has been very good to me, a country boy, and even with all the troubles and mismanagement we have had in high places, it is still the greatest country in the world and is the hope of the world. I want to stay in it and help as long as I can.

A long time ago a poet whom I admire greatly for his works and his friendship remarked that poetry was not my best medium of expression. Never having thought or pretended ever that anything I wrote approached poetry, I was puzzled and still am. However, I end this book with some words I wrote quite a while ago for my own comfort.

> The shafts of light that shone so many years ago
>> Are still the same warm shafts that wakened me from bed
> And played their light on kindly things that other people said
>> Fraught sometimes with happiness, sometimes with woe.
>
> .   .   .   .
>
> This good great world is like a door
>> Where I can touch quite carelessly the knob
> And know that just outside there'll always be some more
>> Of the tug and zest of my never ending job.

APPENDIX

To His Excellency, the Governor of the State of California, and the California Toll Bridge Authority:

Dear Sirs:

The Financial Advisory Committee to the California Toll Bridge Authority was created by Governor Rolph on April 20, 1932, and by request of the Toll Bridge Authority has served continuously since. This committee originally consisted of eighteen citizens of San Francisco and Alameda counties who served without compensation. Through this committee, the original $61,400,000 Reconstruction Finance Corporation loan was negotiated, and through this committee negotiations were carried on with the railroad companies as a preliminary to the present RFC commitment to purchase additional bonds to finance the bridge railway system. Your committee, therefore, again comes before the California Toll Bridge Authority with the following report and recommendations regarding the interurban transportation over the San Francisco Oakland Bay Bridge.

1. Your Committee recommends such service be by electric trains, operating without any change of cars by passengers from a terminal in San Francisco located in the immediate vicinity of Second and Minna Streets over and along existing interurban lines in Alameda County.

In this connection it should be noted that the Reconstruction Finance Corporation limits its loan commitment to electric train service.

2. Your Committee believes that the Authority should be given complete statutory power to acquire, own, operate and lease cars, trains, buses and other equipment over and in connection with the Bridge on a self-liquidating basis similar in principle to the powers possessed by The Water Project Authority of the State of California. This subject is again presented in Section 7 hereof.

However, at this time the most feasible plan appears to be to provide for interurban operation by appropriate contracts with the Southern Pacific Company and subsidiaries and with the Key System, each of which now operates an interurban service between San Francisco and the County of Alameda.

3. Tolls for passage over the Bridge can be fixed only by the Authority. Fares charged by privately owned carriers operating over the Bridge can be fixed only by the Railroad Commission of California.

The cost of interurban transportation must be paid either from fares or from fares plus contributions from other sources. That is fundamental and there is no escape from it.

The cost of transportation is determined primarily by the cost of operation, including wages, cost of supplies, materials and electric power, rentals, cost of maintenance of equipment and their replacements, taxes and the like; and, secondarily by a "return" (comparable to rent) on the physical properties owned by the Carrier and

254

used in the service. The cost per passenger is greatly affected by the total number of passengers and by the regularity or irregularity of the flow of traffic.

As no interurban line can operate over the Bridge for about two years, obviously the costs of their operation at that time can not be definitely established now. It is the opinion of your Committee that, prices then being approximately as they are now, the interurban fares plus bridge tolls of two and one-half cents per ride need not exceed the present interurban fares.

It is possible that agreements may be made with Carriers by which they will stipulate for such an adjustment of fares, effective for a trial period commencing with the opening of the Bridge.

It has sometimes been contended that any Carrier using the Bridge Railroad or the bridge railway equipment should be charged cash rental for such use. Were this done, such rental would enter directly into the Carrier's cost of operation and would adversely affect the passenger fare as fixed by the Railroad Commission. It is simpler and cheaper to repay the cost of the Bridge Railroad and its equipment by tolls paid to the Authority than by the Authority assessing rentals against Carriers who in turn would collect those rentals in the passengers' fares.

The expenditure of money by the Authority for the purchase and reconditioning of equipment also has a direct bearing on interurban fares. If both Carriers were able to borrow money themselves to make these expenditures, they would have to pay interest at approximately 7% as against the Authority's 5% or less and they would be required to repay at least 1/10 of the principal of the loan every year as against the Authority's 1/35 every year. The resulting higher cost per annum would be reflected in fares and would be paid by the passengers.

The best interest of the Public and of the Bridge consists in keeping both fares and tolls at the lowest practicable level. That interest will not be served by making rental or other charges against the Carriers, which immediately become an added expense to the passengers.

Your Committee has knowingly faced the alternatives of (a) assessing the costs of Bridge Railroad interest and amortization apparently against the Carriers and (b) of candidly and openly collecting them in the form of tolls. The first course might have evoked much uninformed applause but its result would have been to complicate the fare problem and to make more complex and difficult the reduction of fares by the Railroad Commission.

In practice both toll and fare will be collected on one ticket, just as fares are now. But the tolls will never confuse the issue of proper and reduced fares. They will be paid in a lump sum monthly by the Carriers to the Authority.

4. The cost of interurban facilities over and in connection with the Bridge which the Authority contemplates furnishing is approximately $15,000,000.00. Your Committee knows of only one source of funds, namely, the Reconstruction Finance Corporation. It has therefore worked to the end that the corporation would agree to make the necessary additional loan to the Authority. On December 18, 1934, the RFC adopted a resolution in the matter of this loan, a copy of which is attached and marked Exhibit "A."

This resolution amounts to an offer by the RFC to the Authority to loan the needed money. If the Authority on or before January 31, 1935, adopts a resolution accepting the offer the loan will have been made effective while the RFC still had legal power to make such loans. After that the Authority will have such time as is reasonably necessary to comply with the conditions of the loan. But as the law now stands, the Authority must actually take from the RFC before June 23, 1939, all the money covered by the loan.

Substantial delays in getting under way with actual construction will result in the Bridge Railroad not being ready when the remainder of the Bridge is opened for public use.

If the Authority, after adopting a resolution accepting the offer of the RFC desires not to meet the conditions set forth in that offer it will be under no compulsion to do so. The passage of an appropriate resolution by the Authority amounts to its acceptance of an option to borrow approximately $15,000,000.00 from the RFC on the terms stated in Exhibit "A." The Authority may negotiate with the RFC for changes in the terms of the loan option as long as the statute empowers the RFC to make loans of this class.

5. Discussions with the Southern Pacific Company and the Key System, the interurban Carriers now operating across the bay and in Alameda County, have been in two distinct parts.

Those having to do with physical plans for the Bridge Railroad, its station or stations and appurtenant facilities, with methods of physical operation, character of equipment and the like have gone on almost continually for more than two years.

Those having to do with possible contractual relations between the Carriers and the Authority were during the period from October, 1932, to October 19, 1934, limited to occasional meetings with executives of the Carriers at which the representatives of Authority vigorously urged that formal negotiations regarding terms of agreement be started.

The principal reason for delay advanced by the Carriers was the noncompletion of arrangements between Southern Pacific Company and the Key System for the unification of the interurban systems in Alameda County of both companies. Both your Committee and the Railroad Commission desired a completely unified interurban operation and the Committee sought to negotiate agreements with one Carrier instead of with two Carriers having conflicting interests.

The delays of the Carriers in commencing contract negotiations were well known to public officials, to the heads of civic organizations and to many interested citizens on both sides of the bay. A copy of a letter addressed to the Carriers on the 5th day of June, 1934, by the President of the Railroad Commission of the State of California is attached hereto and marked Exhibit "B."

On October 19, 1934, the Southern Pacific Company announced that a unified interurban operation was impossible and that it was prepared to negotiate with the Authority separately from the Key System for an abandonment of its interurban ferry service and for rail operation across the Bridge jointly with the Key System. Key System, which had stood ready to negotiate on the basis of a unified system, then opened negotiations separately for operation over the bridge jointly with the Southern Pacific.

6. It was well known that RFC required the performance of sundry conditions before it would make a loan to the Authority to pay the cost of providing interurban facilities over the Bridge. These conditions included (a) abandonment of existing interurban ferry service; (b) contracts with interurban rail carriers to operate exclusively over the Bridge Railway; and (c) approval of these transactions by the Railroad Commission of the State of California.

256

It was also well known that the power of RFC to make loans of this class must, under the law, be exercised on or before January 31, 1935.

Between the above mentioned 19th day of October, 1934, and November 20, 1934, much progress had been made in negotiations with the Carriers over the terms of proposed contracts; and numerous redrafts of agreements evidencing the progress of negotiations had been made. But the negotiations were far from completed and many differences existed (and still exist) between your Committee and the Carriers.

Nevertheless, because of the practical necessity of making formal loan representations to the RFC before the latter part of December, 1934, your Committee on November 20, 1934, determined to make a report to the Authority and to request the Carriers to make their Bridge Applications to the Railroad Commission. The report was in the form of a resolution adopted by your Committee on November 20, 1934, a copy of which is attached hereto and marked Exhibit "C."

7. The Railroad Commission of California commenced its hearing of the Carriers' Bridge Applications on November 27, 1934. Representatives of your Committee attended and testified regarding the subject matter of the applications and regarding the negotiations with the Carriers. Requests were made by interested parties for copies of the then existing drafts of agreements and such requests were complied with.

These drafts represented no completed work of your Committee (see Exhibit "C"). Contracts along the general lines of these drafts were recommended by the Committee, but in numerous respects the drafts were not acceptable to the Committee. They had not yet been considered by the Authority. It should be kept in mind that much public discussion on the subject of agreements with the Carriers has been over drafts of contracts which in important particulars represented only a stage of negotiations.

8. A condition of the RFC's grant of an additional loan for interurban purposes is a discontinuance of the interurban ferry passenger services between San Francisco and Alameda County (see Exhibit "A"). Therefore, it appears necessary for the Authority either to acquire these ferry services or to arrange with their owners, the Southern Pacific Company and the Key System, to abandon them in exchange for the opportunity to move their interurban passengers to and from San Francisco over the Bridge Railroad. Your Committee favors proceeding in the matter by negotiation, as long as it is possible to make adequate progress towards terms that are reasonable and fair.

At the same time your Committee believes that the Authority should have the power, on a self-liquidating basis, to provide and operate means of transportation over the Bridge and in connection with or appurtenant to, or extending the zones of, transportation over the Bridge and also to assist in providing means of such transportation.

To that end it should have power to acquire, own, operate and lease, and also to license the operation of, interurban cars and trains, street cars, buses and other vehicles.

In addition to these powers it should be made certain that the Authority has the legal right to condemn property for Bridge Railroad and related purposes and to grant exclusive rights for the carriage of local interurban passengers over the Bridge.

Consideration should be given to the presentation at the coming session of the Legislature of appropriate bills covering these points.

9. Your Committee calls the attention of the Authority to the advantage it now enjoys by reason of the fact that the RFC resolution (Exhibit "A") contains no statement that railroad companies shall agree to operate interurban services over the Bridge Railroad during the entire life of the RFC loan.

The Authority can, therefore, consider the possibility of negotiating with the Carriers for agreements which can be terminated by either party on notice to the other. Such an arrangement might provide that neither party can terminate the contract during the first five years (for example), but that either party can end the bridge railroad operating arrangement at any time after the initial period by three years (again for example) notice previously given.

10. The Authorities of San Francisco urge more extended and somewhat better situated station and terminal facilities in that city. This is entirely a matter of available funds. Every consideration is being given and should continue to be given to ways and means of meeting these requests. Excellent terminal facilities in San Francisco will be beneficial to all parts of the area served by the Bridge Railroad.

The eastern and central parts of the City of Alameda will be better served in some respects by the Bridge Railroad than by the ferry which now operates between Alameda and San Francisco, but no plan so far developed will give the west end of the City of Alameda as good service as the ferry now affords. Several methods are under discussion to meet the situation. Your Committee recommends that the Authority cooperate as far as possible in solving this very real problem.

11. Your Committee recommends that, despite the declarations of its impossibility, the Authority press the project of a completely unified interurban operation; and that the Authority secure the active cooperation of the Railroad Commission to that end.

Respectfully yours,
Financial Advisory Committee,
California Toll Bridge Authority
By Harrison S. Robinson, *President*
By Leland W. Cutler
By Joseph R. Knowland
Subcommittee

Dated: December 31, 1934.

EXHIBIT A

Meeting of December 18, 1934

RECONSTRUCTION FINANCE CORPORATION

Resolution

Re: Second Self-Liquidating Loan to California Toll Bridge Authority

Whereas, The Board of Directors of this Corporation, on December 20, 1932, authorized the execution of a contract providing for the purchase of bonds of California Toll Bridge Authority, a public corporation of the State of California (hereinafter referred to as the "Authority") in an amount sufficient to obtain SIXTY-ONE MILLION FOUR HUNDRED THOUSAND DOLLARS ($61,400,000) to construct a bridge across the San Francisco Bay between the Cities of Oakland and San Francisco, California (or such portion of that sum as may be required for that purpose); and

Whereas, A Bond Agreement was entered into by and between the Authority and this Corporation, under date of December 15, 1932, containing the terms and conditions of the purchase of such bonds by this Corporation; and

WHEREAS, Under and pursuant to the provisions of said Bond Agreement, this Corporation has acquired and now holds a portion of the bonds of the Authority; and

WHEREAS, Pursuant to the authorization of the Board of California Toll Bridge Authority, contained in a resolution of said Board, adopted on December 8, 1933, a certified copy of which has been forwarded to this Corporation, this Corporation has been requested to increase the loan to be made to the Authority by a sum of not exceeding TEN MILLION DOLLARS ($10,000,000), said additional money, together with such amounts as may be required therefor from the proceeds of the bonds, provided for in said Bond Agreement, to be used for the purpose of acquiring and constructing additional facilities of said bridge and approaches to provide for interurban facilities and terminals between the City and County of San Francisco and the County of Alameda; and

WHEREAS, An investigation has been made by the engineers of this Corporation, as to the relative merits of the different means of mass transportation on said bridge; and

WHEREAS, In view of the facts revealed from such investigation, Mr. Morton Macartney, Chief Engineer Self-Liquidating Division of this Corporation, concurs in the conclusion of Mr. Robert J. Cummins, Special Adviser for this Corporation, that mass transportation over the bridge should be by electric rail facilities, and recommends that such request of the Authority be granted provided such additional loan, together with so much of the loan heretofore authorized as shall be necessary therefor, be used for the purpose of procuring terminals, viaducts, trackage and rail connections, storage yards, signals and interlockers, substation and power supply lines, the purchase of new equipment and alterations to equipment, including cab control, together with all real property necessary therefor, and engineering and legal expenses in connection therewith, and interest charges on the bonds of the Authority during the course of construction; and

WHEREAS, the State of California has enacted legislation providing that no new franchises, permitting ferry service within ten (10) miles of the bridge, may be granted while any of the bonds of the Authority are unpaid and outstanding; and

WHEREAS, Pursuant to authority conferred upon this Corporation by Section 9 of Public Act No. 417 of the 73d Congress of the United States of America, amending and supplementing Section 201 (a) of the Emergency Relief and Construction Act of 1932 as Amended, this Corporation has power to grant said request; and

WHEREAS, It is deemed advisable by the Board of Directors of this Corporation that such request be granted; now, therefore be it

Resolved, That the Treasurer of this Corporation be and is hereby authorized and directed to acquire, for this Corporation, a total principal amount of the bonds of California Toll Bridge Authority, a public corporation of the State of California, in a total principal amount sufficient to make available a sum of money not to exceed SEVENTY-ONE MILLION FOUR HUNDRED THOUSAND DOLLARS ($71,400,000) or such part thereof as may be required for the construction of said bridge and the reimbursement of the State of California, as provided in a Bond Agreement heretofore entered into by and between this Corporation and said California Toll Bridge Authority, and in addition for the purpose of acquiring terminals, viaducts, trackage and rail connections, storage yards, signals and interlockers, substation and power supply lines, the purchase of new equipment and alterations to equipment, including cab control, together with all real property necessary therefor, and engineering and legal expense in connection therewith, and interest charges on the bonds of the Authority during the course of con-

259

struction, and to enter into such contracts or agreements as shall be deemed necessary or advisable by Counsel for this Corporation to carry out the purposes of this authorization, provided said contracts shall be in form satisfactory to the Chief Engineer, Self-Liquidating Division of this Corporation, and General Counsel or Counsel designated by him for such purpose.

Further Resolved, That said Treasurer be and is hereby authorized and directed to exchange the bonds of the Authority, now held by this Corporation or hereafter acquired pursuant to the provisions of said Bond Agreement, for bonds of said Authority hereafter to be issued for the purpose of refunding said bonds and providing funds for such additional contemplated acquisition and construction. Such additional bonds to be authorized and issued by the Authority and acquired by this Corporation shall mature over the same period and in proportionately the same principal installment as the bonds provided for in said Bond Agreement.

Further Resolved, That the bonds of the Authority, now held by this Corporation or hereafter acquired under said Bond Agreement, shall be exchanged for like principal amount of the new bonds to be issued by said Authority, and the additional bonds of the Authority, to be acquired by purchase, shall be bid for, from time to time, at a ratio of prices, coupons and maturities which shall give the respective block of bonds bid for an average yield to maturity of five per centum (5%) per annum, computed in accordance with standard bond tables, excluding, however, from the computation of such yield, the amount of any premium to be paid on redemption of any bond prior to maturity, adjustment shall be made for interest accrued to the date of purchase.

Further Resolved, That all of the terms and provisions of said Bond Agreement, in its present form, shall be applicable to the acquisition and construction of the project of the Authority, enlarged, as herein set forth, and to the bonds to be acquired pursuant to this authorization so far as applicable, unless expressly or impliedly modified by the terms hereof.

Further Resolved, That this Corporation, as the holder of outstanding bonds of the Authority consents that it will exchange all of said outstanding bonds, now held by it or hereafter acquired pursuant to said Bond Agreement for a like principal amount of new bonds of the Authority, with similar maturities, issued for the purpose of refunding said outstanding bonds now held by it or so to be acquired hereafter.

Further Resolved, That this authorization shall be subject to the following additional conditions:

1. The Authority shall, by resolution of its Board, duly adopted, accept and approve all of the terms and provisions of this resolution;

2. The Corporation shall have received satisfactory assurance that any interurban ferry service of Key Terminal Railway, Ltd., Key System, Ltd. (being corporations organized and existing under and by virtue of the laws of the State of California and having their principal place of business in the city of Oakland, County of Alameda, State of California), Interurban Electric Railway Company (a corporation organized and existing under and by virtue of the laws of the State of California and having its principal place of business in the City and County of San Francisco, State of California), Southern Pacific Company (a corporation of the State of Kentucky), Southern Pacific Railroad Company (a corporation of the States of California, Arizona and New Mexico), Central Pacific Railway Company (a corporation of the State of Utah), and South Pacific Coast Railway Company (a corporation of the State of California), between the City and County of San Francisco and the County

of Alameda, shall be abandoned and their franchises shall be canceled and surrendered;

3. That all additional legislation, necessary to enable the Authority to do all things contemplated by this resolution, shall have been procured, and such legislation shall be in form satisfactory to Counsel for this Corporation;

4. That agreements, in form satisfactory to Counsel for this Corporation, shall have been entered into by and between the Authority and responsible railroad companies, vested with the requisite legal powers, for the use of said bridge, and the equipment and facilities to be acquired from the proceeds of this loan;

5. All necessary certificates of convenience and public necessity shall have been issued by the Railroad Commission of the State of California;

6. That at the time of acquiring any of the bonds of the Authority, pursuant to this authorization, Reconstruction Finance Corporation shall be furnished with the final opinion of Messrs. Thomson, Wood and Hoffman, of New York, or other municipal bond counsel, approved by this Corporation, in form satisfactory to Counsel for this Corporation, stating that the bonds, so to be acquired, are valid and binding obligations of the Authority, in accordance with the terms and provisions thereof. Such opinion shall be accompanied by certified transcripts of all relevant proceedings and all other appropriate supporting papers evidencing, to the satisfaction of Counsel for Reconstruction Finance Corporation, the legality by the execution, award, sale or exchange and delivery of such bonds. In the event that delivery of the bond is made elsewhere than in the City of Washington, D.C., an unsigned copy of such opinion, accompanied by preliminary copy, or drafts, or transcripts, of such proceedings and other appropriate supporting papers, containing blanks where necessary, shall be delivered to Reconstruction Finance Corporation, at its office in the City of Washington, D.C., for approval, at least five (5) days before the time of the delivery of the bonds.

7. The filing of detailed plans, specifications, estimated and/or contracts, giving assurance that the adding of adequate electric interurban railway facilities to the bridge, together with terminals in San Francisco and the proper connections with interurban railway facilities now or as may hereafter constructed serving Alameda County, California, together with the necessary additional equipment, including necessary lands and/or rights-of-way for the proper functioning of these facilities, can be accomplished for not to exceed FIFTEEN MILLION DOLLARS ($15,000,000) and that no funds advanced under this commitment shall be used for any other purpose.

Further Resolved, That while it remains in force, unless exception shall be made in the case of the construction of this project by the Authority, it will, in the new construction provided for in this resolution and in all construction contracts hereafter to be let, comply with the requirements of Executive Order No. 6646, of the President of the United States of America, dated March 14, 1934.

Further Resolved, That all bonds so acquired, pursuant to this resolution, shall be subject to the terms and provisions of the resolutions of the Executive Committee of this Corporation, adopted March 24, 1934, and June 26, 1934, adjusting the interest yield to this Corporation on obligations held by it.

Further Resolved, That this resolution shall be and constitute a binding contract between this Corporation and the Authority as soon as the Authority shall, by its Board, adopt a resolution accepting all of the terms and provisions hereof.

Further Resolved, That the Authority shall certify and forward to this Corporation a copy of said resolution as soon as the same shall have been adopted.

Further Resolved, That the Secretary or an Assistant Secretary of this Corporation be and is hereby authorized and directed, in the name and on behalf of this Corporation, to certify a copy of this resolution and deliver such certified copy to the Authority.

The foregoing is a true and correct copy of a resolution of the Board of Directors of this Corporation, adopted on the 18th day of December, 1934.

EXHIBIT B
RAILROAD COMMISSION OF THE STATE OF CALIFORNIA

June 5, 1934

Mr. F. L. Burckhalter
Executive Vice President
Southern Pacific Company
65 Market Street
San Francisco, California

Mr. A. J. Lundberg
President
Key System, Ltd.
2129 Grove Street
Oakland, California

GENTLEMEN:

On Saturday, May 12, 1934, a conference attended by yourselves, Mr. C. H. Purcell, representing the California Toll Bridge Authority, our Transportation Engineer Mr. J. C. Hunter, and myself, was held for the purpose of discussing the matter of public transportation over the San Francisco Oakland Bay Bridge.

At the conference referred to it was agreed by all present that the characteristics of transbay travel are such that multiple unit train operation is indicated as the most suitable means of caring for this traffic. Mr. Purcell stated that unless the California Toll Bridge Authority and your companies can effect an arrangement with this end in view, the State will be under the necessity of giving serious and immediate consideration to the alternative means which may be found to be at its disposal. Further, this Bridge will become a part of the public highway system of the State of California and applications for certificates of public convenience and necessity covering bus service thereon will therefore be matters over which this Commission has jurisdiction. It is our opinion that public convenience and necessity require that immediate steps be taken to assure suitable public transportation over this Bridge.

For more than fifteen years past this Commission has been convinced that a complete unification of the electric railways and ferry lines operated by your companies would be in the public interest. Such unification has been urged in various decisions and studies of this Commission with which you are familiar. At the above mentioned conference we were given to understand that as a result of the negotiations you have heretofore conducted, a basis in principal for the accomplishment of complete unification has been tentatively reached, subject to various approvals and the further working out of various details.

In view of the time which has elapsed since the construction of the Bridge became an assured reality, it is felt that there is some justice in the complaint that your companies have been dilatory in the conduct of the negotiations which we understand have been under way for a long time. The progress of physical construction of the Bridge is now so far advanced that the actual physical work in connection with railway facilities should be under way at this time. Many studies have been made dealing with this matter and a great amount of data is available but in our opinion the whole matter is hinged upon a definite program of future management and to proceed in an expeditious and orderly manner it is in our opinion imperative that the consummation of a plan of unification be decided upon at an early date.

At the conference referred to, and which was held some three weeks ago, it was stated that your companies had reached a general conclusion on the qustion of unification. It is, therefore, the suggestion of the Commission that an agreement on the broad principles of the transaction be promptly reached. If these can be agreed upon, and are approved by this Commission, the transaction can be consummated in so far as the public is concerned. An agreement with the California Toll Bridge Authority may then be made and definite physical preparation for the Bridge transportation undertaken. Ample time may then be taken for the resolution of any number of details which merely affect the respective equities of the companies.

It is requested that you advise the Commission at an early date the status of your negotiations and when we may expect you to file an application seeking authority to consummate the unification plan.

Yours very truly,

Railroad Commission of the State of California
By (Signed) CLYDE L. SEAVEY, *President*

EXHIBIT C

WHEREAS, There have been presented to the Financial Advisory Committee the following drafts of agreement:

1. Agreement between California Toll Bridge Authority and Key System;
2. Agreement between California Toll Bridge Authority and Interurban Electric Railway Company;
3. Agreement between California Toll Bridge Authority and Southern Pacific Company, Southern Pacific Railroad Company, Central Pacific Railway Company, South Pacific Coast Railway Company and Interurban Electric Railway Compny; all of them relating to interurban service over the San Francisco–Oakland Bay Bridge; and

WHEREAS, These drafts evidence the latest stage of the negotiations between the representatives of the Toll Bridge Authority and the representatives of the interurban carriers; and

WHEREAS, It appears that the legal power of the Reconstruction Finance Corporation to loan money to the California Toll Bridge Authority for the financing of interurban facilities over and in connection with the San Francisco–Oakland Bay Bridge will expire by operation of law on January 31, 1935, and that in order to secure favorable consideration by the Reconstruction Finance Corporation any application by the California Toll Bridge Authority should be presented to the Reconstruction Finance Corporation not later than the middle of December, 1934,

Resolved, That the Financial Advisory Committee recommends to the California Toll Bridge Authority favorable action by it upon contracts along the general lines of those submitted at this meeting, upon the ground that the Reconstruction Finance Corporation requires satisfactory evidence that the entire interurban local transbay traffic will, during the life of the proposed interurban loan, be routed exclusively over the San Francisco–Oakland Bay Bridge and upon the further ground that these contracts represent, as to their principal terms, the best results that negotiations with the interurban carriers have been able to produce; and be it

Further Resolved, That the representatives of the California Toll Bridge Authority and of this Committee be advised to continue negotiations with the interurban carriers to the end that sundry provisions of these contracts may be altered to include terms more satisfactory to this Committee and more favorable to the California Toll Bridge Authority; and be it

Further Resolved, That a copy of this resolution be transmitted to the California Toll Bridge Authority.

INDEX